RACIAL SUBORDINATION IN LATIN AMERICA

There are approximately 150 million people of African descent in Latin America yet Afro-descendants have been consistently marginalized as undesirable elements of the society. Latin America has nevertheless long prided itself on its absence of U.S. styled state-mandated Jim Crow racial segregation laws. This book disrupts the traditional narrative of Latin America's legally benign racial past by comprehensively examining the existence of customary laws of racial regulation and the historic complicity of Latin American states in erecting and sustaining racial hierarchies. Tanya Katerí Hernández is the first author to consider the salience of the customary law of race regulation for the contemporary development of racial equality laws across the region. Therefore, the book has a particular relevance for the contemporary U.S. racial context, in which Jim Crow laws have long been abolished and a "postracial" rhetoric undermines the commitment to racial equality laws and policies amid a backdrop of continued inequality.

Tanya Katerí Hernández is a Professor of Law at Fordham University School of Law, where she teaches comparative employment discrimination, critical race theory, intergroup conflict and the law, and trusts and wills. The Fred T. Korematsu Center for Law and Equality awarded Hernández a Non-Resident Faculty Fellowship for 2011–13. She has previously served as a Law and Public Affairs Fellow at Princeton University, a Faculty Fellow at the Institute for Research on Women at Rutgers University, and an Independent Scholar in Residence at the Schomburg Center for Research in Black Culture. In 2011, Hernández was named a Fellow of the American Bar Foundation, and in 2009 she was elected to the American Law Institute. *Hispanic Business Magazine* selected her as one of the 100 Most Influential Hispanics of 2007. Professor Hernández serves on the editorial boards of the *Journal of Legal Education* and the *Latino Studies Journal*. Hernández's scholarly interest is in the study of comparative race relations and antidiscrimination law and her work in that area has been published in the *California Law Review*, *Cornell Law Review*, *Harvard Civil Rights–Civil Liberties Law Review*, and *Yale Law Journal*, among other publications.

Racial Subordination in Latin America

THE ROLE OF THE STATE, CUSTOMARY LAW, AND THE NEW CIVIL RIGHTS RESPONSE

Tanya Katerí Hernández

Fordham University School of Law

CAMBRIDGE
UNIVERSITY PRESS

CAMBRIDGE
UNIVERSITY PRESS

32 Avenue of the Americas, New York NY 10013-2473, USA

Cambridge University Press is part of the University of Cambridge.

It furthers the University's mission by disseminating knowledge in the pursuit of
education, learning, and research at the highest international levels of excellence.

www.cambridge.org
Information on this title: www.cambridge.org/9781107024861

First published 2013
Reprinted 2013 (twice)

A catalog record for this publication is available from the British Library.

Library of Congress Cataloging in Publication data
Hernández, Tanya Katerí.
Racial subordination in Latin America : the role of the state, customary law, and the
new civil rights response / Tanya Katerí Hernández.
  p. cm.
Includes bibliographical references and index.
ISBN 978-1-107-02486-1
1. Race discrimination – Law and legislation – Latin America. 2. Africans – Legal
status, laws, etc. – Latin America. 3. Customary law – Latin America. 4. Civil rights –
Latin America. I. Title.
KG574.H45 2013
342.808′73–dc23   2012017768

ISBN 978-1-107-02486-1 Hardback

For Anani Dzidzienyo,
who made it possible for me to be a scholar of
comparative race relations;
Harlon Dalton, *who made it possible for*
me to be a lawyer; and my
Research Assistants, *who help me bring*
it all together.

CONTENTS

MAPS

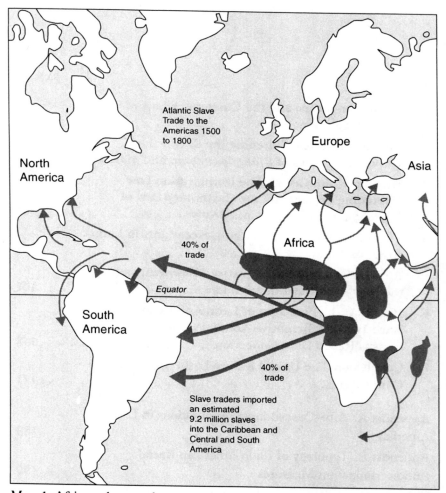

Map 1. African slave trade routes and numbers. From Williams. *Macmillian Encyclopedia of World Slavery, 1E.* © 1998 Gale, a part of Cengage Learning, Inc. Reproduced by permission. www.cengage.com/permissions

MEXICO
■ 103,400
☐ N/A

CUBA
■ 11,224
☐ 62%

THE BAHAMAS
■ 300
☐ 85%

BELIZE
■ 232
☐ 31%

HAITI
■ 7,064
☐ 95%

JAMAICA
■ 2,680
☐ 98%

HONDURAS ■ 6,560
☐ 2%

DOM. REP.
■ 8,721
☐ 84%

GUATEMALA
■ 13,314
☐ N/A

NICARAGUA
■ 5,024
☐ 9%

EL SALVADOR
■ 6,354
☐ N/A

COSTA RICA
■ 3,810
☐ 2%

PANAMA
■ 2,882
☐ 14%

VENEZUELA
■ 22,803
☐ 10%

H GUYANA ■ 698
☐ 45%

SURINAME ■ 436
☐ 41%

COLOMBIA
■ 40,262
☐ 26%

FRENCH ■ 182
GUIANA ☐ 66%

ECUADOR
■ 12,337
☐ 10%

PERU
■ 26,749
☐ 5%

BRAZIL
■ 169,799
☐ 45%

BOLIVIA
■ 5,685
☐ .04%

PARAGUAY
■ 5,884
☐ N/A

CHILE
■ 15,499
☐ N/A

ARGENTINA
■ 37,613
☐ N/A

URUGUAY
■ 3,386
☐ 4%

A: ANTIGUA & BARBUDA
■ 65
☐ 90%

B: SAINT KITTS & NEVIS
■ 43
☐ 98%

C: GUADELOUPE
■ 436
☐ 90%

D: DOMINICA
■ 74
☐ 97%

E: SAINT LUCIA
■ 160
☐ 86%

F: ST. VINCENT & GRENADINES
■ 116
☐ 85%

G: GRENADA
■ 89
☐ 95%

H: TRINIDAD & TOBAGO
■ 1,164
☐ 68%

I: BARBADOS
■ 277
☐ 90%

■ Total Country Population
(in thousands)

☐ Afro-descendants as Percent
of Total Country Population

Map 2. Afro-descendants in Latin America: How many? Reproduced with permission from Inter-American Dialogue.

1 RACIAL INNOCENCE AND THE CUSTOMARY LAW OF RACE REGULATION

I don't think there is much racism in [Latin] America because we are a mix of races of all kinds of Europeans, Africans, Asians, and other races that were or will be; but I understand that in many other parts there is racism, above all in the United States and Europe, is where there is the most racism.[1]

There are approximately 150 million people of African descent in Latin America, representing about one-third of the total population (*see* Maps 1 and 2).[2] Yet, these are considered conservative demographic figures given the histories of undercounting the number of persons of African descent on Latin American national censuses and often completely omitting a racial/ethnic origin census question.[3] At the same time, persons of African descent make up more than 40 percent of the poor in Latin America and have been consistently marginalized and denigrated as undesirable elements of the society since the abolition of slavery across the Americas.[4] Yet, the view that "racism does

---

[1] "Iberoamérica, ¿una región racista?" (Ibero-America: A Racist Region?) BBC Mundo, October 13 2005, http://news.bbc.co.uk/go/pr/fr/-/hi/spanish/latin_america/newsid_4331000/4331708.stm.

[2] Margarita Sánchez and Maurice Bryan, *Persons of African Descent, Discrimination and Economic Exclusion in Latin America* (London: Minority Rights Group International, 2003), 3–4, tbl.1, http://www.minorityrights.org/933/macro-studies/afrodescendants -discrimination-and-economic-exclusion-in-latin-america.html.

[3] Juliet Hooker, "Afro-descendant Struggles for Collective Rights in Latin America: Between Race and Culture," *Souls* 10 (2008), 279, 281.

[4] Gustavo Márquez et al., *Outsiders? The Changing Patterns of Exclusion in Latin America and the Caribbean* (Washington, DC: Inter-American Development Bank, 2007), pp. 15–17; Henry Louis Gates, Jr., *Black in Latin America* (New York: New York University Press, 2011).

not exist" is pervasive in Latin America despite the advent of social justice movements and social science researchers demonstrating the contrary. When the BBC surveyed Latin Americans in 2005 regarding the existence of racism, a significant number of respondents emphatically denied the existence of racism. Many, for instance, made statements such as "Ibero-Americans are not racist," and "Ibero-America is not a racist region, for the simple fact that the majority of the population is either indigenous, creole, or mixed."[5]

Thus the denial of racism is rooted in what many scholars have critiqued as the "myth of racial democracy" – the notion that the racial mixture (*mestizaje/mestiçagem*) in a population is emblematic of racial harmony and insulated from racial discord and inequality. Academic scholarship has in the last twenty years critiqued Latin American "mestizaje" theories of racial mixture as emblematic of racial harmony. Yet, Latin Americans still very much adhere to the notion that racial mixture and the absence of Jim Crow racial segregation are such a marked contrast to the U.S. racial history that the region views itself as what I term "racially innocent." Indeed, the extensive survey data from the Latin American Public Opinion Project's "Americas Barometer 2010" demonstrates that biased Latin American racial ideologies have not completely evolved despite the existing scholarly critiques of *mestizaje* as a trope of racial innocence. For instance, in the Americas Barometer 2010 survey of Bolivia, Brazil, Colombia, Dominican Republic, Ecuador, Guatemala, Mexico, and Peru, the vast majority of the country populations (of all races) agreed with the *mestizaje* notion that "racial mixture is good for the country."[6] In fact, more than 75 percent of all respondents agreed with the statement and largely endorsed the idea of interracial marriages. Yet, the Americas Barometer data also show that for those Latin Americans who did express disagreement with the idea of their children marrying black partners, the opposition level was dramatically greater from white respondents in contrast to black respondents. Specifically, in those countries where the Americas Barometer asked whether there was disagreement with one's

---

[5] "Iberoamérica, ¿una región racista?"

[6] "Americas Barometer 2010," Ethnicity Module of the Project on Ethnicity and Race in Latin America (PERLA), Latin American Public Opinion Project of Vanderbilt University, www.AmericasBarometer.org.

own children marrying a black person, such as Brazil, Colombia, the Dominican Republic, and Ecuador, the opposition by whites to interracial black marriages was on average 60 percent greater than the opposition of blacks to such marriages. (Other countries were asked about marriage to a person of indigenous descent.) These results thus accord with the long-standing data that marriage patterns in Latin America are generally racially endogamous.[7]

The Americas Barometer 2010 data also indicate that white respondents in several Latin American countries are considerably more likely than other groups to state a preference for lighter skin. For instance, in Colombia, Ecuador, and the Dominican Republic, on average 26 percent of white respondents agreed that they would prefer lighter skin, in contrast to the 13 percent average of black respondents who prefer lighter skin. In Mexico and Peru, blacks on average had greater rates of preference for lighter skin (37%) than whites (26%). In Brazil the rate of white preference for lighter skin closely approximated blacks' lighter-skin preference rate. Even socialist Cuba continues to manifest a preference for whiteness and a white opposition to interracial marriage.[8] Moreover, in a 2004 comparison of implicit and explicit racial bias in the United States, Cuba, the Dominican Republic, and Puerto Rico, the rates of both implicit and explicit racial bias were higher in all three Latin American contexts as compared to the United States.[9] Thus despite the overwhelming articulation of mestizaje as an indicator of racial harmony across much of Latin America and the different ways that it is articulated within each country, attitudes of racial distinction and superiority persist beneath the celebration of racial mixture. In part, the absence of a legal critique of the Latin American comparisons to the Jim Crow United States has enabled the Latin American "racial innocence" stance to remain. This book seeks to fill in that gap in the literature and provide the legal critique.

Specifically, this book is about the ways in which the Latin American denial of racism operating in conjunction with the notion that true

---

[7] Peter Wade, *Race and Sex in Latin America* (London: Pluto Press, 2009), pp. 168–73.

[8] Mark Q. Sawyer, *Racial Politics in Post-Revolutionary Cuba* (Cambridge: Cambridge University Press, 2006), pp. 124–6.

[9] Yesilernis Peña, Jim Sidanius, and Mark Sawyer, "Racial Democracy in the Americas: A Latin and U.S. Comparison," *Journal of Cross-Cultural Psychology* 35 (November 2004), 749–62.

racism can only be found in the racial segregation of the United States
veils the actual manifestations of racism in Latin America. I will argue
that an examination of the role of the state after the abolition of slavery
in regulating race through immigration law and customary law disrupts
this picture of Latin America as "racially innocent." I will then assess
the ways in which the contemporary Latin American antidiscrimination laws seek to eradicate the legacy of racial inequality wrought by
the historic racism of the state. Finally, I will conclude the book with
insights as to how the examination of the Latin American context may
be helpful to the U.S. racial justice movement today, given the growing denial of the existence of racism in the United Sates. In doing so, I
shall adopt the term "Afro-descendants," which Latin American race
scholars and social justice movement actors use to encompass all persons of African descent in Latin America who are affected by antiblack
sentiment whether or not they personally identify as "black" or adopt
a mixed-race identity such as mulatto or mestizo. This book will not
focus upon the racial inequality issues of indigenous groups in Latin
America given the extensive literature that already exists regarding that
topic. Instead the analysis will focus upon the particular history of
Afro-descendants' relationship to the state as formerly enslaved subjects seeking visibility as citizens and full participants in the national
identity despite the societal denial of racism.

"¡NO SOMOS RACISTAS!" "WE ARE NOT RACISTS!" THE RACISM-DENIAL CLOAK AROUND ACTUAL DISCRIMINATION

The force of racism denial is so strong in Latin America that even the
ubiquitous utterance and dissemination of racist speech are viewed
as inconsequential. Yet, the very term "negro" (black/negro) is widely
considered derogatory, because persons of African descent are stereotyped and referred to as inherently criminal, intellectually inferior,
overly sexual, and animalistic. Because the racialized stereotypes of
persons of African descent are pervasive, they are commonly understood to smell like animals and, in particular, monkeys. In addition
to these commonalities in antiblack stereotypes across Latin America,

each country in the region has also developed its own subset of derogatory phrases for blacks and blackness.

In Argentina, "negro de mierda"[10] ("shitty negro") is a popular expression, and "negro" is viewed as the worst of insults.[11] As a result, even children's songs in Argentina are replete with antiblack references such as "I like the white, long live the white, let the black die."[12] In fact, a young Argentinean created the Facebook page "Extermination of the (Negros de Mierda) Shitty Negroes."[13] In Brazil, persons of African descent are referred to as "macaco" (monkey), "besta" (animal), "vagabundo" (bum), "filho de puta" (son of a whore), "safado" (insolent person), "ladrão" (thief), and "nega fedorentas" (stinking female nigger).[14] Pointedly, the Brazilian insults are viewed as being coterminous with blackness. This is also unfortunately manifested in Brazilian primary school textbooks, in which black people are consistently depicted as animallike, as socially subordinate, and in other stereotyped manners.[15] In Colombian newspapers, even the polluted air of Cali is blamed on the presumed dirtiness of blacks.[16] In Costa Rica, blacks are typically described as "pigs," "stinking," "unkempt," and "ugly."[17] In Cuba, "doing things like a black person" is a common expression to describe a poorly done task or acts of delinquency.[18]

---

[10] Corina Courtis et al., "Racism and Discourse: A Portrait of the Argentine Situation," in Teun A. van Dijk (ed.), *Racism and Discourse in Latin America* (Lanham: Lexington Books, 2009), pp. 13, 32.

[11] Marina Ari, "Argentina: Empanada, Asado de Vaca y Mucho Racismo," Kaos En La Red, May 22, 2010, http://www.kaosenlared.net/noticia/argentina-empanada-asado-vaca-mucho-racismo.

[12] "Piden que Un Libro Infantil que Fomenta El Racismo sea Quitado de Circulación," MDZ Online, May 27, 2010, http://www.mdzol.com/mdz/nota/212497.

[13] Carlos Neri, "Un Grupo Argentino Exterminación de los Negros de Mierda Indigna en Facebook," Moebius, March 2, 2008, http://enmoebius.com.ar/?p=972.

[14] Teun A. van Dijk, *Racism and Discourse in Spain and Latin America* (Philadelphia: John Benjamins, 2005), pp. 136–7.

[15] Hédio Silva Jr., *Discriminação Racial nas Escolas: entre a lei e as práticas socias* (Brasília: UNESCO Brasil, 2002), pp. 34–8.

[16] Hernando Salazar, "Colombia Contra el Racismo," BBC Mundo, May 23, 2008, http://news.bbc.co.uk/hi/spanish/latin_america/newsid_7415000/7415897.stm.

[17] Marjorie Jiménez Castro, "*Las Máscaras del Chiste Racista,*" *InterSedes: Revista de las Sedes Regionales*, 2 (2001), 43.

[18] Fernando Ravsberg, "Advierten Sobre Racismo en Cuba," BBC Mundo, February 13, 2003, http://news.bbc.co.uk/hi/spanish/latin_america/newsid_2759000/2759775.stm.

In fact, the Cuban Academy of Sciences found in 2003 that dozens of Cuban phrases are used to connect blacks with delinquency and inferiority.[19] This is best exemplified by the popular phrases "It had to be a negro"[20] and "There is no such thing as a good black or a sweet tamarind."[21] In Ecuador, an often-repeated joke is that "a black person running is a thief, a white person running is an athlete."[22] This helps to account for the 2009 survey findings in Ecuador demonstrating that five out of seven Ecuadorians harbor racial prejudice against blacks.[23] Even Ecuadorian state officials are often quite comfortable stating their racialized perspectives. One chief of police publicly stated in 1995, "There is a type of race that is drawn to delinquency, to commit horrible acts ... that is the Black race, which is taking over the urban centers of the country, forming poverty belts that are conducive to delinquency because of their ignorance and their audacity."[24] In Mexico, Afro-Mexicans respond to the stereotypes that they are "ugly" and "dark" with the focus on marrying lighter-skinned partners in the Latin American hope to lighten and thus "improv[e] the race" of their progeny.[25] In Nicaragua, the phrase "100 negroes for one horse" directly compares the inferiority of blacks with the greater value of a single horse,[26] given how blacks are viewed as drug addicts and drunks in Nicaraguan society.[27] In Peru, the common statements

---

[19] Ibid.

[20] T. Avellaneda, "Manifestaciones del Racismo en Cuba: Varias Caras de Un Viejo Mal," Revista Digital Consenso, 2005, http://www.desdecuba.com/02/articulos/11_01.shtml.

[21] Rafael Duharte Jiménez and Elsa Santos García,"'No Hay Negro Bueno Ni Tamarindo Dulce': Cuba, 118 Años Después de la Abolición de la Esclavitud," Matices, http://www.matices.de/18/18pcuba.htm.

[22] José Alfredo Andaluz Prado, "Prácticas Racistas y Discriminatorias Es Castigada Con Prisión," Diario Correo, July 6, 2009, http://www.diariocorreo.com.ec/archivo/2009/07/06/practicas-racistas-y-discriminatorias-es-castigada-con-prision.

[23] Ibid.

[24] Jean Muteba Rahier, "Blackness and the 'Racial' Spatial Order, Migration, and Miss Ecuador 1995–1996," American Anthropologist 100 (1998), 421–30, 424.

[25] Alicia Castellanos Guerrero et al., "Racist Discourse in Mexico," in van Dijk, Racism and Discourse, pp. 217, 233.

[26] K. W. Stephenson, "Michael Campbell: El Racismo Está Enraizado en la Sociedad Nicaragüense," La Brújula Digital, February 25, 2011, http://www.labrujula.com.ni/noticia/159.

[27] Carlos Salinas Maldonado, "Alta Hooker Rectora de la Uraccan 'El Chamán es Sólo la Punta del Iceberg,'" Diario de la Prensa, February 22, 2009, http://archivo.laprensa.

about blacks are that they are criminals, that they can only work in low-level positions, that they only think until midday, that they are delinquents and live badly, that they are a leisurely race, and that black women are prostitutes.[28] A study of Peruvian newspapers from 2008 found a total of 159 different racist adjectives for describing persons of African descent.[29] In Venezuela, despite the national pride in being a mixed-race "café con leche" (coffee with milk) society, the plethora of racist sayings commonly iterated includes the phrase "Kill a negro and live a Pepsi [enchanted] day."[30] The widely circulated racial stereotypes about Afro-Venezuelans include

> [B]lack people are dangerous, they're thieves, they smell bad, they have bad habits, they discredit a company's image ... it's not their fault if they're like that ... black people when they don't do it [make a mess] on the way in they do it on the way out.[31]

Such racialized stereotypes also are repeatedly circulated through Venezuelann popular music with lyrics such as

> Black woman! ... if you were white and had straight hair / My mother told me in distress not to marry a black woman, because when she's asleep, she looks like a coiled snake / A black woman with a big nose doesn't cook for me, because she hides the mouthfuls in her nostrils.[32]

Within Latin America there is also the use of racialized language as terms of endearment, which unconsciously invoke the paternalism of slavery's past. For instance, affection is expressed by stating, "That's my black person" or calling someone "my little black person." Even compliments directed toward those who are black are reserved for

com.ni/archivo/2009/febrero/22/suplementos/domingo/313375.shtml (describing racism in Nicaragua from the perspective of a Caribbean black woman).

[28] van Dijk, *Racism and Discourse,* pp. 159–60.

[29] Centro de Estudios y Promoción AfroPeruanos Lundu, "Informe 2008: Presencia de Afrodescendientes en los Medios Impresos en el Año 2008," 2008, http://lundu.org.pe/web2/informe%20anual%20web/informe %202008.pdf.

[30] Jesús Chucho García, "El Racismo Nuestro de Cada Día," Geledés Instituto da Mulher Negra, March 21, 2010, http://www.aporrea.org/ddhh/a97436.html.

[31] Adriana Bolívar et al., "Discourse and Racism in Venezuela: A 'Café con Leche' Country," in van Dijk, *Racism and Discourse,* pp. 291, 292–3.

[32] Bolívar, "Discourse and Racism in Venezuela," p. 293.

those presumed to "supersede" their blackness by having other "superior" traits. Such racialized compliments include "He is black but has the soul/heart of a white"; "She is black but good looking"; "He is black but well groomed and scented." While such statements are not meant to carry racial malice, they still activate racial stereotypes about the inferiority of blacks. In fact, these perspectives about persons of African descent are so embedded in the social fiber of Latin American societies that persons of African descent's subordinated status in society is viewed as natural and logical. Furthermore, the long-standing notion that "racism does not exist" in Latin America makes those unaffected by hate speech disinclined to acknowledge the harms it causes marginalized groups.

Moreover, when flagrant instances of racist conduct are detailed in the Latin American news media, they are understood as the acts of aberrant individuals who do not represent the greater racial tolerance presumed to be a part of Latin American culture. This dichotomy is well exemplified by a study indicating that while 87 percent of non-black Brazilians manifest racial bias in their response to survey questions, only 10 percent admit to having any racial prejudice.[33] Similarly, while 89 percent of all Brazilians state that racism exists in Brazil, only 4 percent admit to harboring racial prejudice.[34] Thus, despite Brazil's reputation as a land of "cordial" race relations, Brazilians, like others in Latin America, are acutely aware of color distinctions and their hierarchical significance. As one ethnographer who traveled to Brazil to study liberation theology but found racism instead reports:

> The issue of color was, I saw, a constant presence in how men and women looked at each other, chose their lovers and spouses, modeled their bodies. It was there in the daily round of jokes, banter, insults, and accusations. It was there in how people talked to and about each other, in how they touched or did not touch each other.[35]

[33] "Datafolha Revela O Brasileiro," Folha de São Paulo, June 25, 1995, Especial-2, 3, http://almanaque.folha.uol.com.br/racismo02.pdf.

[34] Gevanilda Santos and Maria Palmira da Silva (eds.), *Racismo No Brasil: Percepções Da Discriminação E Do Preconceito Racial Do Século XXI* (São Paulo: Fundação Perseu Abramo, 2005), pp. 141, 145.

[35] John Burdick, *Blessed Anastácia: Women, Race, and Popular Christianity in Brazil* (New York: Routledge, 1998), p. viii.

In fact, Brazilians, like most Latin Americans, cannot imagine an Afro-Brazilian equivalent of Barack Obama being elected their president as a self-professed Afro-descendant.[36] In short, despite the regional differences in racial demography and the prevalence and manner of racial mixture rhetoric, across Latin America there is a common anti-black reality.

Nevertheless, Latin American racial denial is deeply embedded within racially hierarchical environments. This dualism has been historically facilitated by the deployment of strategic comparisons to the U.S. racial regime that are meant to depict Latin America as innocent of perpetrating racism. I call this the rhetoric of "racial innocence." As the Latin American human rights scholar Ariel Dulitzky has stated, "[a] kind of presumption of moral superiority vis-à-vis the United States of America is quite widespread throughout our region. Rarely does a conversation on this issue among Latin Americans take place without mentioning the serious incidence of racism and racial discrimination that exists in the land of our neighbors to the north.[37]" For instance, in the 2005 BBC survey of Latin American racial attitudes, the following invocation of racial innocence was quite prevalent: "I don't think there is much racism in [Latin] America because we are a mix of races of all kinds of Europeans, Africans, Asians, and other races that were or will be; but I understand that in many other parts there is racism, above all in the United States and Europe, is where there is the most racism."[38] In fact, in Suzanne Oboler's study of racism in contemporary Peru, she found that as in most nations of the Americas, the U.S. laws of segregation constitute the ideological definition of racism.[39]

---

[36] Luis Fernando Verissimo, *O Mundo é Bárbaro – E o que Nós Temos a Ver Com Isso* (Rio de Janeiro: Objetiva, 2008).

[37] Ariel E. Dulitzky, "A Region in Denial: Racial Discrimination and Racism in Latin America," in Anani Dzidzienyo and Suzanne Oboler (eds.), *Neither Enemies nor Friends: Latinos, Blacks, Afro-Latinos* (New York: Palgrave Macmillan, 2005), pp. 39, 42–50.

[38] "Iberoamérica, ¿una región racista?"

[39] Suzanne Oboler, "The Foreignness of Racism: Pride and Prejudice among Peru's Limeños in the 1990s," in Dzidzienyo and Oboler (eds.), *Neither Enemies nor Friends*, pp. 75–100.

Indeed, Latin America has long prided itself on the historical absence of state-mandated Jim Crow racial segregation laws that existed in the United States. When assessing contemporary racial conditions, Latin Americans continually make the comparison to the U.S. Jim Crow segregation history with statements such as "There is no violent racism like in other parts of the world like neonazism or the segregation in the south of the United States."[40] "That is a problem of the Americans."[41] Conveniently, the use of the United States as a point of reference has long shielded from view the racial subordination of persons of African descent in Latin America.

Furthermore, the historical absence of official Jim Crow laws of segregation is used as a justification for resisting contemporary black social justice movement demands for racially conscious social policies.[42] For example, in discussing the possibility of workplace affirmative action in Colombia, one commentator warns, "That would be like buying a ticket to a conflict we do not recognize."[43] Another Colombian similarly states, "If we do not want to create a racial conflict that does not exist in this country, we will have to lower the tone of the ethnic complaints and propose universal solutions, like the fight against poverty."[44] Similarly, the Brazilian reaction to the use of affirmative action in some universities is to denounce it as "the replacement of the Brazilian notion of racial democracy with a U.S. style positive discrimination that would generate polarization."[45] Indeed, a widely circulated statement opposing Brazilian affirmative action is entitled "We Are Not Racists: A Reaction to Those Who Want to Transform Us into a Bi-Color Nation."[46] It makes very little difference to such

---

[40] "Iberoamérica, ¿una región racista?"
[41] Oboler, "The Foreignness of Racism," p. 85.
[42] Anani Dzidzienyo, "The Changing World of Brazilian Race Relations?" in Dzidzienyo and Oboler (eds.), *Neither Enemies nor Friends*, pp. 137–55; Hooker, "Afro-descendant Struggles for Collective Rights in Latin America," pp. 279–91.
[43] Catalina Gallo Rojas, "Igualdad Sin Cuotas," *El Tiempo*, July 12, 2009, p. 7.
[44] César Rodríguez Garavito, "En Defensa de las Acciones Afirmativas," *El Espectador*, July 13, 2009, http://www.elespectador.com/columna150499-defensa-de-acciones-a firmativas.
[45] Gonzalo Vega Sfrani, "Universidad Reserva La Mitad de sus Cupos Para Negros y Desata Polémica," *El Mercurio*, October 22, 2006, http://www.ifcs.ufrj.br/~observa/ noticias/elmercurio/discriminacion_22.htm.
[46] Ali Kamel, *Não Somos Racistas: Uma Reação Aos Que Querem Nos Transformar Numa Nação Bicolor* (São Paulo: Nova Fronteira, 2006).

critics that affirmative action actually originated in India and not the United States.

Yet, often overlooked in the national self-serving comparisons to the U.S. Jim Crow past is the role of the state in Latin America in regulating race. Specifically, upon the abolition of slavery Latin American nations enacted restrictive immigration laws and provided state funding explicitly focused on whitening the population and outlawing the immigration of persons of African descent. Through the operation of immigration laws, persons of African descent were recast into their preemancipation status of marginalized peoples. Moreover, customary law (i.e., the enforcement of unwritten laws established by long usage rather than legislative enactment) was also used as a tool of racial exclusion in Latin America.

THE CUSTOMARY LAW OF RACE REGULATION

"We do not have racism – because around here Black people do know their place."[47]

Customary law is particularly relevant to the examination of state racial projects because of the way customary law often arises from the need for social coordination in the reinforcement of social conventions. This may be surprising to contemporary legal scholars who rarely delve into the niceties of customary law and have instead ceded the research domain to anthropologists.[48] And it may be even more surprising in the field of Latin American studies, where the history of customary law has often been obscured, and where there has been a strict aversion to it in the contemporary legal system dominated by civil codes.[49]

Yet, in the Roman law legal traditions of Latin America, customary law is a source of law for the origins of its civil law systems, and thus

---

[47] A Brazilian adage regarding its race relations. Francisco Martins, "Racism in Brazilian Aquarelle – the Place of Denying," *International Journal of Migration, Health and Social Care* 4(2) (October 2008), 37–46, 43.

[48] Martin Chanock, "Law, State and Culture: Thinking about 'Customary Law' after Apartheid," *Acta Juridica*, 1991 (1991), 52–70, 53.

[49] Victor Tau Anzoátegui, *El Poder de la Costumbre: Estudios Sobre el Derecho Consuetudinario en América Hispana Hasta La Emancipación* (Buenos Aires: Instituto de Investigaciones de Historia del Derecho, 2001), p. 13.

I argue that it should not be overlooked as a mechanism of racial control.[50] Specifically, the Roman law concept of *ius non scriptum* (rights from the unwritten) describes the laws that arose from unwritten customary practice and had become binding over time, in contrast to *jus scriptum* (written laws), that is, written laws that were intentionally legislated. The civil law uses of general customary law referred to here adhere to its Roman origins as the tacit agreement of a community deeply rooted through long usage.[51] For instance, various legal scholars have noted that custom was a useful source of law in the development of colonial Spanish legal history with regard to trade and mining,[52] in addition to being generally relevant to the development of Latin American law including Brazilian law.[53] Following the Roman concept of *ius non scriptum*, the civil law traditions of Latin America today still theoretically recognize custom as a source of law distinct from legislative and administrative regulations.[54] While custom has not necessarily been a predominant source of law in Latin America, what is important to note is that customary law has been an acknowledged source of law.

This book's historically rooted vision of customary law for a general population contrasts with the contemporary vision of customary law as the more narrow practice of enforcing the legal norms of a specialized group or subgroup population like indigenous peoples or

---

[50] Herbert Felix Jolowicz, *Historical Introduction to the Study of Roman Law* (Cambridge: Cambridge University Press, 1967); Thomas Glyn Watkin, *An Historical Introduction to Modern Civil Law*, Law of the Nations Series (Aldershot: Ashgate, 1999); Fernando Pinto, *A Presença do Costume e Sua Força Normativa* (Rio de Janeiro: Editora Liber Juris, 1982), p. 126.

[51] Alan Watson, "An Approach to Customary Law," *University of Illinois Law Review* 1984 (1984), 561–76.

[52] M. C. Mirow, *Latin American Law: A History of Private Law and Institutions in Spanish America* (Austin: University of Texas Press, 2004).

[53] Anzoátegui, *El Poder de la Costumbre*; Pinto, *A Presença do Costume*, 45; Ignazio Castellucci, "Law v. Statute, Ius v. Lex: An Analysis of a Critical Relation in Roman and Civil Law," *Global Jurist* 8 (2008), 1–32; German Savastano, "Custom as a Source of Law: Argentinean and Comparative Legal Systems," *ILSA Journal of International and Comparative Law* 15 (2009), 651–67.

[54] John Henry Merryman and Rogelio Pérez-Perdomo, *The Civil Law Tradition: An Introduction to the Legal Systems of Europe and Latin America*, 3rd ed. (Stanford, CA: Stanford University Press, 2007).

African tribes.[55] This dual meaning of customary law also applied in the Roman legal context, where customary law was meant to apply to Roman citizens in general but was also understood as the particular customs of autonomous subgroup populations within the Roman Empire.[56]

The modern conception of customary law particular to indigenous subgroup populations, as discussed by authors like Rachel Sieder and the many anthropologists who call it "traditional law," is not the focus of this book.[57] This is because the contemporary focus on customary indigenous law emphasizes how parallel legal frameworks among a settler majority population and a minority indigenous population can present the danger of a clash of conflicting norms between the state and the customary practices of an indigenous subgroup population, as so dramatically demonstrated by the way customary law in colonial Africa served its white elite administrators.[58] In contrast, this book seeks to elucidate the implicit use of general customary law *by the state* itself to enforce a particular social order, rather than the challenge to the state from the customary practices of specialized groups. This book's use of general customary law then resonates with Bentham's conception of customary law that "cloaks the sinister interests of a dominant elite."[59] In short, customary law can represent the imposition of binding norms advanced by some people in relation to others.[60]

[55] Peter Goodrich, *Reading the Law: A Critical Introduction* (London: Basil Blackwell, 1986), p. 64.

[56] Sir Paul Vinogradoff, *Custom and Right* (Cambridge, MA: Harvard University Press, 1925), p. 23.

[57] Rachel Sieder (ed.), *Multiculturalism in Latin America: Indigenous Rights, Diversity and Democracy* (Houndmills: Palgrave Macmillan, 2002); Peter Fitzpatrick, "Traditionalism and Traditional Law," *Journal of African Law* 28 (1984), 20–7.

[58] Martin Chanock, "Neither Customary nor Legal: African Customary Law in an Era of Family Law Reform," *International Journal of Law and the Family* 3 (1989), 72–88.

[59] Amanda Perreau-Saussine and James Bernard Murphy, "The Character of Customary Law: An Introduction," in Amanda Perreau-Saussine and James Bernard Murphy (eds.), *The Nature of Customary Law: Legal, Historical and Philosophical Perspectives* (Cambridge: Cambridge University Press, 2007), p. 5.

[60] Martin Chanock, *Law, Custom and Social Order: The Colonial Experience in Malawi and Zambia* (Portsmouth: Heinemann, 1985).

Customary law need not be later codified to be viewed as bind-ing.[61] Indeed, Roman sources such as Justinian's Institutes viewed cus-tom as law when communities accepted it as law as evidenced by the enforcement of the law formally or informally.[62] In fact, when cus-tomary law is fully integrated into a society as a matter of state prac-tice, there is little incentive to have the customs codified. What is most salient is whether there is a sense of legal obligation to be bound by the custom and have it enforced. It then follows that the acceptance of a social norm as law is also evidenced by the use of state resources to enforce those norms broadly.[63] In the Latin American context, the deployment of state resources (with policing of racial segregation and dedication of financial incentives for European immigration) is the key factor for transforming social convention into customary law. This is because customary law refers to that subset of social norms "chosen for special enforcement."[64]

Assessing the treatment of Afro-descendants through the lens of customary law helps to elucidate the "law" part of Latin American racial histories. For example, Afro-Brazilian oral testimonies from the postabolition period in southern Brazil repeatedly indicate the entrenched customs of racial segregation in streets, public squares, public gardens, and public parks in both the capital and cities on the periphery ("o interior") that were enforced by the local police, who had a practice of imprisoning Afro-Brazilian violators. Such practices can be characterized as customary law to the extent that they were imposed through physical sanctions and state officials felt obligated to enforce the community norms despite the absence of a written code provision or an explicit state declaration that the customs were law. I call this the "customary law of race regulation" to denote the ways in

---

[61] Leon Sheleff, *The Future of Tradition: Customary Law, Common Law and Legal Pluralism* (London: Frank Cass, 1999), pp. 378, 385.

[62] David J. Bederman, *Custom as a Source of Law* (Cambridge: Cambridge University Press, 2010), p. 17.

[63] Hanne Petersen, "Reclaiming 'Juridical Tact'? Observations and Reflections on Customs and Informal Law as (pluralist) Sources of Polycentric Law," in Hanne Petersen and Henrik Zahle (eds.), *Legal Polycentricity: Consequences of Pluralism in Law* (Aldershot: Dartmouth, 1995), p. 174.

[64] James Bernard Murphy, "Habit and Convention at the Foundation of Custom," in Perreau-Saussine and Murphy (eds.), *The Nature of Customary Law*, p. 76.

which the social norm of racial exclusion effectively operated as a legal regime in which state resources and coercion were utilized to enforce the marginalization of persons of African descent. Thus my use of customary law focuses upon the ways in which the rules of racial exclusion were more than social conventions, but instead the equivalent of law. Considering the role of customary law thus deepens our understanding of the regulation of race in Latin America.

Scholarly discussions of customary law in Latin America often note that many countries in the region will not accord customary law status to those practices that are *contra legem* (against the law), that is, against established legislated law.[65] At the same time scholars also note that several instances of recognized customary law did nevertheless contravene Latin American legislated law.[66] In the specific case of the customary law of race regulation, the only argument for its being *contra legem*, and thus without the status of law, would be with respect to the equality provisions that proliferated in the constitutions in the region post emancipation. That argument, though, can be easily dismissed given the focus of those equality provisions upon the issue of nobility and abolishing the remnants of a monarchy's inequality of status.

For instance, a typical postemancipation equality provision is contained in Argentina's Constitution of 1853, which stated, "The Argentine nation does not recognize prerogatives of blood or of birth; personal, privileges and titles of nobility do not exist. All the inhabitants are equal before the law, and are eligible to all public employments without other consideration than those of fitness."[67] The nineteenth-century limitation of constitutional equality to the issue of nobility is also indicated by the contemporaneous provisions excluding illiterates and paupers from voting as lower-class residents not warranting the full rights of citizenship. To the extent that constitutional equality in nineteenth-century Latin America was limited to

---

[65] Alejandro Guzmán Brito, "El Régimen de la Costumbre en las Codificaciones Civiles de Hispanoamérica y España Emprendidas Durante el Siglo XIX," http://www.restudioshistoricos.equipu.cl/index.php/rehj/article/view/161/155.

[66] Pinto, *A Presença do Costume*, pp. 126–8; Rosembert Ariza Santamaría, "Usos y costumbres en el procedimiento administrativo: Una Administración al servicio de sociedades pluriculturales," in *Procedimiento y Justicia Administrativa en América Latina* (Mexico City: Fundación Konrad Adenauer, 2009), pp. 249–64.

[67] Art. 16, Constitución Nacional (Arg.) (1853).

white males, the customary law of race regulation would not have been viewed as *contra legem* abrogations of the Constitution. Moreover, the nineteenth-century Latin American view of constitutions as political documents with no immediate and direct legal effect absent enabling legislation also dispenses with the question of whether the customs of race regulation would have been considered *contra legem* and thus not enforceable law.

Discussions of customary law typically address how customs as unwritten law can be explicitly applied in courts, or how a subgroup's legal norms can coexist as customary law within a sovereign's larger framework of legislatively enacted laws. This book uniquely examines the implicit use of customary law outside courts by state actors to fortify the apparatus of racial hierarchy in practice. Chapters 2 and 3 examine the postabolition state customary practices of policing public spaces for the maintenance of racial segregation, excluding persons of African descent from places of public accommodation, imposing racist norms in public education, establishing biased regulation of African-based religions, and structuring census enumerations to marginalize persons of African descent, first in Spanish America and then in Brazil.

Examining the large panoply of racially exclusionary customary practices, along with the legislation and funding of restrictive immigration laws, erodes the notion that Latin American states were innocent of racial regulation. To be sure, the particulars of the Latin American legal context cannot be directly equated with the U.S. history of Jim Crow segregation. Nevertheless, it is important to note how state action in Latin American racial subordination had a similar effect in marginalizing persons of African descent in the region. Indeed, the true evil of U.S. Jim Crow racial restrictions emanated not so much from the fact that the laws of segregation were codified into written laws, but from how those laws denoted the participation of the state in racial discrimination. Customary law in Latin America similarly elucidates the pernicious role of the state in regulating race.

While it is true that the region's historical and sociopolitical variation is great, the focus here is to draw out the often overlooked commonalities in how Latin American law writ large constructed racial privilege and continues to yield significant racial disparities across every socioeconomic and political measure detailed in Chapter 4. For this reason, the book focuses on the nineteenth-century establishment of racially exclusionary customary laws and then turns quickly to the contemporary concerns with racial stratification. Less emphasis is placed upon the intervening years, which maintained racial hierarchy unabated, in order to devote more attention to how the legacy of the customary law of race regulation racially positions Afro-descendants today.

As such, this book seeks to disrupt the traditional narrative of Latin America's legally benign racial past and reexamine its salience for the contemporary development of antidiscrimination laws across the region. Given the elite resistance to concrete state-sponsored racial equality public policies, it is important to provide a full accounting of state involvement in the maintenance of racial hierarchy. In turn, the accounting that the book provides yields additional support for the Latin American racial equality policies that are presently being challenged in both courts and the public discourse. In detailing the historic complicity of Latin American states in erecting and sustaining racial hierarchies, the book dispels the Latin American myth of racial innocence and in turn advances the claim of social justice movements for direct state engagement in pursuing racial equality. To be clear, the book's consideration of state action is not limited to the endeavor of justifying the state's contemporary role in initiating policies of racial equality because of the state's historical involvement in causing racial inequality; racial inequality is a pressing concern that should be attended to by state officials without respect to the level of state involvement in historically causing racial inequality. Instead, the book more expansively addresses the rhetorical power of state action for social justice movement actors attempting to dispel the notion of state racial innocence that hinders the national consideration of effectively pursuing racial equality. In this way, the book serves not only as the narrative of how law was involved in the Latin American construction of a racial hierarchy, but also as an assessment of the value of the contemporary state-led initiatives to eradicate racism in the region.

Chapter 5 therefore examines the various legal approaches that have been enacted in Latin America to address racial inequality. Multicultural constitutions, collective land titling laws, employment discrimination laws, public accommodation laws, hate speech laws, and international human rights laws will all be analyzed in the chapter. The particular focus will be on the region's disproportionate reliance upon the criminal law context as a legal response to the long history of marginalization and denial of racism. The potential hindrances to addressing racial discrimination fully within the criminal context will be discussed, along with its exclusive focus on interpersonal forms of racial discrimination rather than broader institutional forms of systemic discrimination.

Chapter 6 will then focus on Brazil's leadership in the use of affirmative action in Latin America. The chapter will detail Brazil's use of race-based affirmative action policies starting in 2001. It will then trace the growing opposition to affirmative action with the growth of race-based affirmative action in the elite institutions of higher education and the legal challenges that have been presented in court to such policies. The chapter will highlight the successes of the programs as a model for the rest of Latin America but will also examine how the region's myopic understanding of the role of the state in racial subordination may hinder broader enactment of affirmative action policies.

The book will conclude in Chapter 7 with insights as to how the examination of the Latin American context may be helpful to the U.S. racial justice movement today. The story of racial regulation in Latin America has a particular salience for the contemporary U.S. racial context. The Afro–Latin American struggle to pierce through the veil of race-transcendent rhetoric that obscures continued racial inequalities may help to elucidate the complex reality of race in the United States today. The successful civil rights movement struggle against Jim Crow segregation now places racial minorities in the United States in a situation comparable to that of persons of African descent in Latin America – struggling against racial hierarchy without formal legal discrimination as a target.

2 SPANISH AMERICA WHITENING THE RACE – THE UN(WRITTEN) LAWS OF *BLANQUEAMIENTO* AND *MESTIZAJE*

Within a short span of time from when Spanish American countries were pronouncing the complete abolition of slavery (primarily across the years 1850–86), they were also confronted with the simultaneous growth of eugenics – a pseudoscientific movement that sought to improve the human race by preserving the genetic purity of whites.[1] Thus any inquiry into the nineteenth-century role of law in regulating race in Latin America must consider the influence of eugenics in the region. This chapter will assess the function of eugenics in Latin American state policies and the resulting racially exclusionary customary practices. In order to demonstrate the regionwide patterns of the customary law of race regulation this chapter will provide a general overview of Latin American eugenics-inspired customary laws. Chapter 3 will then follow with an in-depth case study of Brazil for the purposes of providing greater detail about the development of the customary law of race regulation in the largest country within Latin America with the highest density of Afro-descendants.

European notions of eugenics associated the prevalence of non-whites in Spanish America with the backwardness of mongrel nations.[2] Between 1880 and 1930, intellectuals in Spanish America found support for their own racial elitism in European racial theories like

---

[1] Francis Galton, *Hereditary Genius* (London: Macmillan and Co., 1869).
[2] Lourdes Martínez-Echazábal, "Mestizaje and the Discourse of National/Cultural Identity in Spanish America, 1845–1959," *Spanish American Perspectives* 25 (May 1998), 23–4.

eugenics that asserted the innate inferiority of nonwhites.[3] Given the larger numbers of persons of African and indigenous descent in Spanish America, the region developed its own form of eugenics with the concepts of *blanqueamiento* (whitening) and its correlate *mestizaje* (racial mixing). *Mestizaje* is the belief in the use of racial mixture to lighten the complexion of a nation in the movement toward whiteness and thereby promote racial harmony. Coexisting with this broad-based theoretical understanding of *mestizaje*, which is the focus of this chapter, is the more circumscribed view of *mestizaje* as the racial mixture between whites and indigenous persons that creates the mestizo racial identity.

Blanqueamiento is a concept that has both an individualized personal meaning and a broader national meaning. At the individual level, *blanqueamiento* revolves around the desire for a white appearance and the ambition of having children who are lighter in appearance through the vehicle of interracial intimacy. Lighter children are thought to have greater opportunity for social mobility. At the same time, the individual valorization of whiteness is very much influenced by the national promotion of whiteness, best exemplified by descriptions of interracial intimacy as "improving the race" (*mejorando la raza*). At the national level, *blanqueamiento* is a concept that describes a concrete state-sponsored nation-building campaign to whiten a population and the overarching racial ideology that valorizes whiteness. *Blanqueamiento* is therefore a broader project than the colonial opportunities accorded to select upper-class persons of African descent to change their racial designation officially upon petition and payment to the Spanish Crown for a certificate of whiteness known as a *cédula de gracias al sacar* (governmental concessions of exemption from nonwhiteness).[4] This is because, unlike the individual *cédulas de gracias al sacar*, *blanqueamiento* was meant to benefit the entire nation with a white image, and not just individual persons of African descent seeking access to the legal rights and privileges of colonial whites.

---

[3] Aline Helg, "Race in Argentina and Cuba, 1880–1930: Theory, Policies, and Popular Reaction," in Richard Graham (ed.), *The Idea of Race in Spanish America, 1870–1940* (Austin: University of Texas Press, 1990), pp. 37–8.

[4] James F. King, "The Case of José Ponciano de Ayarza: A Document on Gracias al Sacar," *Hispanic American History Review* 31 (1951), 640–7.

The means through which attempts were made to whiten the population or image of a nation varied across Spanish American nations but were all steeped in the eugenic belief of white superiority. The "scientific" basis for eugenics differed in Spanish America from the European and U.S. approaches. In Europe and the United States, Gregor Mendel's 1866 book *Principles of Heredity* was used to develop a theory for eugenics postulating that successful people had good genetics, while disadvantaged people and groups had bad genetics, which no amount of social development could remedy so that the racial purity of good genes should be protected at all costs.[5] In contrast, the Spanish American approach to eugenics was culturally adapted and instead favored a conceptualization that echoed Jean Baptiste Pierre Antoine Lamarck's earlier understanding of heredity.[6] Lamarck's theory viewed external forces as influencing heredity so that characteristics an individual acquired in adapting to the environment could then be inherited by later generations. Even though Lamarck's theory of genetic acquisition was later disproved, it held great implicit appeal to Spanish American countries seeking to ameliorate disdainful European presumptions that their numerous populations of persons of African and indigenous descent made the nations inferior. Rather than be overwhelmed by the magnitude of "inferior" races that Mendelian eugenics classified as irredeemable, Lamarckism more flexibly considered that with external intervention new characteristics could be acquired and then inherited by one's offspring. As a consequence, many Spanish American countries enacted public hygiene legislation to sanitize and improve their inferior classes.[7] At the same time, legislation requiring prenuptial medical tests was instituted to discourage the reproduction of unfit classes who were viewed as more prone to venereal disease, alcoholism, mental illness, and chronic diseases.[8]

Furthermore, Lamarck's notion of genetic acquisition intuitively provided indirect support for the *mestizaje* concept that interracial

---

[5] Nancy Leys Stepan, *The Hour of Eugenics* (Ithaca, NY: Cornell University Press, 1991), pp. 27–8.
[6] Richard W. Burkhardt, *The Spirit of the System: Lamarck and Evolutionary Biology* (Cambridge, MA: Harvard University Press, 1977).
[7] Stepan, *Hour of Eugenics*, pp. 85–9.
[8] Ibid. at pp. 122–8.

intimacy between a white person and a black person would allow the resulting child to acquire whiteness and all the positive attributes socially associated with whiteness.[9] With this reasoning, over time the presumably "stronger" gene of whiteness would predominate in the population and the numbers of blacks would decrease. For this reason, the Spanish American eugenics notion of constructive racial mixing has been viewed as a unique contribution to a field that traditionally viewed racial mixing as degenerative.[10] This is best captured by the influential Mexican philosopher José Vasconcelos's statement lauding the benefits of a new mixed-race, which he called the "cosmic race," whereby "[t]he lower types of the species will be absorbed by the superior type. In this manner, for example, the Black could be redeemed, and step by step, by voluntary extinction, the uglier stocks will give way to the more handsome."[11]

In short, against the backdrop of the pseudoscience of Lamarckian eugenics, *blanqueamiento* and *mestizaje* operated together and independently to bolster the postemancipation nation-building process of both diminishing blackness and creating a new race diluted of blackness. *Blanqueamiento*, and its gradual approach to the whiteness ideal across generations, provided a means both for removing some of the taint of backwardness and for philosophically opposing European eugenics. In turn, *mestizaje* countered the mongrel nation descriptor with a well-constructed illusion of moral superiority for having solved racial problems by minimizing racial differences and facilitating a racially mixed racial democracy. The manner in which the different Spanish American countries responded to eugenics varied depending upon the extent to which they were able to attract European immigrants, and the size of their indigenous populations. Some nations focused solely on the whitening project of *blanqueamiento* (Argentina, Uruguay, and Chile), and others focused more on the articulation of a *mestizaje/*

---

[9] Edward E. Telles, *Race in Another America: The Significance of Skin Color in Brazil* (Princeton, NJ: Princeton University Press, 2004), p. 28; Ana María Alonso, "Conforming Disconformity: 'Mestizaje,' Hybridity, and the Aesthetics of Mexican Nationalism," *Cultural Anthropology* 19 (2004), 462.

[10] Stepan, *Hour of Eugenics*, p. 170.

[11] José Vasconcelos, *The Cosmic Race: A Bilingual Edition*, Didier T. Jaén (trans.), 2nd ed. (Baltimore: Johns Hopkins University Press, 1997), p. 30.

race mixture pride that included blackness (Colombia, Cuba, and Venezuela), or a "monocultural *mestizaje*" that focused on the mixture of the indigenous with whites to the complete exclusion of blacks (Ecuador and Mexico).[12] Yet as the discussion of the particularities of the various countries will show, all were centrally driven by antiblack sentiment.

ARGENTINA AS THE EPITOME OF *BLANQUEAMIENTO*

Immigration was often the primary playing field for the state promotion of *blanqueamiento* and *mestizaje* nation-building projects. Indeed, debates over immigration policies in Spanish America were often couched in racial language.[13] Argentina is notable for its sole focus on *blanqueamiento* and its extensive use of European immigration to so implement it. Indeed, after the 1853 constitutional emancipation of its slaves, immigration doubled Argentina's population between 1869 and 1895, from 1.8 million to 4 million. By 1914 it had doubled again to 7.9 million – making 30 percent of its population foreign born. Argentina's focus on European immigration in particular is demonstrated by the fact that between 1880 and 1900 alone, almost a million Europeans migrated to Argentina.[14] This number is only exceeded by the rate of U.S. European immigration.[15] The immigration boom in Argentina was not mere happenstance, but instead the result of a concerted effort of the Argentinean government.

Indeed, the original Constitution of 1853 included a provision designed to promote immigration. It stated:

> The federal government shall foster European immigration; and may not restrict, limit or burden with any tax whatsoever, the entry

[12] Jean Muteba Rahier, "Soccer and the (Tri-)Color of the Ecuadorian Nation: Visual and Ideological (Dis)Continuities of Black Otherness from Monocultural Mestizaje to Multiculturalism," *Visual Anthropology Review* 24 (2008), 148–82.
[13] Mary Elizabeth Bletz, "Whiteness of a Darker Color: Narratives of Immigration and Culturation in Brazil and Argentina, 1890–1930," Ph.D. dissertation, New York University (2003), p. 9.
[14] George Reid Andrews, *The Afro-Argentines of Buenos Aires, 1800–1900* (Madison: University of Wisconsin Press, 1980), pp. 20, 178.
[15] Bletz, "Whiteness of a Darker Color," p. 79.

into the Argentine territory of foreigners who arrive for the purpose of tilling the soil, improving industries, and introducing and teaching the arts and sciences.[16]

Moreover, a subsequent constitutional provision explicitly stated:

> Foreigners enjoy within the territory of the Nation all the civil rights of citizens; they may exercise their industry, trade and profession; own real property, buy and sell it; navigate the rivers and coasts; practice freely their religion; make wills and marry under the laws. They are not obliged to accept citizenship nor to pay extraordinary compulsory taxes. They may obtain naturalization papers residing two uninterrupted years in the Nation; but authorities may shorten their term in favor of those so requesting, alleging and proving services rendered to the Republic.[17]

Thereafter, Domingo Sarmiento, president of Argentina from 1868 to 1874, was very open about the governmental interest in European immigration for the purpose of whitening the population when he stated that it would "correct the indigenous blood with new ideas ending the medievalism" of the country.[18] In effect, the *blanqueamiento* of immigration was sought to modernize the nation with an increased white gene pool "capable" of modernization. The constitutional mandate for European immigration even manifested itself in the allocation of public subsidies to lure the immigrants to Argentina.[19]

European immigrants were welcomed into the labor market as Afro-Argentines were simultaneously shut out. By 1914, foreigners in Argentina dominated almost all of the skilled occupational categories despite only representing 30 percent of the population.[20] Italians, who were among the first of the large migration waves and thus dominated the foreign-born population of Argentina, had a large proportion of

---

[16] Constitución de la Confederación Argentina (1853), Art. 25 (emphasis added).
[17] Ibid., at Art. 20.
[18] Andrews, *Afro-Argentines of Buenos Aires*, p. 103.
[19] George Reid Andrews, *Afro-Latin America, 1800–2000* (New York: Oxford University Press, 2004), p. 136.
[20] Herbert S. Klein, "The Integration of Italian Immigrants into the United States and Argentina: A Comparative Analysis," *American Historical Review* 88 (April 1983), 323.

landowners. The 1914 census indicated that 25 percent of Italians twenty or more years of age were property owners (a figure that closely approximated the national norm).[21] In Buenos Aires alone, a 1909 census showed that Italian immigrants owned 38 percent of the commercial establishments in the city despite representing only 22 percent of the city population.[22] The Buenos Aires numbers are particularly relevant given the density of Afro-Argentines in the city up until that time.[23] Indeed, as early as 1887 Italians accounted for 32 percent of the city population, made up 53 percent of the industrial labor sector, and constituted 57.5 percent of the owners of industrial establishments. In contrast, native Argentines, who made up 47 percent of the city population, represented only slightly more than 20 percent of both workers and owners in commerce, 16 percent of the industrial labor sector, and less than 10 percent of the owners of industrial establishments.[24] These strong indicators of how well integrated the Italian immigrants quickly became into the Argentine national economy support the premise that the Argentine elite viewed the European immigration of Italians as the welcome bearer of civilization. With their influx into the population and intimacy with the indigenous population, a "biologically superior population" could be created. Simultaneously, the "vagrant, lazy" Afro-descended populations were replaced in the labor market by the European immigrants. Many of the occupational categories that Afro-Argentines previously filled became dominated by European immigrants. Immigrant replacement of black labor was such a widespread phenomenon that it even extended to the context of the armed forces (an area traditionally open to Afro-descended males).[25] Today, Afro-Argentines make up approximately only 5 percent of the entire national population[26] and are so marginalized that Carlos

---

[21] Ibid. at pp. 318, 321.

[22] Ibid. at p. 321.

[23] Andrews, *Afro-Argentines of Buenos Aires*, pp. 64–200.

[24] Samuel L. Baily, "The Adjustment of Italian Immigrants in Buenos Aires and New York, 1870–1914," *American Historical Review* 88 (April 1983), 284.

[25] Andrews, *Afro-Argentines of Buenos Aires*, pp. 20, 183.

[26] Patricio Downes, "Casi dos Millones de Argentinos Tienen Sus Raíces en el Africa Negra," Clarín, June 9, 2006, http://edant.clarin.com/diario/2006/06/09/sociedad/s-03801.htm.

Menem, the president of Argentina in 1989–99, once stated, "No, we have no blacks. Brazil has that *problem*."[27]

STATE SUPPORT FOR EUROPEAN IMMIGRATION ACROSS SPANISH AMERICA

While Argentina certainly provides the most stark example of European immigrant displacement of Afro-descended peoples in the labor market, it is certainly not an aberration in Spanish America and the Caribbean. As a result of various legislative efforts and public discourse encouraging European immigration, Brazil, Cuba and Uruguay, along with Argentina, received more than 90 percent of the 10–11 million Europeans who arrived between 1880 and 1930.[28] Early on, the Congress of Gran Colombia (constituting what is now Colombia, Ecuador, Panama, and Venezuela until its dissolution in 1830) sought to encourage European immigration through grants of public land.[29]

In Uruguay, the migration of European immigrants between 1880 and 1930 was 580,000 (while its total 1880 population was only 520,000).[30] In the large city of Montevideo, the city's population growth from 58,000 to 309,000 between 1880 and 1908 is directly attributed to the influx of European immigration. In fact, by 1908 foreign-born residents represented 30 percent of the city's population, and their proportion among city workers was even higher.[31] By 1925, government publications proclaimed Uruguay "totally of European origin," despite the simultaneous existence of a vibrant collection of operating black newspapers publishing for the Afro-Uruguayan community.[32]

---

[27] Rosario Gabino, "¿Hay Negros en Argentina?" BBC Mundo, March 16, 2007, http://news.bbc.co.uk/hi/spanish/specials/2007/esclavitud/newsid_6455000/6455537.stm.

[28] Andrews, *Afro-Latin America*, pp. 129, 136.

[29] Frank Safford, "Race, Integration, and Progress: Elite Attitudes and the Indian in Colombia, 1750–1870," *Hispanic American Historical Review* 71 (1991), 2.

[30] George Reid Andrews, *Blackness in the White Nation: A History of Afro-Uruguay* (Chapel Hill: University of North Carolina Press, 2010), p. 8.

[31] Ibid. at pp. 40–2.

[32] Ibid. at pp. 3–5.

In fact, those black newspapers are central to the documentation of the Uruguayan state's role in racial segregation after the abolition of slavery. Afro-Uruguayan newspapers reported on the frequency with which public schools did not admit Afro-descended children and the racial exclusion of many state employment positions including law enforcement.[33] Notably, the state failed to intervene to prevent the racial exclusion of Afro-Uruguayans from public facilities such as hotels, theaters, restaurants, dance halls, and cafes.[34] As late at 1956, Afro-Uruguayans recognized their racial context as explicitly segregated and could state that "[s]egregation is what concerns us and what we want to abolish."[35]

In Venezuela after the emancipation of its slaves in 1854, the government and its leading intellectuals became very vocal about expressing their desire for European immigration to effectuate a "transfusion of blood."[36] The preferred immigrants were from Ireland, Germany, the Canary Islands, and later Italy.[37] Government attempts to transport European immigrants were later followed by 1891 legislation that excluded all nonwhites from entering the country.[38] The selective immigration policy was then made part of the Constitution in 1906 with its prohibition of any African-descended immigration.[39] The Venezuelan government was also very overt in its official statements regarding its opposition to black immigration, as exemplified by the following Commerce Department bulletin language:

[J]ust the idea of such a thing, even if it might be a rumor, justifies our alarm. The introduction of individuals of this race, under the

[33] Ibid. at pp. 83–96.
[34] Ibid. at pp. 105, 109.
[35] Ibid. at p. 110 (quoting Suárez Peña, 1956 president of the Afro-Uruguayan organization Asociación Cultural y Social Uruguay).
[36] Winthrop R. Wright, "Race, Nationality, and Immigration in Venezuelan Thought, 1890–1937," *Canadian Review of Studies in Nationalism* 6 (1979), 3.
[37] Raquel Álvarez de Flores, "Evolución Histórica de las Migraciones en Venezuela: Breve Recuento," *Aldea Mundo* 22 (November 2006–April 2007), 90.
[38] Iliana París García, *Ideología y Proceso de Blanqueamiento una Aproximación Construccionista a su Posible Influencia en la Identidad y la Autoimagen de Tres Mujeres Negras Venezolanas* (Caracas: 2002), p. 27.
[39] Winthrop R. Wright, "Café con Leche: A Brief Look at Race Relations in Twentieth Century, Venezuela," *Maryland Historian* (1970), 22.

conditions by which they would come, constitutes a true immigration, and this is not the class of immigrant that Venezuela needs.[40]

Accordingly, even the arrival of Afro-American seamen was viewed as dangerous and shore leave petitions to enter Venezuela were often denied.[41] The Venezuelan legal ban on nonwhite immigration was reaffirmed with the 1936 immigration legislation that also instituted a commission of immigration to function as an intermediary between Venezuelan mining, industrial, and agricultural interests and emigration authorities in various European countries.[42]

Like Venezuela, in 1862 Costa Rica instituted a legal ban on the immigration of persons of African descent (and Chinese descent as well) while attempting to promote European immigration with an 1896 decree authorizing the executive annual funding of European immigration incentive programs.[43] Colombia, Mexico, and Peru would also enact similar legislation with the aim of encouraging white immigration and preventing the immigration of blacks, Asians, and indigenous peoples.[44] In this way, Latin America's racially restrictive immigration laws paralleled the aims of the U.S. Immigration Act of 1924. The U.S. law similarly restricted immigration on the basis of national origin and set quotas that favored immigration from Northern and Western Europe.[45]

Colombia, Peru, and Venezuela actually subsidized European immigrants with travel funds and tax breaks.[46] In the Dominican Republic,

[40] Winthrop R. Wright, "Elitist Attitudes toward Race in Twentieth-Century Venezuela," in Robert Brent Toplin (ed.), *Slavery and Race Relations in Spanish America* (Westport, CT: Greenwood Press, 1974), pp. 325–47.
[41] Ibid. at p. 337.
[42] Wright, "Race, Nationality, and Immigration in Venezuelan Thought," pp. 8–9.
[43] Ronald Soto Quirós, "Desafinidad con La Población Nacional: Discursos y Políticas de Inmigración en Costa Rica," *Istmo*, July 24, 2003, pp. 2, 4.
[44] Moisés González Navarro, "Mestizaje in Mexico during the National Period," in Magnus Mörner (ed.), *Race and Class in Spanish America* (New York: Columbia University Press, 1970), pp. 145–69; Mário C. Vásquez, "Immigration and Mestizaje in Nineteenth-Century Peru," in Mörner (ed.), *Race and Class in Spanish America*, pp. 73–95; Peter Wade, *Blackness and Race Mixture: The Dynamics of Racial Identity in Colombia* (Baltimore: Johns Hopkins University Press, 1993), pp. 11–12, 15.
[45] Immigration Act of 1924, ch. 190, 43 Stat. 153 (1924).
[46] Frederic Martínez, "Apogeo y Decadencia del Ideal de la Inmigración Europea en Colombia, siglo XIX," *Boletín Cultural y Bibliográfico* 34 (1998), 3; Andrews, *Afro-Latin America*, p. 284.

government memos overtly stated that Europeans were the "desired" immigrants.[47] As a result, government labor contracts were made and land was distributed to European immigrants.[48] Furthermore, the Dominican government instructed its first ministers in France, Holland, and Germany to promote immigration to Santo Domingo. In Ecuador, in addition to awarding extensive land grants and funding the cost of travel from Europe, the government passed legislation allowing European settlements a significant degree of autonomy over their own municipal jurisdictions.[49]

Similarly, post independence Cuba sought immigrants from Spain and provided them with subsidies to encourage their migration, along with land grants and tax relief.[50] The campaign for European immigration in Cuba was forcefully carried by leading Cuban intellectuals such as José Antonio Saco who wanted superior "white race" immigrants to settle in Cuba.[51] Cuban essayists of the time urged that white immigration be promoted and that nonwhite immigrants be strictly prohibited. Indeed, one pamphlet entitled "La extinción del negro" (The Extinction of the Negro), projected a "bright future" for Cuba once "the black race will have disappeared from our environment" with the increase of immigration.[52] Nearly 1 million Spaniards went to Cuba after independence, more than in the four centuries of colonial rule by Spain, representing 95 percent of the total number of persons entering the country by the 1920s.[53] As a result, census data from the

---

[47] Kimberly Elson Simmons, *Reconstructing Racial Identity and the African Past in the Dominican Republic* (Gainesville: University of Florida Press, 2009), p. 26.

[48] Harry Hoetink, "The Dominican Republic in the Nineteenth Century: Some Notes on Stratification, Immigration, and Race," in Mörner (ed.), *Race and Class in Spanish America*, pp. 96–121.

[49] Nicola Foote, "Race, State and Nation in Early Twentieth Century Ecuador," *Nations and Nationalism* 12 (2006), 265.

[50] Richard Gott, *Cuba: A New History* (New Haven, CT: Yale University Press, 2005), p. 54.

[51] Gema Rosa Guevara, "Founding Discourse of Cuban Nationalism: La Patria, Blanqueamiento and La Raza de Color," PhD dissertation, U.C. San Diego (2000), p. 50.

[52] Gustavo Enrique Mustelier, *La Extinción del Negro: Apuntes Político-Sociales* (Havana: Imprenta y Papelería de Rambla, Bouza y Cía, 1912).

[53] Marianne Masferrer and Carmelo Mesa-Lago, "The Gradual Integration of the Black in Cuba: Under the Colony, the Republic, and the Revolution," in Toplin (ed.), *Slavery and Race Relations in Spanish America*, pp. 348–84.

period 1899 to 1943 reflect the overrepresentation of blacks in the lowest and worst paid sectors of the economy, such as agriculture and personal services.[54] During this time, Afro-Cubans were also systematically excluded from the academic and electoral processes.[55]

When disaffected Afro-Cubans attempted to form their own political party in 1910 entitled "el Partido Independiente de Color," its leaders were arrested and prosecuted for allegedly conspiring to impose a "Black dictatorship."[56] The Cuban senate then passed legislation known as the Morúa law, prohibiting the formation of political parties along racial lines.[57] When the black group organized a political party to repeal the Morúa law, the government suppression, in what came to be called the "Race War of 1912," was violent, massive, and enmeshed in the *blanqueamiento* national focus.[58] Afro-Cuban protesters demonstrated their frustration with their poor economic status by damaging property, including sugar mills and company stores. Although the protest focused on damaging property and not harming individuals, the Cuban armed forces retaliated by killing Afro-Cubans and Haitian contract workers indiscriminately.[59] One Afro-Cuban scholar recalled:

> I still remember how I listened, wide-eyed and nauseated, to the stories – always whispered, always told as when one is revealing unspeakable secrets – about the horrors committed against my family and other blacks during the racial war of 1912. ... Chills went down my spine when I heard stories about blacks being hunted day and night; and black men being hung by their genitals from the lampposts in the central plazas of small Cuban towns.[60]

[54] Alejandro de la Fuente, *Race and Inequality in Cuba, 1899–1981*," *Journal Contemporary History* 30 (1995), 155.

[55] Helg, "Race in Argentina and Cuba, 1880–1930," p. 53.

[56] Aline Helg, "Race and Black Mobilization in Colonial and Early Independent Cuba: A Comparative Perspective," *Ethnography* 44 (1997), 63.

[57] Luis E. Aguilar, "Cuba, c. 1860–c. 1930," in Leslie Bethell (ed.), *Cuba: A Short History* (Cambridge: Cambridge University Press, 1993), pp. 21, 44.

[58] Aline Helg, *Our Rightful Share: The Afro-Cuban Struggle for Equality, 1886–1912* (Chapel Hill: University of North Carolina Press, 1995), p. 193.

[59] Louis A. Pérez, Jr., "Politics, Peasants, and People of Color: The 1912 'Race War' in Cuba Reconsidered," *Hispanic American History Review* 66 (1986), 537.

[60] Lourdes Casal, "Race Relations in Contemporary Cuba," in Anani Dzidzienyo and Lourdes Casal (eds.) *The Position of Blacks in Brazilian and Cuban Society* (London: Minority Rights Group, 1979), p. 12.

A direct observer has also noted that the army "was cutting off heads, pretty much without discrimination, of all Negroes found outside the town limits."[61] There was also an onslaught of white civilian volunteers, who formed militias and offered their services "to defend the government" against Afro-Cuban political protesters.[62] As such, the Race War of 1912 can be considered a national project of *blanqueamiento*. Indeed, at least one contemporary noted that the massacre had been an attempt by whites to realize their century-long dream of eradicating blacks from Cuba.[63] Thus, the decade after independence found Afro-Cubans in worsened economic conditions and with no improvements in political participation for which they had fought the Spaniards.

Even countries that were less dependent upon slave labor, such as Chile, participated in *blanqueamiento* national projects. Despite the fact that Chile abolished slavery as early as 1823, the government established an immigration agency in Europe in 1882. The agency was directed to promote the promise of land grants to willing immigrants, as facilitated by an 1824 law encouraging European immigrants to establish workshops in urban centers and communities in sparsely populated areas.[64] Many of the immigrants were from Britain, Switzerland, and the German states. Similarly, the Paraguayan government actively sought European immigrants, who were allowed to form their own colonies. For instance, in 1894, 600 settlers from Australia immigrated to Paraguay to establish "the New Australia" colony, and Germans arrived in 1886 to establish "Nueva Germania"/New Germany.[65] Likewise, in Uruguay, the state actively supported European immigration.[66] One source notes that the wave of European immigration started in 1830, and within 100 years more than 1,000,000 Europeans immigrated to the country.[67]

[61] Pérez, Jr., "Politics, Peasants, and People of Color," p. 537.
[62] Helg, *Our Rightful Share*, p. 203.
[63] Lino D'Ou, "El fantasma histriónico," *Labor Nueva*, February 27, 1916.
[64] Richard Gott, "Spanish America as a White Settler Society," *Bulletin of Spanish American Research* 26 (2007), 283, 286.
[65] Gott, "Spanish America as a White Settler Society," p. 287.
[66] Andrews, *Blackness in the White Nation*.
[67] Carlos M. Rama, "The Passing of the Afro-Uruguayans from Caste Society into Class Society," in Mörner (ed.), *Race and Class in Spanish America*, pp. 28–50.

REGIONAL HINDRANCES TO THE *BLANQUEAMIENTO* IMMIGRATION PROJECT

The demographic effects of the whitening project of European immigration in many Spanish American countries were mitigated by a number of factors. European immigrants did not favor Spanish American
destinations that were less developed and poorer than larger nations
like Argentina and Brazil. Most other countries in Spanish America
and the Caribbean lacked the resources to attract large waves of
European immigrants consistently with significant government subsidies and land grants. The involvement in foreign wars also hindered
European immigration. Peru, for example, suffered ten military inva-
sions between 1821 and 1895.[68] During wartime all the proffered
inducements for European immigrants were countered by wartime
fiscal constraints that denied privileges and guarantees to foreigners.[69]

   Moreover, in countries like Costa Rica, Cuba, the Dominican
Republic, Panama, and Venezuela, where dominant U.S. industrial
entities were disdainful of Spanish American aspirations to whiteness
when they clashed with their desire for a readily available low-wage
worker population, a large importation of more readily available West
Indian workers occurred. Thus despite the legal mandates against
nonwhite immigration in Venezuela, the industrial sector annually
imported 6,000–11,000 black Antillean seasonal laborers. The Spanish
American opposition to West Indian immigration manifested itself in
the political arena and even in some national legislation banning black
immigration as existed in Panama. The Panamanian legislation of 1926
also required that workforces of Panamanian enterprises be at least 75
percent native-born rather than foreign-born residents.[70] In Cuba, the
government decreed in 1933 that 50 percent of all employees were to
be native Cubans and not foreign-born residents.[71] In Costa Rica, the
U.S. entrepreneur and miner Cooper Keith, who was contracted in
1871 to construct a railroad system, defied the Costa Rican legal ban

---

[68] Felipe de la Barra, *Invasiones militares de Lima: Desde la Conquista hasta la República*
   (Austin: University of Texas Press, 2008) (digitized 1959 manuscript), pp. 11–19.
[69] Vásquez, "Immigration and Mestizaje in Nineteenth-Century Peru," p. 79.
[70] Andrews, *Afro-Latin America*, p. 140.
[71] Masferrer and Mesa-Lago, "Gradual Integration of the Black in Cuba," p. 362.

on black immigration in order to recruit West Indian workers, who he claimed were "more resistant to the hardships of working in the tropics."[72] But because of the Costa Rican distaste for black immigrants, the government refused to recognize them as citizens or to give them legal rights over the land that they farmed once settled in Costa Rica.[73] In fact, black immigrants in Costa Rica did not receive citizenship rights until as late as 1949.

In the absence of *blanqueamiento* inspired legislation, one national leader went so far as to sanction the outright military slaughter of its residents of African descent, as occurred in 1937 under the dictator Rafael Leónidas Trujillo in the Dominican Republic, in his campaign against Haitian immigrants. After an international inquiry Trujillo was compelled to pay a 1938 reparation settlement of $525,000 to Haiti for the killings. (This was less than $30 for each of the approximately 20,000 victims.)[74] At the same time that Trujillo was expelling and exterminating Haitian immigrants, he also launched a large-scale agricultural colonization program to encourage the migration of European immigrants. As a result, a Jewish enclave was established in Sosúa during the 1930s.

The Spanish American desire for European immigration only waned as the influx of European immigrants in particular countries came to be viewed as the unwelcome harbinger of labor movement demands.[75] Thus, for example, even in Argentina, the site of the most successful Spanish American *blanqueamiento* project, its legislature passed the Law of Residency in 1902, which authorized the expulsion or denial of entry to foreigners who threatened the public order.[76] Under this law any immigrant who participated in a labor union could be deported. Similarly, Argentina's 1910 Law of Social Defense associated immigrants with labor agitation and identified all terrorists as

---

[72] Ronald N. Harpelle, "The Social and Political Integration of West Indians in Costa Rica: 1930–50," *Journal of Spanish American Studies* 25 (February 1993), 104, 111.

[73] Ronald N. Harpelle, "Ethnicity, Religion and Repression: The Denial of African Heritage in Costa Rica," *Canadian Journal of History* 29 (April 1994), 98.

[74] Madison Smartt Bell, "A Hidden Haitian World," *New York Review of Books*, July 17, 2008, 41.

[75] Bletz, "Whiteness of a Darker Color," pp. 91–4, 201.

[76] Ibid. at 95–6, 201.

foreigners. But even as immigrants were being marginalized as threats to elite economic interests, European immigrants who assimilated were integrated into the national picture of Argentineans, in way not offered to Afro-Argentines.[77] Thus, *blanqueamiento* continued to be idealized as the mechanism for understanding racial hierarchy in Argentina and throughout Spanish America.

THE *MESTIZAJE* COMPLEMENT TO *BLANQUEAMIENTO*

Argentina, Chile, Uruguay, and southern Brazil were the few regions that were able to use an influx of European immigration to "whiten" the appearance of their populations significantly and to diminish the proportion of persons of visible African descent. In contrast, other nation-states in Spanish America with their larger proportions of black and indigenous populations more heavily relied upon the discourse of *mestizaje* to maintain white privilege. *Mestizaje* literally refers to the act of miscegenation and to the production of a mixed-race mestizo racial identity but also encompasses the broader discursive practice of preferring a particular racial, gender, and class hierarchy for racial mixture. Central to *mestizaje* is the notion that African ancestry is inferior and needs to be mixed with whiteness in order to be ameliorated. Thus with *mestizaje*, whiteness continues to be the ideal and the presumed locus of power and leadership even in the midst of purported national "celebrations" of racial mixture.[78]

The white supremacist underpinnings of *mestizaje* are made evident when one considers the gender and class specificity regarding the discourse of racial mixture. White elite women are completely precluded from the idealization of racial mixture. Their racial purity and class status are not implicated in *mestizaje*. Indeed, they are meant to continue the production of an elite white class. Instead, it is the intimacy of black women with white men that is the focus of *mestizaje* and its presumed ability to decrease the black presence within

---

[77] Bletz, "Whiteness of a Darker Color," pp. 137–8.
[78] J. L. Salcedo-Bastardo (ed.), *Simón Bolívar, The Hope of the Universe* (Paris: UNESCO, 1983), p. 118.

a nation. And while interracial sexual intimacy was viewed as the pre-
rogative of all white men, only immigrant or working-class white men
were viewed as the appropriate marriage partners of black women.[79]
Nineteenth-century Cuban law reflected this gendered approach to
mestizaje with its prohibition of marriage between white women and
men of color, while permitting marriage between mixed-race women
and white men.[80] *Mestizaje* thus served nineteenth-century Spanish
America's *blanqueamiento* imperative with the second best alternative
of promoting those who were "white, but not quite."[81]

Thus, after their failed attempts to whiten the population directly,
many Spanish American countries took the very racial mixture that
was viewed by nineteenth-century Europeans as emblematic of a backward society and reinterpreted it to be an emblem of national pride.[82]
Chapter 3 will discuss how Brazil also deployed *mestizaje* in the service of promoting a national identity of inclusion while justifying white
racial privilege. Spanish American nations had a ready source of
reference for the promotion of *mestizaje* in the publications of their
well-known intellectuals including the Cuban abolitionist José Saco,[83]
the Cuban independence revolutionary José Martí,[84] Simón Bolívar in
Venezuela,[85] and José Vasconcelos in Mexico.[86] While Saco, Martí, and
Bolívar presented *mestizaje* as a source of national unity in the face
of struggles for independence against Spain, Vasconcelos deployed it
as a defense against the racialized rhetoric of imperialism from the

[79] Gema R. Guevara, "Inexacting Whiteness: Blanqueamiento as a Gender-Specific
    Trope in the Nineteenth Century," *Cuban Studies Journal* 36 (2005), 105–28, 109.
[80] Marilyn Grace Miller, *Rise and Fall of Cosmic Race: The Cult of Mestizaje in Spanish
    America* (Austin: University of Texas Press, 2004), p. 51.
[81] Homi K. Bhabha, "Of Mimicry and Man: The Ambivalence of Colonial Discourse,"
    October 28(1) (Spring 1984), 132.
[82] Alexandra Isfahani-Hammond, "Introduction: Who Were the Masters in the
    Americas?" in Alexandra Isfahani-Hammond (ed.), *The Masters and the Slaves:
    Plantation Relations and Mestizaje in American Imaginaries* (New York: Palgrave
    Macmillan 2004), p. 2.
[83] Graham (ed.), *Idea of Race in Spanish America*, p. 39.
[84] José Martí, Deborah Shnookal (ed.), and Mirta Muñiz (ed.), *José Martí Reader:
    Writings on the Americas* (Melbourne: Ocean Press, 1999), pp. 161–7.
[85] Harold A. Bierck, Jr. (ed.), *Selected Writings of Bolívar*, vol. I, *1800–1822*, Lewis
    Betrand (trans.) (New York: Colonial Press, 1951), p. 110.
[86] José Vasconcelos, *La Raza Cósmica: Misión de la raza Iberoamericana, Notas de Viajes
    a la América del Sur* (Paris: Agencia mundial de librería, 1925).

United States that depicted Latin America as an inferior region of nonwhites.[87] With independence from Spain (obtained between 1810 and 1898), *mestizaje* also served Caribbean and Spanish American governments seeking an inclusive discourse with which to consolidate the nation-state while maintaining a racial hierarchy that would constrain the integration of all the newly emancipated African slaves and their descendants, and the many black soldiers recruited to fight wars of independence in the name of egalitarianism.[88] Thus, for example, in Cuba, José Antonio Saco, the most prominent nineteenth-century Cuban intellectual, in anticipating the challenge to white supremacy that a newly emancipated black citizenry would present, advocated European immigration along with miscegenation between white men and black women because they would provide "the great link by which the African race ascends to mix itself with the white race."[89]

In the Dominican Republic, *mestizaje* operated through a myth of vibrant indigenous ancestry, in order to do the work of not only distancing the country from a black identity, but also distinguishing the country from its black neighbor, Haiti. This was done by elevating the role of the Dominican Republic's indigenous ancestors as the genetic link to brown skin (despite the fact that the vast majority of the indigenous population was killed within fifty years of Columbus's arrival in 1492). The 1882 publication of the novel *Enriquillo* represented the growing national identity with an indigenous past purported to be of more significance than the genetic influence of the large-scale African population.[90] The novel describes an indigenous leader who heads a 1519 insurrection against the Spanish colonizers and garners a peaceful negotiation for a form of self-government in exchange for the return of runaway slaves. As a consequence of the Dominican promotion of indigenous ancestry, *indio* became the preferred term for identifying a

[87] Miller, *Rise and Fall of Cosmic Race*, p. 43.
[88] Peter Blanchard, "The Language of Liberation: Slave Voices in the Wars of Independence," *Hispanic American History Review* 82 (2002), 499–523, 521.
[89] José Antonio Saco, *Colección de Papeles Científicos, Históricos y Políticos Sobre la Isla de Cuba*, vol. 3 (Paris: Impr. de d'Aubusson y Kugelmann, 1858), p. 208; Martínez-Echazábal, "Mestizaje and the Discourse of National/Cultural Identity," p. 29.
[90] Manuel de Jesús Galván, *Enriquillo* (Santo Domingo: G. Hermanos, 1882).

mixed-race person, despite the fact that few if any nineteenth-century Dominicans could trace their origins to actual indigenous ancestors.[91] *Indio* is a purposefully ambiguous term that corresponds to what other Spanish American countries refer to as mulatto but that invokes the invented indigenous past to elide the significance of derided African ancestry.[92] *Indio* became an institutionalized myth during the Trujillo dictatorship (1931–61), when all official documents reified the mythic figure of the *indio*. In fact, Trujillo ordered that history textbooks be rewritten to erase the recognition of Dominican African ancestry.[93]

Yet, unlike the Dominican Republic, some countries in Spanish America had and continue to have a sizable population of indigenous peoples. In those countries in the region with a smaller proportion of blacks and larger numbers of actual indigenous peoples *mestizaje* was also used to center the racial mixture of whites with those of indigenous ancestry in the figure of the mestizo, in ways that simultaneously worked to eviscerate those of African ancestry from the national imaginary. The anthropologist Jean Muteba Rahier, refers to this as the national process of "monocultural mestizaje."[94] For instance, in Mexico the elevation of the indigenous mestizo who assimilated to European cultural mores as the national symbol was done in concert with the denigration of blackness.[95] As noted earlier in this chapter, the key Mexican intellectual figure of *mestizaje*, José Vasconcelos, promoted the idea of a miscegenated "cosmic race" that would allow mestizos of white and indigenous ancestry to modernize the nation while the "lower stock" of blacks would vanish from the population. With the exclusion of blacks from the Mexican conceptualization of *mestizaje*, it is not surprising that in Bobby Vaughn's study of contemporary Afro-Mexican identity, he "found no evidence among Blacks of the dominant Mexican view that indigenous heritage is central to

---

[91] M. Fennema and T. Lowenthal, *La Construcción de raza y nación en la República Dominicana* (Santo Domingo: Editoria Universitaria, 1987), p. 28.

[92] David Howard, *Coloring the Nation: Race and Ethnicity in the Dominican Republic* (Oxford: Signal Books, 2001), p. 41.

[93] Simmons, *Reconstructing Racial Identity*, p. 29.

[94] Rahier, "Soccer and the (Tri-) Color of the Ecuadorian Nation," pp. 148–82.

[95] Ángel Rosenblat, *La Población Indígena y el Mestizaje en América* (Buenos Aires: Editorial Nova, 1954), vol. II, pp. 32–5.

one's heritage."[96] *Mestizaje* similarly operated to marginalize blackness while promoting the assimilation of the indigenous in such countries as Ecuador,[97] Guatemala,[98] and Honduras[99] (with their use of the ambiguous mixed-race term *ladino* to distinguish assimilated nonwhites with social capital from denigrated indigenous peoples and blacks excluded from the national image).

Inasmuch as *mestizaje* racial terms such as "mulatto" or "mestizo" are used to identify those perceived to be racially mixed, the terms can be viewed as tools of *blanqueamiento* to the extent that the numbers of persons of African ancestry are "whitened" with their categorical ascendancy from a "negro" racial classification to a "mulatto or mestizo" racial classification.[100] Thus, the whitening aspects of *mestizaje* are particularly evident in the governmental deployment of census taking and the frequent choice to omit racial data on the census entirely.

THE CENSUS AS AN INSTRUMENT OF *BLANQUEAMIENTO* AND *MESTIZAJE*

Historical analyses that have been done of the census and other demographic data in Argentina for the early part of the nineteenth century persuasively suggest that census enumerators reclassified large segments of the Afro-Argentine population out of the "pure" black

[96] Bobby Vaughn, "Afro-Mexico: Blacks, Indigenas, Politics, and the Great Diaspora," in Anani Dzidzienyo and Suzanne Oboler (eds), *Neither Enemies nor Friends: Latinos, Blacks, Afro-Latinos* (Houndmills: Palgrave Macmillian, 2005), pp. 117–36, 123.

[97] Norman Whitten, Jr., "El Mestizaje: An All Inclusive Ideology of Exclusion," in Norman Whitten, Jr. (ed.), *Cultural Transformation and Ethnicity in Modern Ecuador* (Urbana: University of Illinois Press, 1981), pp. 45–94.

[98] Isabel Rodas Núñez, "Identidades y la Construcción de la Categoría Oficial 'Ladino' en Guatemala," Working Paper No. 29, Centre for Research on Inequality, Human Security and Ethnicity (October 2006), pp. 4–7.

[99] Darío A. Euraque, "The Banana Enclave, Nationalism and Mestizaje in Honduras, 1910s–1930s," in Avi Chomsky and Aldo Lauria (eds), *At the Margins of the Nation-State: Identity and Struggle in the Making of the Laboring Peoples of Central America and the Hispanic Caribbean, 1860–1960* (Durham, NC: Duke University Press, 1998).

[100] Andrew Juan Rosa, "El Que No Tiene Dingo, Tiene Mandingo: The Inadequacy of the 'Mestizo' as a Theoretical Construct in the Field of Spanish American Studies – the Problem and Solution," *Journal of Black Studies* 27(2) (November 1996), 278.

racial category of "moreno" and instead transferred them over to the categories of *pardo* (mixed-race person also known as *mulatto*), and white.[101] Because the rate at which the numbers in the *moreno* category decreased while the numbers in the *pardo* category increased exceeds the biological possibilities for production of mixed-race children, it appears that many *morenos* were simply reclassified as *pardos* over time during an era in which census enumerators selected a respondent's racial category on the basis of a visual inspection rather than the self-classification of the individual.[102] The strategic reclassification of *morenos* into *pardos*, and *pardos* into white, thus served to whiten the statistical representation of the nation. While *negros* and *pardos* together were consistently counted as at least 25 percent of the Argentine population in 1810, 1822, and 1838, by 1887, they were counted as only 1.8 percent of the population.[103] Once the Argentine nation constitutionally committed itself to whitening the country with the influx of European immigration, the census forms discontinued the use of the racially ambiguous category of *pardo*. Instead all persons of any African descent were placed into the "de color" (people of color) category. The year 1887 was the last time that the Argentine census included a racial question in any form until the census of 2010.[104]

Similarly, neighboring Uruguay discontinued including a racial category question on its census after 1852 and only reinstituted the question in 1996.[105] In Colombia, a census racial category question was omitted after 1843, and not reinstituted until 1993.[106] In Costa

[101] Andrews, *The Afro-Argentines of Buenos Aires*, pp. 64–92.
[102] Doreen S. Goyer and Eliane Domschke, *The Handbook of National Population Censuses: Spanish America and the Caribbean, North America, and Oceania* (Westport, CT: Greenwood Press, 1983), pp. 41–9.
[103] "Casi dos millones de argentinos tienen sus raíces en el Africa negra," *Clarín*, June 9, 2006, http://www.clarin.com/diario/2006/06/09/sociedad/s-03801.htm.
[104] Ibid.
[105] Marisa Bucheli and Wanda Cabela, *Encuesta Nacional de Hogares Ampliada 2006: Perfil demográfico y socioeconómico de la población uruguaya según su ascendencia racial* (Montevideo: Instituto Nacional de Estadística, 2006), p. 2, http://www.ine.gub.uy/enha2006/Informe%20final%20raza.pdf.
[106] Yolanda Bodnar, "Colombia: Apuntes sobre la diversidad cultural y la información sociodemográfica disponible en los pueblos indígenas," presentation at "Pueblos indígenas y afrodescendientes de América Latina y el Caribe: relevancia y pertinencia de la información sociodemográfica para políticas y programas," United Nations Economic Commission for Spanish America and the Caribbean, Santiago

Rica, since the inception of the decennial census in 1861, a race-related question has only been included in the census years of 1927, 1950, and most recently in the 2000 census.[107] The contemporary shift toward once again including racial classifications in the census in some Spanish American countries has been the result of lobbying by black social movement organizations and the international organizations that support them. With census racial classifications, socioeconomic data can be aggregated to demonstrate statistically the concrete racial disparities that exist.

Nevertheless, the strategic whitening actions of government sponsored census enumerators have been particularly well documented in the case of Puerto Rico. While Puerto Rico has been a territory of the U.S. government since 1898, its cultural practices and racial politics emanate more directly from the historical Spanish colonial legacy of *blanqueamiento* and *mestizaje*.[108] For this reason its census whitening practices elucidate much about the Latin American operation of *blanqueamiento* and *mestizaje*. The recent release of public use microsamples of the 1910 and 1920 censuses in Puerto Rico made it possible for the first time to document empirically the role of the census in statistically whitening the population. The analysis of the data indicates that the dramatic increase by 7.5 percentage points in the white population from 1910 to 1920 (an increase more than twice that of any other single decade in the twentieth century) could not have been solely attributable to natural increase factors like fertility and migration. Instead, demographers have shown that the whitening of the Puerto Rican

de Chile (April 2005), p. 14, http://www.eclac.cl/mujer/noticias/noticias/5/27905/ YBodnar.pdf.

[107] Donald Allen, "La Experiencia de Costa Rica," presentation at "Todos Contamos: Los Grupos Étnicos en los Censos," Interamerican Development Bank, Cartagena de Indias, Colombia (November 2000); Susana Schkolink and Fabiana del Popolo, "Los censos y los pueblos indígenas en América Latina: Una metodología Regional," presentation at "Pueblos indígenas y afrodescendientes de América Latina y el Caribe: relevancia y pertinencia de la información sociodemográfica para políticas y programas," United Nations Economic Commission for Spanish America and the Caribbean, Santiago de Chile (April 2005), p. 12, http://www.eclac.cl/celade/ noticias/paginas/7/21237/FdelPopolo-SScholnick.pdf.

[108] Arlene Torres, "La Gran Familia Puertorriqueña 'Ej Preta de Beldá,'" in Arlene Torres and Norman E. Whitten, Jr. (eds), *Blackness in Spanish America and the Caribbean* (Bloomington: Indiana University Press, 1998), vol. II, pp. 285–306.

population was almost entirely due to racial reclassification by census enumerators across censuses.

> Thus, if miscegenation was the principal source of Puerto Rico's whitening in this period, we would expect the census results from 1920 to show a decline in the proportion of the population classified as black, coupled with an increase in the proportion of the population classified as mulatto. Instead, we see a decline in both the mulatto and black shares of the population, alongside the dramatic increase in the proportion of whites.[109]

With a cultural shift in how whiteness was socially defined, census enumerators were 60 percent more likely to classify a child of nominally interracial parents as white in 1920 than in 1910 despite the fact that the mixed-race category of *mulato* was still an official designation on the census. After the 1920 census, each census thereafter continued the whitening trajectory until racial classifications were discontinued in 1952 (and only reinstated with the 2000 census).

The U.S. control over Puerto Rico after the Spanish American War in 1898 ironically provides a clearer demonstration of the Spanish American/Caribbean operation of *blanqueamiento*. While the U.S. Census Bureau has organized the enumeration of the Puerto Rican census since 1899, the U.S. government preference for precision regarding racial categories had been subverted by the implementation of native Puerto Rican enumerators. Because it was only with the 2000 census that respondents were asked to self-classify their racial identity, the role of the census enumerator in racially classifying the Puerto Rican population has been significant. Historically, the U.S. Census Bureau assigned a North American agent to direct the Puerto Rico enumeration and the post hoc editing of the census returns for "racial accuracy." Special agents were selected among Puerto Rico's "better classes" to aid in the post hoc editing process.[110] In 1920, the

---

[109] Mara Loveman and Jerónimo O. Muñiz, "How Puerto Rico Became White: Boundary Dymanics and Intercensus Racial Reclassification," *American Sociological Review* 72 (December 2007), 915–39.

[110] D. A. Skinner, *Porto Rico: Report from Supervisor of the Census for the District of Porto Rico, to the Hon. E. Dana Durand, Director of the Census* (Washington, DC: United States Census Bureau, July 26, 1910).

overwhelming majority (88% of the 16,965 forms) of post hoc edits reclassified individuals as *mulatos* primarily from the white category (13,225), with much fewer from the black category (1,665).[111] In short, the U.S. controlled post hoc editing process with its more strict enforcement of the boundaries of whiteness highlights the manner in which the unedited forms reflected the operation of Puerto Rican *blanqueamiento*. In other words, Puerto Rican enumerators responded to the Puerto Rican *blanqueamiento* and *mestizaje* ideology shared with Spanish America by increasingly classifying lighter-skinned mixed-race Puerto Ricans as white across censuses. Indeed, the U.S. Census Bureau itself directly conceded the role of *blanqueamiento* when it reported in 1938 that the decline in the nonwhite share of the Puerto Rican population "was without doubt the result of the gradual change in the concept of the race classifications as applied by census enumerators" in Puerto Rico.[112] Thereafter, as Puerto Rico gained additional features of self-rule, the local government success-fully lobbied to have the race question eliminated from the census with the justification that the Puerto Rican racial mixture made such a question unimportant. Just as the rest of Spanish America resisted the implications of racial inferiority asserted by nineteenth-century eugenics, Puerto Rico turned to *blanqueamiento* and *mestizaje* as tropes of modernization and regional unity in the aftermath of the 1898 Spanish American War control by the United States and the 1917 allocation of U.S. citizenship to Puerto Ricans on the island.[113] In 2000, the census reinstated the race question and found that at 80.5 percent, the proportion of self-identified whites exceeded that of the United States by 5.4 percent, in ways that strongly suggested the continuing salience of *blanqueamiento* and *mestizaje*.[114] For the 2010 census, Puerto Rican respondents continued to select the single

[111] Loveman and Muñiz, "How Puerto Rico Became White," 923 (2,075 of the 1910 edited forms had original classifications that were illegible).
[112] *Censo de Puerto Rico: 1935 Población y Agricultura* (Washington: Adminstración de Reconstrucción de Puerto Rico, 1938), p. 17.
[113] Torres, "La Gran Familia Puertorriqueña 'Ej Preita de Beldá,'" pp. 285–306.
[114] Isar Godreau, Hilda Lloréns, and Carlos Vargas-Ramos, "Employing Incongruence at Work: Employing U.S. Census Racial Categories in Puerto Rico," *Anthropology News* (May 2010), 11–12.

white category disproportionately at 75.1 percent (with only 3.2% selecting more than one racial category, 7.8% selecting "some other race," and 12.3% selecting black).

While Puerto Rico was certainly extreme in its articulation of *blanqueamiento* through the census, other Spanish American and Caribbean nations also used the census for the operation of their racial ideologies. For instance, the widespread choice to omit racial data from the census is the predominant way in which the census is strategically used to promote *blanqueamiento* and particularly *mestizaje*. It is important to note that even while many Spanish American countries were omitting questions about race or color on the census, they often included questions about indigenous ancestry, as was the case in Chile,[115] Mexico,[116] Panama,[117] and Venezuela.[118] Thus, the removal of racial data from census forms cannot be viewed as simply a national belief in color blindness, but rather a strategic avoidance of acknowledging the national presence of blackness. This is particularly evident in the case of Guatemala, where as late as 1940, the decennial census included a black ("Negro") racial classification. Yet when in 1950, Guatemala omitted the black racial classification, it retained the census ethnic categories of indigenous or nonindigenous ("Indígena o no Indígena/Ladino"), thereby deleting any statistical recognition of the Afro-Guatemalan population.[119] In fact, one historical study persuasively suggests that the paper trail disappearance of the Afro-Guatemalan population began in the colonial era, when large

---

[115] Marylee Mason Mandiver, "Racial Classifications in Spanish American Censuses," *Social Forces* 28 (December 1949), 138–46, 141.

[116] Kif Augustine-Adams, "Making Mexico: Legal Nationality, Chinese Race, and the 1930 Population Census," *Law and History Review* 27 (2009), 113–44; Woodrow Borah, "Race and Class in Mexico," *Pacific Historical Review* 23 (1954), 331–42; Goyer and Domschke, *Handbook of National Population Censuses*, p. 246.

[117] Deyanira Avilés Bósquez, "Los Grupos Étnicos en los Censos: Experiencia de Panamá," presentation at "Todos Contamos: Los Grupos Etnicos en los Censos," Cartagena de Indias, Colombia, Nov. 2000 (on file with the Interamerican Development Bank, Washington, DC).

[118] Mandiver, "Racial Classifications in Spanish American Censuses," p. 145.

[119] Marco Antonio I. Aguirre, "Los Grupos Étnicos en los Censos de Guatemala," presentation at "Todos Contamos: Los Grupos Étnicos en los Censos," Cartagena de Indias, Colombia (November 2000) (on file with the Interamerican Development Bank, Washington, DC).

numbers of African-descended Guatemalan mulattos were counted as mestizos of indigenous ancestry or whites in the census.[120]

Mexico also provides an interesting case of a country in which with its independence from Spain in 1821, it legislated the prohibition of the classification of persons by race in all official government documents. The Mexican Sovereign Constituent Congress enacted the Plan de Iguala prohibiting the classification of persons by race in official government documents.[121] Yet this legal prohibition had no influence on the various government entities that continued to differentiate the Mexican population according to race[122] and viewed the indigenous population as more intelligent than those of African descent. As Countess Paula Kolonitz, a member of the Mexican political elite in 1864, stated: "Los indios son mucho más inteligentes que los negros y su carácter tiene un fondo más noble." [The Indians are much more intelligent than the Negroes and their character is more deeply noble.][123]

Indeed, even the national census enumeration of the population that immediately followed the Mexican Revolution (1910–20) contained racial classifications of pure indigenous, indigenous mixed with white, and white ("indígena pura, mezclada con blanca, blanca") for the 1921 census.[124] Only the black/*negro* category was omitted. Racial classification still mattered, but blackness was viewed as no longer salient to the national identity of the country. Nevertheless, some state governments conducting their own census enumeration continued to include racial classifications, such as the 1890 Oaxaca census inclusion of Indians, blacks, mestizos, and whites ("indios, negros, mestizos y blancos").[125] In the Oaxacan state census of 1890, Afro-Mexicans

[120] Christopher H. Lutz, *Santiago de Guatemala 1541–1773: City, Caste, and the Colonial Experience* (Norman: University of Oklahoma Press, 1994).

[121] Moisés González Navarro, "Mestizaje in Mexico during the National Period," pp. 145–69.

[122] Taunya Lovell Banks, "Mestizaje and the Mexican Mestizo Self: No Hay Sangre Negra, So There Is No Blackness," *Southern California Interdisciplinary Law Journal* 15 (2006), 199–234.

[123] Ethel Correa, "Indios, Mestizos, Negros y Blancos en un municipio de la Costa Chica, Oaxaca a través de un censo de 1890," *Suplemento del Boletin Diario de Campo* (March–April 2007), 80–95.

[124] Augustine-Adams, "Making Mexico," p. 124.

[125] Correa, "Indios, Mestizos, Negros y Blancos," p. 95.

below the age of fifteen were counted as 20 percent of the population. It is highly improbable that this entire 20 percent of the youthful population of Oaxaca was extinguished in the thirty-one years that elapsed before the 1921 census. In other words, Afro-Mexicans were still present in the population despite the national disinclination for including them in the count of the population.

The removal of racial data collection from the decennial census forms in Spanish America was often accompanied by a strong government rhetoric of *mestizaje*. For example, when the Mexican government definitively omitted all official racial classifications on the national census of 1930 it did so with much public fanfare (while still including the indigenous proxy inquiry into language spoken and continuing in the 1940–70 census years to enumerate the indigenous with an inquiry into language spoken). The National Statistics Department of Mexico stated that census racial classifications were no longer necessary by 1930, because the population was now racially mixed and social stratification was a matter of economic class rather than racial identity.[126] What is also particularly noteworthy is the manner in which the Mexican government overtly promoted the census as a vehicle for creating the nation. The posters that were disseminated by the census bureau in preparation for the 1930 census boldly stated, "Take the census; make the country. Let's do both together," along with "Taking a census will make the country."[127] With those words, the Mexican census bureau ironically represented the Spanish American aspiration for having the census enumeration create a modern nation through its reflection of an idealized national citizen distanced from blackness.

In short, after the emancipation of slaves, Spanish America as a region sought to whiten its population as a vehicle of modernization. Some countries, such as Argentina, were successful in their use of immigration laws and government subsidies to actually whiten the population with the influx of European immigration. Other Spanish American countries less successful in whitening their populations through the vehicle of European immigration more heavily relied upon the strategic presentation of government census data to veil

---

[126] Augustine-Adams, "Making Mexico," p. 125.
[127] Ibid. at p. 114.

the demographic presence of African-descended populations. These efforts were also coupled with various national promotions of *mestizaje*. In effect, the written immigration laws and the unwritten laws for census enumeration practices and *mestizaje* national identity campaigns, all sought to marginalize and constrain the fully realized citizenship of Afro-descendants. Like Jim Crow segregation laws in the United States, Spanish American *blanqueamiento* and *mestizaje* campaigns similarly "kept Negroes in their place" in the absence of slavery.[128]

This Spanish American history of the racialized use of legislated law in the immigration context disrupts the racial innocence narrative that has long obstructed contemporary racial equality efforts. Similarly, the involved role of the state in its census politics of whitening can be viewed as a related customary law of race regulation. To the extent that the state had an entrenched unwritten customary practice of deploying the census to whiten its population counts and thereby marginalize its Afro-descendant citizenry, the state's policies also coalesced into a customary law of race regulation. Yet Brazil stands out as a jurisdiction where the development of a customary law of race regulation was more extensive and more documented than in the rest of Latin America. For this reason, the Brazilian customary law of race regulation warrants closer examination in the next chapter.

---

[128] Donald Hugh Smith, "Civil Rights: A Problem in Communication," *Phylon* 27 (1966), 379–87, 380.

3 BRAZILIAN "JIM CROW": THE IMMIGRATION LAW WHITENING PROJECT AND THE CUSTOMARY LAW OF RACIAL SEGREGATION – A CASE STUDY

Brazil was the last country in the Americas to emancipate its slaves, in 1888. Yet, with the abolition of slavery, Brazil shared a Latin American disinterest in fully integrating or according substantive citizenship rights to its black occupants. This was a deeply troubling issue for Brazilian elites given the significant numbers of slaves who had been imported into the nation. Indeed, more than 90 percent of the approximately 10 million enslaved Africans taken to the Americas were brought to Latin America and the Caribbean, whereas only 4.6 percent were taken to the United States.[1] One historian estimates the total number of African slaves imported into Brazil as 3.6 million.[2] In contrast, U.S. historians estimate that only 500,000 African slaves were imported into the United States and British North America.[3] Brazil's response to the fear of a newly freed black population was like the rest of Latin America's – an attempt to whiten its population.

In Brazil, the whitening philosophy was called *branqueamento* and directly paralleled Spanish America's whitening philosophy of *blanqueamiento*. Like *blanqueamiento* in Spanish America, *branqueamento* in Brazil was both an ideology and a set of practices for whitening the Brazilian population and presumably modernizing the nation. The efforts to whiten the population were so extensive across the region

[1] S. W. Mintz, *Caribbean Transformations* (Chicago: Aldine, 1974).
[2] Carlos Augusto Taunay, *Manual do Agricultor Brasileiro* (São Paulo: Companhia das Letras, 2001).
[3] Hugh Thomas, *The Slave Trade: The Story of the Atlantic Slave Trade: 1440–1870* (New York: Simon & Schuster, 1997), p. 500.

that one scholar describes Latin America as having a "white settler culture" that continues to exert influence today in the opposition to the recognition and fuller inclusion of nonwhites.[4] But Brazil stands out among Latin American countries as the nation with the most extensive legislative network of racial restrictions to regulate race after the abolition of slavery and thus serves as a useful case study for providing greater detail about the development of the customary law of race regulation.

THE LEGAL ENACTMENT OF RACIAL REGULATION – IMMIGRATION LAW

The first step in the national whitening campaign was legislating restrictive immigration laws designed, first, to encourage European immigration and, second, to prohibit or severely discourage the immigration of peoples of African, Asian, and Indigenous ancestry. As early as the 1850s, with the growing international pressure to disengage from the slave trade and abolish slavery completely, the legislature took decisive steps to encourage European immigration.[5] A statute passed that year provided generous land grants to immigrants designed to encourage more European immigration.[6] The same statute also denied land title to residents of *quilombos*, land that had been occupied by the descendants of runaway slaves for generations. The provincial government of São Paulo then heavily funded the Society for the Promotion of Immigration.[7]

After the final emancipation of slaves in 1888, and the dissolution of the Brazilian Empire in 1889, the legal preference for white immigrants

[4] Richard Gott, "Latin America as a White Settler Society," *Bulletin of Latin American Research* 26 (2007), 269–89, 287.
[5] Kim D. Butler, *Freedoms Given, Freedoms Won: Afro-Brazilians in Post-Abolition São Paulo and Salvador* (New Brunswick, NJ: Rutgers University Press, 1998), pp. 26–7.
[6] Eunice Aparecida de Jesus Prudente, *Preconceito Racial e Igualdade Jurídica No Brasil* (Campinas: Julex Livros, 1989), pp. 129–31.
[7] Thomas P. Holloway, "Immigration and Abolition: The Transition from Slave to Free Labor in the São Paulo Coffee Zone," in Dauril Alden and Warren Dean (eds.), *Essays Concerning the Socioeconomic History of Brazil and Portuguese India* (Gainesville: University Press of Florida, 1977), p. 163.

would become more overt because of the distaste Brazilian elites had for the vision of African-descended peoples as paid laborers.[8] Indeed, in official gatherings of the planter class anticipating the end of slavery, meeting minutes recorded the preference for white immigrants over the "indolence" of the native population then laboring in servitude as a "decrepit race."[9] Understanding the preference for European immigrants as racially motivated is especially clear when one observes that the Europeans who were recruited were not skilled laborers, and many were illiterate rural dwellers.[10] Moreover, during the postemancipation period when European immigrants were being sought, the wage labor positions available were for low-skilled laborers without education or professional training that could have been easily filled by the newly emancipated Brazilians had they not been viewed as racially "unfit" for wage labor.[11] Indeed, newspaper classified advertisements explicitly stated, "Whites preferred."[12] These racialized attitudes about the ability to work as wage labor were then reflected in regional legislative assemblies, such as that of São Paulo in 1888, where the desirability of white foreign workers was discussed along with the proposal to provide land grants to encourage their immigration.[13]

Accordingly, one of the first enactments of the new republic was Immigration Decree No. 528 promulgated on June 28, 1890, by the provisional president, Manoel Deodoro da Foneseca.[14] His decree excluded all members of the indigenous populations of Asia and Africa from immigrating to Brazil. This was at a time when overall immigration was at its height and immigrants from other continents like Europe

---

[8] Cecilia Maria Marinho de Azevedo, *Onda Negra, Medo Branco: O Negro No Imaginário Das Elites Século XIX* (São Paulo: AnnaBlume, 1987), p. 252.

[9] *Congresso Agrícola do Rio de Janeiro* (Rio de Janeiro: Tipografia Nacional, 1878), pp. 155–9.

[10] Petrônio Domingues, *Uma História Não Contada: Negro, racismo, e branqueamento em São Paulo pós-abolição* (São Paulo: Editora Paz e Terra, 2004), pp. 89–91.

[11] Lúcio Kowarick, *Trabalho e Vadiagem: A Origem Do Trabalho Livre No Brasil* (São Paulo: Editora Paz e Terra, 1987), p. 118.

[12] Domingues, *Uma História Não Contada*, pp. 109–10.

[13] Relatório apresentado à Assembléia Legislativa Provincial de São Paulo pelo presidente da Província Exmo. Sr. Dr. Francisco de Paula Rodrigues Alves, no dia 10 de janeiro de 1888 (São Paulo: Tipografia a vapor de Jorge Seckler & Comp., 1888), p. 32.

[14] Prudente, *Preconceito Racial*, pp. 151–2.

were allowed entry without a fee. In 1921, the Brazilian Congress passed a similar law, which specifically prohibited black immigrants from entering Brazil.[15] When blacks sought to do so, they were simply denied visas.[16] This preceded the U.S. National Origins Quota Immigration Act of 1924, which explicitly based U.S. immigration on racial and ethnic origin. However, one of the decree provisions was relaxed two years later, when a statute passed in October 1892 permitted the entry of Chinese and Japanese immigrants.[17] Large waves of immigration in Brazil coincided with the abolition of slavery in 1888, making European immigration a national policy by the late nineteenth century with migrant numbers only exceeded by Argentina.[18] In fact, in 1889 Brazil enacted a law to grant automatic naturalization to the immigrants who migrated from Europe.[19]

Furthermore, the government expended funds to encourage European immigration with the payment of transportation costs. European transportation costs to Brazil were paid by the Brazilian national government from 1851 to 1909 and then by the São Paulo province (and later state) from 1881 to 1927.[20] São Paulo administrative law also provided for state funded housing where food and hospital care would be supplied,[21] along with a cash grant that varied by the age of the European immigrant.[22] São Paulo state funded immigration expenditures also included proimmigration lobbying in European countries, farming tools, and the waiver of military service for the children of immigrants.[23] In 1888, just months before the final emancipation of the slaves, the São Paulo Provincial Assembly authorized

---

[15] Decree No. 4247, art. 5, de 6 janeiro 1921, Diario Oficial Da União [D.O.U.] (Bra.).

[16] Teresa A. Meade, *"Civilizing" Rio: Reform and Resistance in a Brazilian City, 1889–1930* (University Park: Penn State University Press, 1996), p. 31.

[17] Prudente, *Preconceito Racial*, pp. 153–4.

[18] Mary Elizabeth Bletz, "Whiteness of a Darker Color: Narratives of Immigration and Culturation in Brazil and Argentina, 1890–1930," PhD dissertation, New York University (2003), pp. 22–3, 30.

[19] Ibid. at pp. 157–8.

[20] Regulamento para o Serviço de Imigração da Província de São Paulo (São Paulo: Tipografia do Correio Paulistano, 1887), art. 17, p. 7.

[21] Ibid.

[22] Ibid.

[23] Domingues, *Uma História Não Contada*, p. 69.

the government to allocate this plethora of immigration subsidies to a minimum of 100,000 immigrants.[24] The dedication of governmental funds to the whitening project of European immigration was so significant that by 1895 immigration subsidies took up 14.5 percent of São Paulo's annual budget, 10 percent of its 1896 budget, and 10.8 percent of its 1901 budget.[25]

While the floodgates were opened for European immigrants, the continued ban on immigrants from the continent of Africa was broadly interpreted so as to exclude U.S. tourists of African descent who had never set foot in Africa let alone had citizenship status in a country on the African continent. Furthermore, the Brazilian government continued to exclude U.S. citizens of African descent despite its flagrant breach of the 1828 Peace, Friendship, Trade, and Navigation Agreement between Brazil and the United States. This treaty stated that "the citizens and subjects of both countries may travel throughout the other, with right to reside and do business. ... There will be a perfect, fixed, and inviolable peace and friendship between [the United States and Brazil] in all their possessions and territories ... without distinction of people and places."[26]

The racial restriction on Brazilian immigration law continued with the government of Getúlio Vargas (1930–45). In 1934, his new constitution would effectively limit immigration to whites.[27] This was done by capping the annual number of immigrants to 2 percent of those of each national origin who had arrived in Brazil within the last fifty years. Because Africans were not allowed to immigrate to Brazil in the prior fifty years, the 2 percent annual quota effectively prohibited all African immigration without ever having to be racially specific in its terminology.[28] The Brazilian Constitution also went on effectively to prohibit settlements by blacks or Asians regardless of their country

[24] Telésforo de Sousa Lobo, *São Paulo na Federação: problemas sociais, questões racias, política imigrantista e estudos econômicos* (São Paulo: s/ed., 1924), p. 219.

[25] *Boletim da Diretoria de Terras, Colonização e Imigração*, no. 1, São Paulo, 1941, pp. 6–22.

[26] Jeffrey Lesser, "Immigration and Shifting Concepts of National Identity in Brazil during the Vargas Era," *Luso-Brazilian Review* 31 (Winter 1994), 23–44.

[27] Prudente, *Preconceito Racial*, pp. 155–6.

[28] Constituição da República Dos Estados Unidos do Brasil de 16 julho de 1934, art. 121, para. 6.

of origin, by forbidding a concentration of immigrants anywhere in the country that would conflict with the law to regulate the selection of immigrants and their assimilation.[29] This measure was presumably designed to curtail their immigration from other Latin American nations.[30] Provisions in the Brazilian Constitution designed to allow the government to prevent nonwhite immigrants from entering the country were reenacted in the 1946 Constitution and in a 1969 decree by the military government.[31]

The *branqueamento* immigration project was so successful that in less than a century of subsidized European immigration, Brazil imported more free white labor than black slaves imported in three centuries of the slave trade (4,793,981 immigrants arrived from 1851 to 1937 as compared with the 3.6 million slaves forcibly imported).[32] In São Paulo, where European immigration was the most intense, the population of African descent (*mulato* and *negro* counted together) decreased from 47 percent in 1811 and 1836 to 16 percent by 1928.[33]

With the overt racialization of the immigration policy, Brazilian legislators and elite stakeholders were quite explicit about the desire to use immigration to eradicate blacks. Like Spanish America's *blanqueamiento* projects, Brazilian white immigration was rooted in eugenics discourse that reinforced preexisting Brazilian beliefs about the inferiority of Africans and their eventual extinction.[34] For instance, in 1879, the parliament member Joaquim Nabuco stated, "As the black man and the white live together in the same society for hundreds of years, the former's blood will tend to be absorbed into that of the latter, or it will disappear altogether as the one race gives up the field to the other, better prepared for the struggle of life."[35]

[29] Ibid. at para. 7.
[30] Prudente, *Preconceito Racial*, pp. 155–6.
[31] Constituição da República Dos Estados Unidos do Brasil de 18 septembre de 1946, art. 162.
[32] Sales Augusto dos Santos and Laurence Hallewell, "Historical Roots of the 'Whitening' of Brazil," *Latin American Perspectives* 29 (January 2002), 70.
[33] Samuel Lowrie, "O elemento negro na população de São Paulo," *Revista do Arquivo Municipal* 48 (June 1938), 12.
[34] Dos Santos, "Historical Roots of the 'Whitening' of Brazil," p. 75.
[35] Joaquim Nabuco, *Discursos Parlamentares* (Brasília: Câmara dos Deputados, Centro de Documentação e Informação, Coordenação de Publicações, 1983), p. 182.

As the numbers of European immigrants increased, so did the public intellectual support for eugenics. In 1912, the intellectual elite João Batista Lacerda, who was a presenter at the 1911 First Universal Racial Conference, predicted that by 2012, the Brazilian population would be 80 percent white, 3 percent *mestiço* (mixed), and 17 percent Indian, and there would be no blacks.[36] Lacerda's prediction was seemingly supported by an official analysis of Brazilian census taking. Despite the fact that a race/color question was omitted from both the 1900 census and the 1920 census, the prominent social theorist Oliveira Vianna authored an official census publication in 1920 declaring that there had already been a rapid decrease of the "inferior blood coefficient" in the Brazilian gene pool.[37] Thereafter, the census and other governmental collections of statistical data would be the sites for whitening the national image. The symbolic whitening of the population was facilitated by Minister of Finance Rui Barbosa's December 14, 1890, decree ordering the destruction of all Ministry of Finance documents pertaining to slavery (ownership papers, ship logs, religious documents).[38] The National Congress endorsed the Barbosa decree on December 20, 1890. As an abolitionist, Minister Barbosa wanted to remove the "black stain" of Brazil's slave owning past.[39] Yet the decree simultaneously obstructed the ability to trace the African origins of many "white" Brazilians.

Given this highly racialized construction of immigration law and policy, how does one then explain the massive number of Japanese immigrants who immigrated to Brazil starting in 1908? Indeed, nearly a quarter of a million Japanese settled in Brazil in the sixty-year period of 1908–68.[40] The population stands as the largest settlement of

---

[36] Thomas Skidmore, *Black into White: Race and Nationality in Brazilian Thought* (New York: Oxford University Press, 1974), p. 67.

[37] Oliveira Vianna, *O Povo Brasileiro e Sua Evolução do Brasil 1920* (Rio de Janeiro, 1922).

[38] Americo Jacobina Lacombe, Francisco de Assis Barbosa, and Eduardo da Silva, *Rui Barbosa E a Queima Dos Arquivos* (Rio de Janeiro: Fundação Casa de Rui Barbosa, 1988).

[39] Ministro Rui Barbosa, Circular No. 29, 14 de maio 1891 (Brazil).

[40] Tomoko Makabe, "Ethnic Hegemony: The Japanese Brazilians in Agriculture, 1908–1968," *Ethnic and Racial Studies* 22 (July 1999), 702–23.

Japanese outside Japan except for Manchuria.[41] With their settlement
primarily in the São Paulo area, their presence was clearly noticeable
yet did not accord nicely with the prevailing eugenics discourse. How
did this population shift nonetheless occur?

The concurrence of the coffee-plantation economic demand for
low-wage labor and the Japanese socioeconomic crisis of the 1920s,
along with the 1907 U.S. ban on admitting Japanese immigrants, all
influenced the migration of massive numbers of Japanese immigrants.[42]
With the 1917 exclusion of the Japanese from migrating to the United
States, the Japanese government sought alternative destinations for its
agricultural workers, such as Argentina, Peru, and Mexico, in addition
to Brazil.[43] The Japanese government paid for their transport and other
expenses to Brazil, in addition to arranging for plantation employment
and housing of entire family units. Brazilian regulations required that
at least three able-bodied farmworkers in a family migrate together to
ensure immediate dedication to agricultural production.[44]

The coffee-plantation economic interest in Japanese agricultural
labor was so great that some characterized the migrants as culturally
white in their superiority to "native" Afro-Brazilians. For instance in
1925, the congressional representative Oliveira Botelho stated:

> The Turks and Syrians of white skin and good physical appearance,
> immigrants of their own accord, concern themselves only with
> business and do not venture outside the cities. Agriculture clamors
> for strong arms and will not ever forgive us if, on futile pretexts, we
> impede its development. ... [I]f the thirty million Brazilians pro-
> duced the same proportion as the thirty thousand Japanese work-
> ing here, Brazil would be the richest country in the world.[45]

Indeed, even with Vargas's 1934 constitutional limitations on the immigration of nonwhites, one federal deputy asserted that "the Japanese
colonists are even whiter than the Portuguese [with their contribution to

[41] Daniel M. Masterson and Sayaka Funada-Classen, *The Japanese in Latin America*
   (Urbana: University of Illinois Press, 2004), p. 73.
[42] 1907 Gentlemen's Agreement; Immigration Act of 1917, ch. 29, 39 Stat. 874 (1917);
   Immigration Act of 1924, ch. 190, 43 Stat. 153 (1924).
[43] Masterson and Funada-Classen, *Japanese in Latin America*, p. 5.
[44] Makabe, "Ethnic Hegemony," p. 721 n. 4.
[45] Butler, *Freedoms Given, Freedoms Won*, p. 37.

the whiteness of economic growth and domestic production]."[46] Such perspectives were aided by the Japanese immigrants' own investment in the media promotion of their whiteness. Newspapers, magazines, and books regularly published photographs of "Brazilian-looking" children who were the children of Japanese and white Brazilian parents.[47] Such photographs seemed to suggest that the Japanese were ideal candidates for a *mestiçagem*/racial mixture that could more immediately result in whiteness. The Japanese were not literally viewed as white, but the landowners who supported their entry certainly considered them superior to Afro-Brazilian laborers.[48]

To be sure, during the World War II period, the voices of those who had previously objected to the nonwhite immigration of the Japanese were accorded greater public space. Nevertheless, Brazil did not implement a mass evacuation or resettlement of its Japanese residents, as did the United States during the war. Japanese Brazilians were permitted to continue their occupational activities and businesses without disruption, because by that time much of the nation relied upon their agricultural production.[49] Rather than communitywide internment, an official campaign was launched to "Brazilianize" the Japanese residents. Foreign language schools and newspapers were banned, laws forbade the use of the Japanese language in public places, and Japanese first names were required to be Christianized.[50] In short, while a complex array of circumstances account for the large-scale migration of the Japanese to Brazil, their presence never undermined the national valorization of whiteness. By 1975, a major Brazilian bank launched an advertisement campaign with the caption "We need more Brazilians

[46] Jeffrey Lesser, "Negotiating National Identity: Middle Eastern and Asian Immigrants and the Struggle for Ethnicity in Brazil," Working Paper No. 8, Center for Comparative Immigration Studies Working Papers University of California, San Diego (April 2000), pp. 1–12.

[47] Jeffrey Lesser, *Negotiating National Identity: Immigrants, Minorities, and the Struggle for Ethnicity in Brazil* (Durham, NC: Duke University Press, 1999), p. 105.

[48] Lesser, "Immigration and Shifting Concepts of National Identity in Brazil during the Vargas Era," pp. 23–44.

[49] Makabe, "Ethnic Hegemony," p. 709.

[50] John P. Augelli, "Cultural and Economic Changes of Bastos, a Japanese Colony on Brazil's Paulista Frontier," *Annals of the Association of American Geographers* 48 (March 1958), 3–19.

like this Japanese."[51] The advertisement was well received and thus
continued to run for more than twenty-five years.

SEGREGATION OF THE LABOR MARKET

While blacks were not completely eradicated from the entire Brazilian
population, the *branqueamento* immigration policy was successful to the extent that newly freed slaves and their descendants were
purposely displaced from the labor market by the importation of
European immigrants. No support or social guarantees of any kind
were provided to former slaves to help them enter the free labor system after their release. While it is true that the northeastern state
of Bahia did enact a color-blind distributive land law in 1897 that
could theoretically enable postabolition Afro-Brazilians and others
to garner legal title to small parcels of farmland, freed slaves encountered many obstacles that hindered their ability to obtain such titles
in great numbers.[52]

Furthermore, Afro-Brazilians were systematically excluded from
the labor market. For instance, the postemancipation naval services
were well known for excluding Afro-Brazilians from the rank of officer
to such an extent that the popular press commonly referred to whiteness as a prerequisite. The newspapers of 1910–23 are replete with
accounts of the military service preference for candidates who were
"as white as possible."[53]

Similarly, in a 1928 São Paulo legislative session discussing the
eventual 1928 enactment of a law to lift the prohibition against the
entry of Afro-Brazilians to the local police force, it was noted that
Afro-Brazilians were prohibited from employment as prison guards and

[51] Lesser, "Negotiating National Identity," p. 11.
[52] Mary Ann Mahony, "Afro-Brazilians, Land Reform, and the Question of Social
Mobility in Southern Bahia, 1880–1920," in Hendrik Kraay (ed.), *Afro-Brazilian
Culture and Politics: Bahia, 1790's to 1990's* (Armonk, NY: M. E. Sharpe, 1998),
pp. 90–116.
[53] Álvaro Pereirado Nascimento, "Um Reduto Negro: Cor e Cidadania na Armada
(1870–1910)," in Olívia Maria Gomes da Cunha and Flávio dos Santos Gomes
(eds.), *Quase-cidadão: Histórias e Antropologias da Pós-Emancipação no Brasil* (Rio de
Janeiro: Editora FGV, 2007), pp. 283–311.

military police.[54] And even with the 1928 legally mandated prohibition against the exclusion of Afro-Brazilians from the local police force, whiteness was still included as an official requirement for applicants in solicitation documents.[55] Afro-Brazilians were only nominally able to enter the São Paulo police force after 1932.

In an 1894 listing of occupations after abolition in São Paulo (where more than 50 percent of the immigrants settled) foreign workers represented 82.5 percent of those occupations essential to rapid urban expansion and industrialization (manufacturing, crafts, transport, commerce) while blacks were relegated to domestic sphere employment. In São Paulo alone 71.2 percent of the workers at that time were foreigners.[56] Furthermore, in rural locations that were able to attract sufficient immigrant workers, they too were preferred to emancipated slaves and displaced them as free labor. Indeed, the Minister of Agriculture Antonio Prado proposed measures to promote the establishment of immigrants in agriculture.[57] The preference for white immigrants is also demonstrated in Sam Adamo's study of Rio de Janeiro employment practices of the 1930s. Adamo found that lower-skilled white immigrants were preferred to better-educated Afro-descendants even though the Afro-descendants were typically paid less.[58]

RACIAL SEGREGATION BY CUSTOMARY LAW: THE CONSTRUCTION OF WHITE SPACES

In São Paulo, the heart of the immigration *branqueamento* national project, Afro-Brazilians encountered racial exclusion and segregation by law and custom. The desire for white spaces accompanied the project of whitening the population. Unlike in the Northeast, where

[54] Anais da Câmara dos Deputados de São Paulo, vol. 1, 1928, 13 Sessão Ordinária em 31 julho, p. 351.
[55] Domingues, *Uma História Não Contada*, p. 137.
[56] George Reid Andrews, "Black and White Workers: São Paulo, Brazil, 1888–1928," *Hispanic American Historical Review* 68 (August 1988), 491–524.
[57] Florestan Fernandes, *The Negro in Brazilian Society*, Jacqueline D. Skiles, A. Brunel, and Arthur Rothwell (trans.) (New York: Simon & Schuster, 1971), p. 19.
[58] Sam C. Adamo, "Race, Health, and Justice in Rio de Janeiro, 1890–1940," PhD dissertation, University of New Mexico (1983), pp. 62–80.

Afro-Brazilians were consistently a significant portion of the population, in São Paulo and other southern regions of Brazil, Afro-Brazilians were a minority. São Paulo's Afro-Brazilian population in 1886, two years before abolition, was reported as 24 percent and decreased to 16 percent by 1928.[59] In contrast, Salvador, Bahia, a representative northeastern city, reported its 1890 population as 61.4 percent Afro-Brazilian and its 1940 population as 64.9 percent Afro-Brazilian.[60] Even if the census numbers are to be taken with a grain of salt given their political malleability, the contrast between the North and South remains constant with regard to the relative proportion of Afro-Brazilians by region. As such, São Paulo and the other southern regions with fewer Afro-Brazilians were better positioned to use customary law to segregate Afro-Brazilians from whites.

This occurred in the 1920s with the verbal designation of separate São Paulo streets for whites and blacks.[61] Collections of oral testimony from Afro-Brazilians alive during the postabolition period in southern Brazil (made possible by the late date of 1888 for complete emancipation) repeatedly indicate the entrenched customs of racial segregation in streets, public squares, public gardens, and public parks in both the capital and cities on the periphery ("o interior"). These customary laws regarding racial segregation in public spaces were enforced by the local police, who had the practice of imprisoning Afro-Brazilian violators.

Absent from the oral history depositions are any descriptions of court cases challenging such police detention practices. To the extent any Afro-Brazilian dared to challenge police detentions for segregation violations, such challengers would have faced the difficult obstacle of Brazilian law's long-standing enforcement of customary law. Legislated into law during the colonial period, the "Law of Good Reason of 1769" authorized the legal enforcement of social customs with long usage.[62] Such customs had the force of law[63] and continued

[59] Domingues, *Uma História Não Contada*, p. 188.
[60] Butler, *Freedoms Given, Freedoms Won*, p. 134.
[61] Domingues, *Uma História Não Contada*, pp. 157–62.
[62] Nuno Espinosa Gomes da Silva, *História Do Direito Português* (Lisboa: Fundacão Calouste Gulbenkian, 1991), p. 360 (discussing Lei da Boa Razão 18.08.1769); Thomas H. Reynolds and Arturo A. Flores, *Foreign Law: Current Sources of Codes and Basic Legislation in Jurisdictions of the World, Brazil* (Littleton, CO: Fred B. Rothman, 1989 & August 2004 Release), vol. I, p. 6.
[63] José Homem Corréa Telles, *Comentário Crítico à Lei da Boa Razão* (Lisboa: 1824).

to do so through Brazil's independence and today as well.[64] Detaining
Afro-Brazilian trespassers of socially designated white spaces was a
custom with the force of law. Accordingly, the popular vision of Brazil
as a nation without a version of U.S. Jim Crow segregation should be
revised to account for the regional experiences of racial segregation
and their customary law status.

Places of public accommodation also practiced racial segregation.
São Paulo restaurants would simply refuse to serve Afro-Brazilians who
dared to enter socially designated white restaurants. Housing advertisements would state, "No people of color accepted" or the racially coded
phrase "Foreigners preferred." To the extent that Afro-Brazilians
were documented as living in proximity to whites, it reflected the
numerous immigrant families who rented rooms and basements to
Afro-Brazilians for additional income.[65] Afro-Brazilian newspapers of
the time reported the failure to serve Afro-Brazilian patrons in barber-
shops, hospitals, and many other places of public accommodation and
retail businesses. In nearby Campinas, "Whites only" signs were used
in movie theaters and other public places.[66] Similar accounts of racial
segregation appear in Rio de Janeiro's interior towns.

Rio de Janeiro police records from the time of the 1888 abolition
of slavery through the 1890s reveal numerous cases of Afro-Brazilians'
being detained by police simply for walking around at night.[67] A large
percentage of reported crimes at this time were public order offenses
such as vagrancy that were used to marginalize Afro-descendants.[68] The
police records also indicate that vagrancy charges were aimed not at
conviction but at labeling Afro-descendants as "criminal individuals."[69]
Similarly, in the city of Rio Claro, vagrancy law was used to contain the
presence of nonwhites in "white" public spaces in the effort to keep

[64] Emmanuel Gustavo Haddad, "*O Costume Como Parâmetro da Aplicação da Justiça e
da Criação da Lei*," *Jus Navigandi* 11 (February 6, 2007), n. 1315.
[65] Butler, *Freedoms Given, Freedoms Won*, p. 76.
[66] Elisa Larkin Nascimento, "Aspects of Afro-Brazilian Experience," *Journal of Black
Studies* 11 (1980), 206.
[67] Sidney Chalhoub, "Medo Branco de Almas Negras: Escravos, Libertos e
Republicanos na Cidade do Rio," *Revista Brasileira de Historia* 8 (1988), 83–105.
[68] Adamo, "Race, Health, and Justice in Rio de Janeiro," pp. 228, 242.
[69] Olivia Maria Gomes da Cunha, "The Stigmas of Dishonor: Criminal Records,
Civil Rights, and Forensic Identification in Rio de Janeiro, 1903–1940," in Sueannn
Caulfield and Sarah C. Chambers (eds.), *Honor, Status, and Law in Modern Latin
America* (Durham, NC: Duke University Press, 2005), pp. 295–315.

newly freed slaves in a subjugated status.[70] The newly freed were residentially segregated in the Rio Claro town center and were prohibited from promenading around the Rio Claro town square.

In Vasalia, a small town in Rio de Janeiro's northwestern interior, residents recall "Jim Crow–like segregation of the main street, stores, public sidewalks, social clubs, dances, and beauty contests that was a fact of life as recently as 1985."[71] In Rio de Janeiro itself, the government undertook to redesign the city so as cleanse it of its Afro-Brazilian dwellers. With the 1902–6 "First Plan for the Beautification and Sanitation of Rio de Janeiro," the capital city was reconstructed to create a "tropical Paris."[72] Seven hundred and sixty buildings were destroyed in the central parishes to move Afro-Brazilian to less visible locations. The Rio de Janeiro government did not want Afro-Brazilians living in the space meant to resonate with "white" Europe. The racialization of space began decades of slum clearance that cast Afro-Brazilians out to the periphery, where public services and utilities were absent.[73] In effect, Rio became two separate cities divided along race and class lines. Similarly, the federal government encouraged the racialization of space as well. It used a "whites only" policy in recruiting diplomats and special envoys for missions abroad to present Brazil as a whitelike nation.[74]

STATE WHITENING PROJECT THROUGH PUBLIC EDUCATION

Just as the state's immigration policy was informed by notions of eugenic racial hierarchy, the state's postabolition model of education was similarly influenced. The work of Jerry Dávila details the way in which a national elite of scientists associated with eugenics headed and

[70] Warren Dean, *Rio Claro: A Brazilian Plantation System, 1820–1920* (Stanford, CA: Stanford University Press, 1976), p. 151.

[71] France Winddance Twine, *Racism in a Racial Democracy: The Maintenance of White Supremacy in Brazil* (New Brunswick, NJ: Rutgers University Press, 1998), p. 120.

[72] Paul Christopher Johnson, "Law, Religion, and 'Public Health' in the Republic of Brazil," *Law and Social Inquiry* 26 (Winter 2001), 23.

[73] Meade, *"Civilizing" Rio.*

[74] Thomas E. Skidmore, "Racial Ideas and Social Policy in Brazil, 1870–1940," in Richard Graham (ed.), *The Idea of Race in Latin America, 1870–1940* (Austin: University of Texas Press, 1990), p. 12.

implemented the various local school initiatives that sought to mitigate
the degeneracy of Afro-Brazilian and indigenous children from 1917
to 1945.[75] Despite the fact that the development of a public education system was viewed as a mechanism to equip all children equally
to modernize the nation, the system itself replicated preexisting racial
hierarchies while attempting to whiten the population culturally. School
administrators and teachers received education in the cultural and
behavioral theories that explained racial deficiencies and the eugenic
policies that would address them. The racial biases of Brazil's educators could be quite overt, such as those of Everardo Backheuser, who
in 1926 stated that racial diversity in elementary schooling would be
detrimental to the country.[76]

The eugenic structuring of public education began in the Rio de
Janeiro capital in 1917, then the largest school system. It served as a
model and was adopted by other regions, which often received federal resources to do so. The Rio de Janeiro Department of Education
circulated their findings in a quarterly journal distributed to teachers throughout the country. Furthermore, the federal Ministry of
Education and Public Health gave the eugenicists in Rio de Janeiro
free reign to develop policies and programs they thought scientifically
based. The eugenic educational policies included segregation of students by IQ and "health status," in addition to the implementation of
"health brigade" inspection teams. In 1958, the eugenic reforms of
the public school system were codified into national law with the Law
of Directives and Bases in Education, which were retained with slight
modifications by the Brazilian legislature in 1996.[77]

To begin with, students were segregated into different classrooms
according to their intellectual capacity as measured by the racially
infused standardized IQ testing of the time. (The IQ tests developed
in the United States were used in Brazil.) Low-capacity children were
not taught to read in the first grade but were taught how to "adapt to
school life" with instruction on personal hygiene. This then trapped

[75] Jerry Dávila, *Diploma of Whiteness: Race and Social Policy in Brazil, 1917–1945*
(Durham, NC: Duke University Press, 2003), p. 25.
[76] Jens R. Hentschke, *Reconstructing the Brazilian Nation: Public Schooling in the Vargas
Era* (Baden-Baden: Nomos, 2007), p. 209 n. 164.
[77] Lei no. 9 394 de 20 de dezembro de 1996 (Brazil).

Afro-Brazilian students in the first grade because the lack of academic instruction meant they had to keep repeating the grade until they learned to read in some manner or simply dropped out in frustration.

Students were also segregated or simply removed from school altogether by virtue of their compromised "health status" in ways that also excluded Afro-Brazilian children from adequate schooling or any schooling at all. Poor health included syphilis, parasites, adenopathy, anemia, and indifference to education or antisocial behavior resulting from presumed hereditary or cultural causes. Such students were often excluded from school under the pretense that they would jeopardize the health of those who were deemed ready to learn. Grade repetition itself was considered a symptom of illness.

The few Afro-Brazilian children who managed to surmount the barriers to entry and daily exclusion were then exposed to programs that sought to ameliorate their degenerate racial status and culturally whiten them. The most significant of those programs were the "health brigades" that set out to improve them eugenically. Health brigades organized each classroom with a student assigned the task of inspecting the hygiene of classmates daily and recording it on a classroom chart posted on the door. Those students with poor hygiene (inevitably Afro-Brazilian) were then sent to the principal's office for an additional lecture on hygiene, rather than staying in the classroom for academic instruction. Instead school hours were devoted to teaching the students how to wash their faces, ears, and hair and brush their teeth, trim their nails, and polish their shoes. In effect, Afro-Brazilian children were provided rudimentary literacy skills, if any, only through the third grade while educators focused on teaching hygiene habits intended to racially improve them for society. In addition, European musical programs were instituted to civilize the nonwhite students and encourage them to abandon degenerate African-based carnival music.

For those Afro-descended children actually exposed to an academic curriculum, their education included being assaulted with racially biased textbooks.[78] For example, as late as 1964, the

---

[78] Carmen Nava, "Lessons in Patriotism and Good Citizenship: National Identity and Nationalism in Public Schools during the Vargas Administration, 1937–1945," *Luso-Brazillian Review* 35 (Summer 1998), 39–63.

official textbook for geography and history of Brazil stated that "of all the races, the white race is the most intelligent, persevering and enterprising ... the negro race is much more retarded than others."[79]

The whitening of education also entailed the exclusion of Afro-Brazilians as teachers. While there were Afro-descended teachers during the first two decades of the twentieth century who had been educated by religious charities, this was altered by the Rio de Janeiro–led governmental educational reforms. Beginning in 1917, specialized courses of study modeled upon the college study of social sciences were required to be a schoolteacher. Previously a high school degree was sufficient for teaching elementary school anywhere in Brazil. Yet Afro-Brazilians encountered barriers to obtaining the newly required specialization. The professional training offered in the "normal school" equivalent to Columbia Teachers College, upon which it was modeled, required an entrance examination so rigorous that applicants of means took a year-long daily private school preparatory course for it. Such preparatory courses were financially out of reach for most Afro-Brazilians, thereby resulting in poor test results confirming the presumed deficiency of the Afro-Brazilian applicants. Psychological testing of the candidates was also viewed as confirming their racial deficiency as educators. Furthermore, candidates were also required to meet weight and height standards set at a narrow eugenic ideal favoring European body types. As a result, the public school educator norm became a white middle-class woman trained to view her students as racially formed.[80]

The few Afro-descended students fortunate enough to locate white patrons to pay for a private school education could still be denied admission because of administrative concerns that other parents would remove their children in protest.[81] In that manner, private schools could retain their white exclusivity and Afro-descended children remained segregated in the problematic public primary schools.

---

[79] Hentschke, *Reconstructing the Brazilian Nation*, p. 142.
[80] Dávila, *Diploma of Whiteness*.
[81] Hentschke, *Reconstructing the Brazilian Nation*, p. 143.

REGULATION OF AFRICAN-BASED RELIGIONS AS
BRANQUEAMENTO

As in the operation of the public education system, the Brazilian government also implemented its *branqueamento*/whitening project through
the vehicle of oppressive regulation of African-based religious practices. After independence and the abolition of slavery, Brazil enacted
the Decree Separating Church and State on January 7, 1890. Article
II of the decree stated, "All religious sects have an equal right to exercise their forms of worship according to their faith, and shall not be
molested in their private or public forms of worship."[82] Yet, despite the
decree, African-based religious groups found themselves the subject of
intense government scrutiny through criminal law and administrative
law practices. This did not change when the decree's religious freedom
provision was incorporated into the Constitution of 1891.

The Penal Code of 1890 contained new articles that were used
to undercut the efficacy of religious freedom for African religious
groups.[83] Article 157 prohibited the "practice of spiritism, magic and
its sorceries, the use of talismans and cartomancy to arouse sentiments
of hate and love, the promise to cure illness, curable and not curable;
in sum, to fascinate and subjugate public belief." Article 158 forbade
"administering, or simply prescribing any substance of any of the natural domains for internal or external use, or in any way prepared, thus
performing or exercising the office denominated as curandeiro [spiri-
tual healer]." In addition, Law No. 173, enacted in 1893, granted legal
rights only to those religious associations that registered with the state
and did not promote "illicit" or "immoral" ends. All of these legal provisions were used in combination effectively to ban African-based religious practice as socially dangerous and a threat to public health under
the auspices of the Service of Administrative Hygiene of the Union.
This was in accord with the general conception of Afro-Brazilians as
constituting a social hygiene problem for the country.[84]

---

[82] Johnson, "Law, Religion, and 'Public Health' in the Republic of Brazil," p. 23.

[83] Yvonne Maggie, *Medo do Feitiço: Relações Entre Magia e Poder no Brasil* (Rio de
Janeiro: Arquivo Nacional, Orgão do Ministério da Justiça, 1992), pp. 22–3.

[84] Michael R. Trochim, "The Brazilian Black Guard," *Americas* 44 (January 1988),
285–300.

African religions were treated as illegal magic and effectively defined out of the concept of valid religion, thereby constructing Brazil's official religious practices as white and its national identity as white as well. As a consequence, police forces invaded and destroyed African-based religious centers (Candomblé terreiros, and related centers of Macumba, Ubanda, Xango, Tambor de Minas, and Spiritism), in addition to harassing and arresting the practitioners and confiscating their icons and ritual implements.

Even the Afro-Brazilian-dominated Northeast region witnessed police persecution.[85] And in Bahia, government officials in 1902 went so far as to outlaw African-based *batuque* candomblé drumming in secular carnival musical processions.[86] The Bahian elite long harbored a concern about being nationally viewed as "brancos da Bahia" ("whites of Bahia"), that is, less white because of the national suspicion of racially mixed ancestors in the predominantly black Northeast. It is likely that this elite Bahian insecurity regarding the national questioning of their whiteness exacerbated the elite desire to dissociate themselves from African-based religion and culture.[87]

The regulation of African-based religions altered only slightly under the regime of Getúlio Vargas (1930–45), which sought a facial image of national unity. While Vargas's presidential law decree 1202 recognized the legitimacy of "traditional" houses of candomblé to practice, it left to the police the responsibility to distinguish those groups that were not "traditional" and thus practitioners of illegal sorcery, magic, and fraudulent healing. The requirement that the religious groups register with the state made them particularly vulnerable to police regulation and harassment. (Similarly, 1932 Bahian laws declaring performers of *capoeria*, the Afro-Brazilian martial art, "dangerous delinquents" subjected Afro-Bahians to police harassment.)[88] Indeed,

[85] Roger Bastide, *The African Religions of Brazil: Toward a Sociology of the Interpenetration of Civilizations*, Helen Sebba (trans.) (Baltimore: Johns Hopkins University Press, 1978), p. 164.

[86] Peter Fry, Sérgio Carrara, and Ana Luiza Martins-Costa, "Negros e Brancos no Carnaval da Velha Republica," in João José Reis (ed.), *Escravidão e a Invencão da Liberdade: Estudos sobre o Negro no Brasil* (São Paulo: Brasiliense, Brasilia: CNPQ, 1988), p. 259.

[87] Butler, *Freedoms Given, Freedoms Won*, p. 185.

[88] Ibid. at p. 187.

an entire police department ("Polícia de Costumes") was established by Vargas in 1934 to regulate and distinguish between legitimate and illegal religious practices. The national mandate to register with the Department of Customs was not lifted until 1974, thereby marginalizing African religious practitioners from the image of a white nation, as depicted by the famous white Christ statue atop Corcovado in Rio de Janeiro since 1931.

The culmination of all the various facets of the government *branqueamento* project was a visibly whitened southern region of Brazil. Nevertheless, the interest in continuing to seek European immigrants waned with growing alarm about immigrant labor union activity. European immigrant labor union activity was significant and strike movements numerous in 1917–20.[89] While governing elites were reluctant to deport the immigrants they had invested so much capital in drawing to Brazil, they did finally discontinue the immigrant recruitment program in 1927.[90] This was followed in 1931 by the federal government's placing restrictions on immigration into the country, as well as on the employment of foreign nationals in commerce and industry, pursuant to Decree 20.921.[91]

THE SHIFT FROM *BRANQUEAMENTO* TO *MESTIÇAGEM*

Without the influx of additional European immigrants, Brazil continued to have a national population with visible African and indigenous ancestry. The nation-state's desire to promote an international image of civilization (despite the presence of those they considered racially uncivilized) prompted the government interest in the theories of the Brazilian sociologist Gilberto Freyre, an elite white son of the racially mixed Northeast region.

---

[89] Sheldon L. Maram, "Urban Labor and Social Change in the 1920's," *Luso-Brazilian Review* 16 (1979), 215–23.

[90] Sheldon L. Maram, "Labor and the Left in Brazil, 1890–1921: A Movement Aborted," *Hispanic American Historical Review* 57 (1977), 254–72.

[91] Decreto 20.921, de August 25, 1931, Diario Oficial dos Estados Unidos do Brasil, pp. 13, 552–8.

Freyre's published works of 1930–70 made a conceptual shift away from *branqueamento* without ever challenging the belief in white superiority.[92] Freyre described the development of Brazil as a set of intimate encounters between races that had resulted in the creation of a new race. Through *mestiçagem* – racial mixture – there was now a "Brazilian race," which in turn presumably indicated the absence of racial discord in the society. Brazilian culture was also a result of racial mixture, but Freyre viewed the European contribution as the most evident and important. In this way, *mestiçagem* parallels the discourse of Spanish America's *mestizaje* and José Vasconcelos's description of a racially mixed but white-focused "cosmic race" discussed in the preceding chapter.

While Freyre did use the term "racial democracy" in some lectures and statements for English-speaking audiences to describe the path Brazil was on by virtue of *mestiçagem*, he did not coin the term. Indeed, the noted historian George Reid Andrews has observed that Brazilian writers and intellectuals have been debating the issue of racial democracy since the 1880s.[93] Yet it is perhaps the sociologist Florestan Fernandes's Brazilian publications in 1965 that were later translated into English in 1971, challenging the "myth of racial democracy," that gave the term a wider scholarly circulation.[94] Nevertheless, Freyre is widely credited with the racial mixture thesis now commonly termed "racial democracy."[95] It may well be that the Brazilian government's enthusiasm for Freyre's ideas led to the association between Freyre and the term "racial democracy."

The Getúlio Vargas regime's (1930–45) populist discourse converged nicely with Freyre's *mestiçagem* ideology and was directly incorporated into the government's nation-building projects. *Mestiçagem*

[92] Gilberto Freyre, *Casa Grande e Senzala* (Rio de Janeiro: Maia & Schmidt, 1933) (later published in English as *The Masters and the Slaves*); Gilberto Freyre, *Sobrados e Mucambos: Decadência do Patriarchado Rural no Brasil* (São Paulo: Companhia Editora Nacional, 1936) (later published in English as *The Mansions and the Shanties*).

[93] George Reid Andrews, "Brazilian Racial Democracy, 1900–90: An American Counterpoint," *Journal of Contemporary History* 31 (1996), 488.

[94] Fernandes, *The Negro in Brazilian Society*, p. 137.

[95] David Lehmann, "Gilberto Freyre: The Reassessment Continues," *Latin American Research Review* 43 (2008), 209–10.

was credited as Brazil's true nationality ("a verdadeira nacionalidade") and was promoted in public proclamations, schools, universities, and the national media.[96] When Vargas consolidated his power to be a dictator in 1937, he abolished all political parties, including the racially conscious Frente Negra Brasileira (Black Brazilian Front), which had organized as a political party in 1930 and then officially registered as one in 1936.[97] In addition, the census again became the venue for validating the government's racial ideology.

Just as census data were deployed for validating the *branqueamento* project of whitening the population, with the shift to *mestiçagem*, census data were deployed to tout the prominence of racial mixture. This was often done without any reliance on the actual statistical data regarding the population by race. For instance, with the 1940 census, the results were presented with an elaborate report extolling the progress of the new Brazilian race.[98] Yet, the new mixed Brazilian race was celebrated in the census report as a barometer for how "Negroes and Indians are continuing to disappear ... in the constant process of biological and social selection and that immigration, especially that of a Mediterranean origin, is not at a standstill, the white man will not only have in Brazil his major field of life and culture in the tropics, but be able to take from old Europe – citadel of the white race."[99] The accuracy of the census report's comparative predictions of course could not be verified given the absence of a census in 1930 and 1910 and the absence of the color/race question on the 1920 census. Furthermore, at least one demographer has suggested that racial statistics in Brazil have at times been directly altered to indicate a whiter population. For instance, in a 1940 publication Samuel Lowrie noted that in absolute terms the black population of São Paulo was actually increasing despite the fact that many of its members were being statistically transferred from black to white racial categories.[100]

[96] Andrews, "Brazilian Racial Democracy," p. 488.
[97] Thomas Skidmore, *Politics in Brazil 1930–1964: An Experiment in Democracy* (New York: Oxford University Press, 1967).
[98] Fernando de Azevedo, *Brazilian Culture: An Introduction to the Study of Culture in Brazil,* William Rex Crawford (trans.) (New York: Macmillan, 1950), 33 (English translation of original 1940 census text published in 1943).
[99] Ibid. at p. 41 (emphasis added).
[100] Samuel H. Lowrie, "The Negro Element in the Population of São Paulo, a Southernly State of Brazil," *Phylon* 3 (1942), 398–416.

With the 1950 census change from using enumerators to designate the "appropriate" color categories to using a self-classification method instead, the ability to whiten symbolically was in the hands of the citizenry. It was thus no surprise when the 1950 census indicated a 3.6 percent decrease in the number of blacks from 1940, along with a 5.3 percent increase in the number of *pardos* (a category that then included not only mixed-race persons but also those of indigenous descent).[101] Again, the published census report for the 1950 census celebrated the progress the nation was making in whitening its population through *mestiçagem*.[102]

While the 1960 census racial data were never fully released, the military regime that took over in 1964 and ruled until 1985 was so entrenched in the ideology of racial democracy that it characterized any critique of racial democracy as an "act of subversion."[103] In addition, the formation of black-identified groups was forbidden as segregationist and racist. The military's intolerance of any critique of racial democracy was furthered by its decision to omit a color or racial category question on the 1970 census. Ironically, it turns out that the military regime really had no cause to fear a color/racial census question. For when a 1976 National Household Survey Supplement on Social Mobility and Color was conducted with an open-ended color question, the population responded with 135 different colors.[104] In short, the cult of *mestiçagem* already had a stronghold on the racial identities of Brazilians seeking any category but black to pick. Yet, the military still wanted to omit a color or racial question on the 1980 census. Only with the gradual political liberalization process ("abertura"), which began in the late 1970s, were social scientists and black activists able to lobby for the restoration of a color question on the 1980 census. Yet the restoration of a color question on all subsequent census questionnaires

[101] Melissa Nobles, *Shades of Citizenship: Race and the Census in Modern Politics* (Stanford, CA: Stanford University Press, 2000), p. 105.

[102] *Estudos de estatística teórica e aplicada, contribuções para o estudo da demográfica do Brasil* (Rio de Janeiro: Instituto Brasileiro de Geográfia e Estatística, 1970), p. 169 (reprint of IBGE's 1956 census analysis report).

[103] Thales de Azevedo, *Democracia Racial* (Petrópolis: Editora Vozes, 1975), p. 53 n. 27.

[104] Instituto Brasileiro de Geográfia e Estatística, Departamento de Estatísticas de População e Socias, "Resultados da apuração de Boletim Especial l.02 da PNAD 76," Vol. I (1976).

did not disrupt the national racial democracy mind-set so carefully cultivated by the government.

Early on with Getúlio Vargas's *brasilidade* campaign, Brazilians were exposed to a variety of governmental media projects promoting Brazilianess and national *mestiçagem* as the only appropriate identity. This included the daily radio program *Hora do Brasil* (the Brazil Hour).[105] The government's *brasilidade* influence was also disseminated through its strict guidelines regarding curriculum and required texts. Primary school teachers were instructed to explain the formation of the Brazilian people as the combination of "the white, contributing with language, the customs, the religion; the black bequeathing us gentleness and the spirit of sacrifice of the African, the indigenous, transmitting the use of the characteristics of love for liberty and attachment to the earth, which are innate feeling of the Brazilian."[106] This indoctrination continued in secondary school and the university with the use of Gilberto Freyre's book *Casa Grande e Senzala* (published in English as *The Mansions and the Shanties: A Study in the Development of Brazilian Civilization*), as a "classic text" (in which he characterized Brazilian slavery as milder because of the colonial Portuguese presumed ability to accept and intermarry with other races and cultures).

The national attachment to the ideology of racial democracy was also facilitated by the Latin American concern with imperialism. To be sure, Brazil was further removed from the political involvement of the United States (unlike Cuba and Puerto Rico post independence). Yet, the desire for foreign investment to spur modernization and industrialization was accompanied by apprehension of being considered an inferior mongrel nation subject to external interference and influence. The national eye to external opinions thereby encouraged all Brazilians to consider themselves united in opposition to any imposed inferiority from abroad. Indeed, Brazil and Spanish America have been described by the scholar Darién Davis as having an "inferiority complex" for which patriotism was the defense that then resulted in the co-optation

---

[105] Darién J. Davis, "The Mechanism of Forging a National Consciousness: A Comparative Approach to Modern Brazil and Cuba, 1930–1964," Ph.D. dissertation, Tulane University (1992), p. 249.
[106] Ibid. at pp. 252–3.

of ethnic minorities.[107] The concept of *mestiçagem*'s racial democracy in Brazil (and *mestizaje* in Spanish America) served as a useful source of national pride vis-à-vis the Jim Crow segregation of the United States.

At the same time, the state-supported racialization of spaces permitted regional identities to stand in for the role of race-based identities without being viewed as contradicting the notion of racial democracy. For instance, in São Paulo, the "Paulista" identity by 1930 was associated with the whiteness of modernity, industry, and economic progress.[108] The Paulista identity and that of the southern region as a whole were racially coded as white in juxtaposition to the blackness and backwardness of the Northeast region of Brazil. Indeed, soon after Getúlio Vargas first gained power in 1930, the São Paulo state government declared war on the central government because of Vargas's appointment of a "backward" northeastern-born interim governor of the state. For eighty-three days starting July 9, 1932, São Paulo state troops struggled with federal troops. The War of São Paulo was characterized at the time as a fight to defend "its white man's culture" against the populism of Vargas's *dictanegra* (black dictatorship).[109] Outnumbered and ill equipped, the Paulistas negotiated a settlement with the central government but maintained their conviction that São Paulo was to be more highly valued within the nation-state because of its more civilized culture. More importantly, the racialized regional differences were understood nationwide as coexisting with a racial democracy that depicted harmony against a backdrop of presumed hierarchical difference. This in turn helps explain the long-standing phenomenon of a high rate of color endogamy in intimate relationships within the midst of a presumed racial democracy.[110]

---

[107] Ibid. at pp. 230, 253–60.
[108] Barbara Weinstein, "Racializing Regional Difference: São Paulo versus Brazil, 1932," in Nancy P. Applebaum, Anne S. Macpherson, and Karin Alejandra Rosenblatt (eds.), *Race and Nation in Modern Latin America* (Chapel Hill: University of North Carolina Press, 2003), pp. 237–62.
[109] Ibid. at pp. 246–7.
[110] Sueann Caulfield, "Interracial Courtship in the Rio de Janeiro Courts, 1918–1940," in Applebaum, Macpherson, and Rosenblatt (eds.), *Race and Nation in Latin America*, 163–86; Samuel H. Lowrie, "Racial and National Intermarriage in a Brazilian City," *American Journal of Sociology* 44 (March 1939), 684–707.

Indeed, a significant feature of *mestiçagem*'s racial democracy is its power to negate the articulation of racial differences while supporting the existence of racial hierarchy and socioeconomic exclusion as a matter of color-blind class distinctions. The decades of *branqueamento* state-sponsored policies have ensured a subordination of Afro-Brazilians that *mestiçagem*'s racial democracy normalizes as mere happenstance. For that reason, it is only in recent years that the potency of the myth of racial democracy has begun to be challenged in Brazil and Spanish America as well. While the Brazilian immigration laws and customary laws of segregation cannot be directly equated to the U.S. Jim Crow context, taking note of the parallel aims and effects of the two forms of racial regulation erodes the mythology of Brazil as a nation innocent of governmental racial regulation. In the chapters that follow, I shall detail the legacy of Brazilian *mestiçagem* and *mestizaje* in Latin America and its impediment to racial equality throughout the region, which also resonates with the legacy of racial disparities wrought by Jim Crow segregation in the United States.

4 THE SOCIAL EXCLUSION OF AFRO-DESCENDANTS IN LATIN AMERICA TODAY

"Where are all the black people?" Jean Paul Sartre asked during his visit to a university in Rio de Janeiro.[1]

Despite the history of having participated in significant numbers in the struggles for independence from Spain and thereafter continuing to struggle for the abolition of slavery, persons of African descent in Latin America are still viewed as a marginalized group today. Survey research throughout the region indicates that antiblack stereotypes pervade the society unabated since slavery.[2] The research also demonstrates that these stereotypes are widely held among members of the working class and upper class alike.

While the constitutions of Latin America universally promote formal equality, persons of African descent have achieved a very small measure of socioeconomic progress since emancipation.[3] Indeed,

---

[1] Francisco Martins, "Racism in Brazilian Aquarelle – the Place of Denying," *International Journal of Migration, Health and Social Care* 4(2) (October 2008), 37–46, 42.

[2] George Reid Andrews, *Afro-Latin America, 1800–2000* (New York: Oxford University Press, 2004), p. 178.

[3] Art. 16, Constitución Nacional of 1994 (Arg.), http://pdba.georgetown.edu/ Constitutions/Argentina/argentina.html;

República de Bolivia Constitución Política del Estado, art. 6 (2009), http://pdba. georgetown.edu/Constitutions/Bolivia/bolivia.html;

Constitución Política de la República de Chile, art. 19 (1980 with 2005 reforms), http://pdba.georgetown.edu/Constitutions/Chile/chile05.html; Constitución Política de Colombia, tit. II, ch. 1, art. 13, in Gisbert H. Flanz, in *4 Constitutions of the Countries of the World*, Release 95–4, Peter B. Heller and Marcia W. Coward (trans.) (1995), pp. 164–5; Constitución Política de la República de Costa Rica, Art. 33 (1949 with 2003 reforms), http://pdba.georgetown.edu/Constitutions/Costa/costa.html; Constitución, ch. VI, arts. 42–3 (1992) (Cuba), in Inter-Univ. Assocs., Inc., Republic

Afro-descendants are a significant presence in much of the region yet have a highly limited presence in politics and government.

Throughout the region, African descendants are disproportionately living in poverty and illiteracy, with limited access to education and employment opportunities, all resulting in shorter life expectancies.[4] Most African descendants live in rural areas and suffer a lack of infrastructure and utilities, with no health services, few schools, high unemployment, and low income.[5] In fact, scholars attribute the slow economic growth of Latin American and Caribbean countries to their discriminatory exclusion of Afro-descendants.[6] In addition,

of Cuba, *5 Constitutions of the Countries of the World*, Release 2000–1 (2000), pp. 12–3; Constitución de la República Dominicana, art. 8 (2002), http://pdba.georgetown. edu/Constitutions/DomRep/dominicanrepublic.html; Constitución Política, tit. II, ch. 1, art. 11 (2008) (Ecuador), http://pdba.georgetown.edu/Constitutions/Ecuador/ ecuador08.html#mozTocId666824;

   Constitución, tit. II, ch. I, art. 3 (El Sal.), in Inter-Univ. Assocs., Inc., Republic of El Salvador, in *6 Constitutions of the Countries of the World*, Reka Koerner (trans.), Release 98–5 (1998), p. 1; Constitution of Guatemala, art. 4 (1985 with 1993 reforms), http://pdba.georgetown.edu/Constitutions/Guate/guate.html; Constitución, tit. III, ch. 1, art. 60 (Hond.), in Gisbert H. Flanz and Jefri Jay Ruchti, in *8 Constitutions of the Countries of the World, Republic of Honduras,* Reka Koerner (trans.), Release 97–2 (1997), p.16; Constitución Política de los Estados Unidos Mexicanos, art. 1, 3 (1917 with 2008 reforms), http://pdba.georgetown.edu/Constitutions/Mexico/textovi-gente2008.pdf; Constitución Política de la República de Nicaragua, tit. IV, ch. 1, art. 27, in Inter-Univ. Assocs., Inc., Republic of Nicaragua, *13 Constitutions of the Countries of the World*, Anna I. Vellvé Torras (trans.), Release 98–5 (1998), p. 6; Constitución Política, tit. III, ch. 1, art. 19 (Pan.), in Jorge Fabrega P. and Jefri Jay Ruchti, Republic of Panama, in *14 Constitutions of the Countries of the World*, Jorge Fabrega P. (trans.), Release 95–8 (1995), p. 105; Constitution of Paraguay, art. 88 (1992), http://pdba. georgetown.edu/Constitutions/Paraguay/paraguay.html; Constitución Política, tit. I, ch. I, art. 2, cl. 2 (Peru), in Peter B. Heller, Peru, in *14 Constitutions of the Countries of the World*, Release 95–1 (1995), p. 113; Constitución, tit. III, ch. 1, art. 21, cl. 1 (Venez.), in Gisbert H. Flanz, Bolivarian Republic of Venezuela, in *20 Constitutions of the Countries of the World*, Release 2000–3 (2000), p. 4.
4 Bryce Pardo, "Members of Congress Discuss Challenges Facing Afro-Descendants in Latin America," *Inter-American Dialogue*, April 9, 2008.
5 Margarita Sánchez and Maurice Bryan, *Afro-descendants, Discrimination and Economic Exclusion in Latin America* (London: Minority Rights Group International, May 2003), p. 3, http://www.minorityrights.org/933/macro-studies/afrodescendants-discri mination-and-economic-exclusion-in-latin-america.html.
6 Jonas Zoninsein, "The Economic Case for Combating Racial and Ethnic Exclusion in Latin America and the Caribbean Countries," in Mayra Buvinic, Jacqueline Mazza, and Ruthanne Deutsch (eds.), *Towards a Shared Vision of Development* (Washington, DC: Inter-American Development Bank, 2001).

they attribute Latin America's lower economic standing as compared to East Asia and Eastern Europe to its exclusion of the rural poor (many of whom are Afro-descendants) from social protections and services.[7] Despite the variation in demographic density and political histories, studies of the region show a remarkable similarity in the marginalization of Afro-descendants and the racial discrimination they encounter.[8]

In much of the region, Afro-descendants are considered to be the "poorest of the poor." When poverty rates are estimated by race, Afro-descendants constitute 30 percent of Latin America's population but represent 40 percent of the region's poor.[9] The picture for Afro-descendants is particularly bleak when one considers that Latin America is the region with the most unequal income distribution in the world. Furthermore, the social exclusion of Afro-descendants remains consistent even when income level is controlled for in statistical analyses.

Consider the Colombian context. In Colombia, the country in Spanish America with the largest Afro-descended population (10–17 million), 80 percent of Afro-descendants live below the poverty line.[10] Ninety-eight percent of black communities in Colombia lack basic public utilities, whereas only 6 percent of white communities are similarly deprived. There are also racial disparities in the delivery of health care services. While 40 percent of white Colombian communities have health service coverage, only 10 percent of black communities do.[11] Low salaries in Afro-descendant Colombian communities further limit

[7] Robert Kaufmann and Stephan Haggard, *Development, Democracy and Welfare States: Latin America, East Asia and Eastern Europe* (Princeton, NJ: Princeton University Press, 2008).

[8] *Forum on Poverty Alleviation for Minority Communities: Communities of African Ancestry in Costa Rica, Honduras, Nicaragua, Argentina, Colombia, Ecuador, Peru, Uruguay, Venezuela* (Washington, DC: Inter-American Development Bank, 1996).

[9] Gustavo Márquez et al., *Outsiders? The Changing Patterns of Exclusion in Latin America and the Caribbean* (Washington, DC: Inter-American Development Bank, 2007), pp. 15–17.

[10] Diego Cevallos, "Latin America: Afro-Descendants Marginalized and Ignored," Inter Press Service News, May 19, 2005, http://ipsnews.net/africa/interna.asp?idnews=28752.

[11] Sánchez and Bryan, *Afro-descendants, Discrimination and Economic Exclusion in Latin America*, p. 5.

access to health care because medicine and consultation services are not provided free of charge. As a result, the infant mortality rate in the Afro-descendant population is nearly twice the Colombian national average.[12] In another country with a large density of Afro-descendants, Cuba (estimated at 34–65%), Afro-descendants are largely relegated to the worst housing and poorest paid jobs and their situation has only worsened within the last ten years.[13]

While, Colombia, Cuba, and Brazil are all countries with large Afro-descended populations and significant racial inequality, black subordination also exists in nations with smaller numbers of Afro-descendants and larger proportions of marginalized indigenous populations. For instance, in Peru, while Afro-descendants are estimated to be only 1.5–10 percent of the population and are disproportionately urban dwellers, their rate of poverty exceeds the national rate, and their average income is lower than the national average.[14] Their access to health care is also lower than the national average as a result of the discriminatory treatment at health centers.[15] For instance, Afro-Peruvians are made to wait longer for medical attention, and when they finally access a medical professional they are cursorily examined and quickly dispatched. Afro-Peruvian women also note that during medical interviews, medical personnel often refer to them with racialized sexual terms rather than by name.[16] Similarly, in Ecuador, 81 percent of Afro-descendants live below the poverty line, and their infant mortality rate for children below the age of five is 48.3 percent as compared to the 30.8 percent for the white population.[17]

---

[12] Inter-American Commission on Human Rights of the Organization of American States, "Preliminary Observations of the Inter-American Commission on Human Rights after the Visit of the Rapporteurship on the Rights of Afro-Descendants and against Racial Discrimination to the Republic of Colombia," March 27, 2009, Observation no. 36.

[13] Cuban Academy of Sciences 2003 Study.

[14] "Los Afrodescendientes en el Perú: Una Aproximación a su Realidad y al Ejercicio de sus Derechos," Informe de Adjuntía No. 003–2011-DP/ADHPD, Defensoría del Pueblo del Perú (February 2011), pp. 44, 108–9.

[15] Ibid. at pp. 48–53.

[16] Ibid. at pp. 51–3.

[17] "Quest for Inclusion: Realizing Afro-Latin Potential," Organization of Africans in the Americas, Position Paper, vol. 1 (2000), p. 6; *Pueblos Indígenas y Afrodescendientes de América Latina y el Caribe: Información Sociodemográfica para Políticas y Programas* (New York: Comisión Económica para América Latina y el Caribe, 2006), p. 437.

In addition, the Afro-Ecuadorian rate for telephone line connection is half that of the rest of the Ecuadorian population. In Uruguay, while Afro-descendants were reported by the 2006 census as 9.1 percent of the population, their rate of poverty is double that of white Uruguayans.[18]

Geographic segregation also influences the marginalization of Afro-descendants in Latin America. In residential areas where Afro-descendants are concentrated, the quality of housing and access to public services are disproportionately deficient.[19] Moreover, government's investment in infrastructure in these areas is inadequate. As a result Afro-descendants have lower rates of access to public utilities in Latin America. For example, in Colombia, the areas that are densely populated by Afro-Colombians are extremely poor.[20] Indeed, the municipality with the highest percentage of Afro-Colombians has the lowest per capita level of government investment in health, education, and infrastructure.[21] In fact, the lower levels of access to and quality of public services for Afro-Colombians are the main determinants of their lower levels of well-being in the nation. While geographic segregation in Latin America is certainly influenced by the correspondence between African ancestry and indigent status, there is also evidence of informal regulation to maintain spaces as "white." Journalists have noted the rise of racist skinhead gangs who attack Afro-descendants who enter upper-class neighborhoods, restaurants, and nightclubs in Colombia, Uruguay, and Venezuela.[22]

---

[18] George Reid Andrews, *Blackness in the White Nation: A History of Afro-Uruguay* (Chapel Hill: University of North Carolina Press, 2010), p. 160.

[19] Cristina Torres Parodi, *Equidad en Salud: Una Mirada desde la Perspectiva de la Etnicidad* (2001), p. 14, http://ciss.insp.mx/migracion/site_library/raza17.doc; Fernando Urrea Giraldo and Hector Fabio Ramírez Echeverry, "Cambios en el Mercado de Trabajo de Cali (Colombia), Reestructuración Económica y Social del Empleo de la Población Negra en la Década del 90: Un Análisis de Segregación Socio-Racial a Partir de las Transformaciones Más Recientes del Mercado de Trabajo," Presentation, Third Latin American Congress on the Sociology of Work, Buenos Aires, Argentina (May 2000), p. 1, http://www.alast.org/PDF/Marshall2/MT-Urrea.PDF.

[20] Olivier Barbary and Fernando Urrea (eds.), *Gente Negra en Colombia: Dinámicas Sociopolíticas en Cali y el Pacífico* (Medellín: Editorial Lealon, 2004).

[21] Gustavo Márquez et al., *Outsiders?* pp. 22–4.

[22] Andrews, *Afro-Latin America*, p. 195.

Furthermore, the majority of Afro-descendants in Latin America have little to no access to adequate primary or secondary education.[23] This deprivation stands in marked contrast to the constitutional right to an education that the Latin American national constitutions assert.[24] The inferior education offered Afro-descendants evidences itself in the dilapidated educational facilities and lack of high-quality teachers and educational materials. Students of African descent are relegated to underfinanced public schools for primary and secondary education, while economically privileged white children attend private schools with many more resources.[25] Even the selection of faculty members is racially stratified.[26]

[23] *Right to Education of Afro-descendant and Indigenous Communities in the Americas, Report Prepared for a Thematic Hearing before the Inter-American Commission on Human Rights* (Washington, DC: Robert F. Kennedy Memorial Center for Human Rights, March 12, 2008), p. 3, http://scm.oas.org/pdfs/2008/CP21371E.pdf.

[24] Art. 5, 75, paras. 17, 19, Constitución Nacional (Arg.); República de Bolivia Constitución Política del Estado, art. 177, para. I–III, art. 180; Constitución Política De La República De Chile, art. 10, 11; Constitución Política de Colombia, arts. 44, 64, 67–9; Constitución Política de la República de Costa Rica art. 79; Cuba (Constitution), art. 39, para. B; Constitución Política, art. 23, para. 20, art. 49, 53, 63 (Ecuador); Constitución Política de la República Dominicana, art. 8, para. 16; Constitución Política de la República de El Salvador, art. 35, 53, 56, 58; Constitución Política de la República de Guatemala, art. 71, 73, 74; Constitución Política de los Estados Unidos Mexicanos, art. 2, para. B, § II, art. 3, para. IV, V, art. 4; Constitución de Nicaragua, art. 105, 119, 121, 125; Constitución Política de Panamá art. 52, 87, 90, 91, 96, 104; Constitución de la República de Paraguay, art. 73, 74, 76, 77; Constitución Política del Perú art. 13, 16, 17; Constitución de la República Oriental del Uruguay, art. 68, 70–1; Constitución de la República Bolivariana de Venezuela, pmbl., art. 102, 103, 121.

[25] Laurence Wolff and Claudio de Moura Castro, *Secondary Education in Latin America and the Caribbean: The Challenge of Growth and Reform* (Washington, DC: Inter-American Development Bank, 2000), p. 10 (describing the class divide between public and private school settings in Latin America and the Caribbean); Michael Smith, "Educational Reform in Latin America: Facing a Crisis," International Development Research Center Report, February 19, 1999, http://web.idrc.ca/en/ev-5552-201-1-DO_TOPIC.html.

[26] Orlando Albornoz, *Education and Society in Latin America* (Pittsburgh: Macmillan, 1993), p. 26; Allison L. C. de Cerreno and Cassandra A. Pyle, "Educational Reform in Latin America P7," Working Paper, Council on Foreign Relations (1996), http://www.ciaonet.org/wps/cea01/; Pablo Gentili, "Educación y Ciudadanía: Un Desafío para América Latina," in Jenny Assael et al. (eds.), *Reforma Educativa y Objetivos Fundamentales Transversales* (Programa Interdisciplinario de Investigaciones en Educación, 2003), http://www.piie.cl/seminario/textos/ponencia_gentili.pdf.

As a result, across Latin America, Afro-descendants are disproportionately illiterate and subject to incomplete educations with barriers
to both primary and secondary education. This racial disparity in levels of education is paralleled by the de facto racial segregation of the
Latin American educational system.[27] The intentionality of the educational segregation is highlighted by the statement "No 'cholo' – a native
Peruvian – would be found in any of the elite universities in Lima, and
no 'negro' would be found in the same type of university in Caracas."[28]
These racialized attitudes that pervade Latin America may in turn help
explain the reasons for the neglect of public primary and secondary
education by Latin American governments.[29]

The racial inequality of the Latin American educational systems is
exemplified by the significant racial disparity in educational outcomes.
For instance, in Colombia 31.3 percent of Afro-Colombians are illiterate, a rate nearly three times that of the rest of the population.[30] Only 13
percent of Afro-Colombians who are more than eighteen years old have
completed primary education.[31] At the postgraduate level only 7.07 percent of enrolled students are Afro-descendants.[32] In the Pacific region,
where the majority of Afro-Colombians reside, for every 100,000 students who finish secondary school, only 2 enroll in a university.[33] And
of those who do manage to enroll in a university, many are unable to
complete their education. Similarly, in Ecuador, the Afro-Ecuadorian
rate of enrollment in secondary school is 36.7 percent as compared to
the white rate of 55 percent. At the university level, Afro-Ecuadorian

[27] Albornoz, *Education and Society in Latin America,* pp. 6, 141.

[28] Ibid. at p. 141.

[29] Ruth Sautu, "Poverty, Psychology, and Dropouts," in Laura Randall and Joan B.
Anderson (eds.), *Schooling for Success: Preventing Repetition and Dropout in Latin
American Primary Schools* (Armonk, NY: M. E. Sharpe, 1999), pp. 23, 27.

[30] Enrique Sánchez and Paola García, "*Más Allá de los Promedios: Afrodescendientes en
América Latina*" (Washington, DC: ACNUR, 2006), pp. 16, 38, www.acnur.org/bib-
lioteca/pdf/4558.pdf.

[31] *El Derecho a la Educación: La Educación en la Perspectiva de los Derechos Humanos,*"
(Colombia: Procuraduría General de la Nación, 2006), p. 159.

[32] Colombian Vice Minister of Preschool, Basic and Medium Education, Ministry of
Education, "Direction of Order and Equity" (2007), www.mineducacion.gov.

[33] "The Judicial System and Racism against People of African Descent: The Cases of
Brazil, Colombia, the Dominican Republic and Peru," *Judicial Studies Centers of the
Americas* (March 2004), n. 50.

enrollment is at 5.5 percent while the white rate is 16.8 percent.[34] The illiteracy rate for Afro-Ecuadorians is 10.3 percent as compared to the white rate of 4.7 percent. In Peru, Afro-Peruvians have disproportionately lower rates of matriculation in elementary, secondary, and university education.[35] In Uruguay, the Afro-Uruguayan rate of enrollment in universities is nearly half that of white Uruguayans. Even more telling is the fact that returns to education are higher for whites than Afro-Uruguayans: that is, Afro-Uruguayans are paid less than whites for each year of education they obtain.[36]

The hierarchical nature of the Latin American educational system ensures that the majority of Afro-descendants cannot use education as a gateway to upward mobility. Yet, studies of industries in which little racial disparity exists in the educational level of the employees, still demonstrate that Afro-descendants are paid a lower wage.[37] Thus the racially skewed educational system and labor market discrimination both combine to subordinate Afro-descendants. For example, various studies in Colombia have demonstrated that regardless of the educational advantage that an Afro-Colombian job applicant may have in terms of degrees, racial discrimination depresses his or her job opportunities and wages.[38]

Indeed, racial discrimination in the labor market is prevalent throughout the region and plays a significant role in determining job placement and career opportunities. This is evident even within occupational contexts in which formal education is not a prominent requirement for selection. Studies of hiring patterns across the region have found employers very reluctant to hire Afro-descendants for managerial, professional, or technical positions; for white-collar clerical jobs; or even for low-level jobs in retail commerce and sales.[39] The small black middle class that exists in Latin America is primarily employed by national government agencies. Once hired, Afro-descendants are located in low-status positions, with lower rates of promotion and advancement but higher rates of dismissal.

[34] *Pueblos Indígenas y Afrodescendientes*, p. 435.
[35] "Los Afrodescendientes en el Perú," pp. 56–62.
[36] Andrews, *Blackness in the White Nation*, pp. 150, 161.
[37] Gustavo Márquez et al., *Outsiders?* pp. 24–6.
[38] Barbary and Urrea, *Gente Negra en Colombia*, pp. 145–7.
[39] Andrews, *Afro-Latin America*, p. 179.

Racial stereotyping as detailed in Chapter 1 also facilitates the exclusion of Afro-descendants because racialized views have become so embedded in the social fiber of Latin American societies that the subordinated status of Afro-descendants in the labor force is naturalized and viewed as logical.[40] For example, in Peru the preference for lighter skin is so pervasive that blacks are only viewed as attractive when their appearance denotes racial mixture with white or indigenous ancestry.[41] This in turn is manifested in the data showing a statistically significant pattern of race influencing earnings and shaping occupational segregation.[42] Indeed, 40 percent of Afro-Peruvians work in low-skill jobs. Most Afro-Peruvians are employed in low-status positions such as drivers, porters, pallbearers, or babysitters. Moreover, Peruvian help-wanted advertisements seeking drivers, cooks, doormen, butlers, and maids often state a preference for nonwhites (*negros* or *morenos*). Afro-Peruvians do not generally hold leadership positions in government or business, and it is widely believed that the navy and air force "follow unstated policies that exclude blacks from the officers corps."[43]

Similarly, in socialist Cuba, Afro-Cubans are systematically excluded from jobs in the tourist sector as employers demand a "good [aka white] appearance" as a job prerequisite, just as employers in Peru, Venezuela, and elsewhere in Latin America do.[44] In studies that control for educational level, the Cuban preference for whiteness in the labor market continues.[45] In many locations with vibrant tourist economies such as Colombia, Costa Rica, Cuba, and Venezuela,

---

[40] Peter Wade, "Afro-Latin Studies: Reflections on the Field," *Latin American and Caribbean Ethnic Studies* 1 (April 2006), pp. 105–24.

[41] Tanya María Golash-Boza, *Yo Soy Negro: Blackness in Peru* (Gainesville: University of Florida Press, 2011), p. 158.

[42] *Reporte ante el comité para la eliminación de la discriminación racial* (last visited on March 27, 2001), www.cnddhh.org.pe/publications; Calvin Sims, "Peru's Blacks Increasingly Discontent with Decorative Role," *New York Times*, August 17, 1996, p. 2.

[43] "1999 Country Reports on Human Rights Practices," U.S. Department of State, Bureau of Democracy, Human Rights, and Labor, February 25, 2000, http://www.state.gov/www/global/human_rights/1999_hrp_report/peru.html.

[44] Andrews, *Afro-Latin America*, pp. 179, 194.

[45] Mark Q. Sawyer, *Racial Politics in Post-Revolutionary Cuba* (Cambridge: Cambridge University Press, 2006), pp. 138–45.

Afro-descendants find that they can only earn higher wages through paid sex work or drug dealing.

In Ecuador, Afro-Ecuadorians have the highest rate of unemployment in the country.[46] Those Afro-Ecuadorians who are employed are primarily maids, security guards, porters, drivers, or temporary workers in the informal economy.[47] In Uruguay, the Afro-Uruguayan unemployment rate is 50 percent higher than that of whites, and their earnings 60 percent of whites'.[48] Even where formal education is not a prerequisite, Latin American studies have revealed evidence of racial discrimination. For instance, Afro-descendants in the Uruguayan national soccer league have experienced racial discrimination.

Moreover, Afro-descendant access to the protections of the formal labor market are also racially constrained. For example, in Colombia, economists have noted that despite the existence of protective labor laws, the vast majority of Afro-descended women who access domestic service positions through Cali employment agencies are relegated to ill-serving exploitative contracts that flagrantly violate the labor laws.[49] In addition, although the employment agencies place many Afro-descended women in domestic service positions, they rarely negotiate written employment contracts on their behalf. Instead the work contracts are most often verbal and offer even fewer protections than the unilateral contracts that are the norm for the written employment contracts.[50] The empirical study of the Cali domestic service context also observes that because many of the employers are disinclined to hire dark-skin Afro-descended women, they reason that only the lowest of salaries and job protections are warranted.

Given the struggles that Afro-descendants encounter in seeking sustainable work, it should not be surprising that their presence

---

[46] *Pueblos Indígenas y Afrodescendientes*, p. 435.

[47] Carlos de la Torre, "Afro-Ecuadorian Responses to Racism: Between Citizenship and Corporatism," in Anani Dzidzienyo and Suzanne Oboler (eds.), *Neither Enemies nor Friends: Latinos, Blacks, Afro-Latinos* (New York: Palgrave Macmillan, 2005), p. 63.

[48] Andrews, *Blackness in the White Nation*, p. 150.

[49] Jeanny Posso, "Mecanismos de Discriminación Étnico-Racial, Clase Social y Género: La Inserción Laboral de Mujeres Negras en el Servicio Doméstico de Cali," in María del Carmen Zabala Arguelles (ed.), *Pobreza, Exclusión Social y Discriminación Étnico-Racial en América Latina y el Caribe* (Bogotá: Siglo del Hombre Editores y Clasco, 2008), pp. 215–38.

[50] Ibid. at p. 227.

within political spheres has also been limited. In fact, the social exclusion of Afro-descendants has been seemingly intractable in Latin America, because of their simultaneous exclusion from the political sphere. Indeed, a significant number of Latin American countries did not abolish literacy requirements for voting until almost a century after emancipation.[51] Because Latin American political and electoral systems exclude Afro-descendants, this in turn reduces the ability of Afro-descendants to influence public policies and programs that could alleviate their marginalization. For example, in Nicaragua as of 2007, there was not a single Afro-descendant in the national assembly even though Afro-descendants make up 9 percent of the country's population.[52] In Costa Rica, in 2006, there was only one black member in the fifty-seven-seat legislative assembly and no black member in the cabinet.[53] While the Afro–Costa Rican public figure Epsy Campbell did make a historic run for president in May 2009, she only received 19

[51] Argentina: 1912 (removing literacy and property requirements); Bolivia: 1952 (removing literacy requirements); Brazil: 1988 (removing literacy and property requirements); Chile: 1970 (removing literacy and property requirements); Colombia: 1936 (removing literacy and property requirements); Costa Rica: 1913 (removing literacy requirements), 1949 (removing both literacy and property requirements); Cuba: 1901 (removing literacy requirements); Ecuador: 1978 (removing literacy requirements); El Salvador: 1945 (removing literacy requirements); Guatemala: 1945 (removing literacy requirements); Honduras: 1894 (removing literacy requirements); Nicaragua: 1948 (removing literacy requirements); Panama: 1904 (removing literacy requirements); Peru: 1979 (removing literacy and property requirements); Uruguay: 1918 (removing literacy and property requirements); Venezuela: 1946–7 (removing literacy and property requirements). Stanley L. Engerman and Kenneth L. Sokoloff, "The Evolution of Suffrage Institutions in the New World," *Journal of Economic History* 65 (December 2005), 912–13 (discussing the removal of literacy requirements in Argentina, Brazil, Chile, Colombia, Costa Rica, Ecuador, El Salvador, Guatemala, Mexico, Peru, and Uruguay); Paul W. Drake and Mathew D. McCubbins, *The Origins of Liberty: Political and Economic Liberalization in the Modern World* (Princeton, NJ: Princeton University Press, 1988), p. 134 (discussing the removal of literacy requirements in Argentina, Bolivia, Brazil, Chile, Colombia, Costa Rica, Cuba, Dominican Republic, Ecuador, Guatemala, Honduras, Mexico, Nicaragua, Panama, Paraguay, Peru, and Venezuela); Leslie Bethell (ed.), *Latin America: Politics and Society since 1930* (New York: Cambridge University Press, 1998), p. 36 (discussing the removal of literacy and property requirements in Argentina, Brazil, Chile, Colombia, Costa Rica, Peru, Uruguay, and Venezuela).

[52] Gustavo Márquez et al., *Outsiders?* pp. 27–8.

[53] *Costa Rica, Country Reports on Human Rights Practices 2006* (Washington, DC: Department of State, Bureau of Democracy, Human Rights, and Labor, March 6, 2007), http://www.state.gov/g/drl/rls/hrrpt/2006/78886.htm.

percent of the vote.[54] The 19 percent vote return is modest when one considers that a Costa Rican survey found her to be "the woman with the most presidential possibilities in Costa Rica."[55]

In marked contrast to the context of gender barriers to political participation, the majority of Latin American governments have not proactively addressed the issue of Afro-descendant exclusion. By 2005, eleven of eighteen Latin American nations had adopted quotas to increase women's representation in government bodies.[56] On average, women's presence in congress has jumped by 9 percentage points in those countries with gender quotas. The dearth of such government intervention for Afro-descendants makes a striking counterpoint.

One recent exception is Colombia. A law passed in 1993 granted Afro-descended communities the right to two representatives in the lower house pursuant to a specially designed "virtual" district. The effects of the measure have been muted by the fact that reservations for Afro-Colombians make up only 1.2 percent of the congressional seats, despite the fact that they are estimated to be one-quarter of the Colombian population.

Despite this plethora of data displaying the pervasive exclusion of Afro-descendants across the region, Latin American elites attribute the plight of Afro-descendants solely to their low socioeconomic status. Such a justification presumes that the long-standing pattern of Afro-descendant poverty exists in isolation from the pejorative view of blackness. Moreover, the narrow focus on class status ignores the growing number of studies that demonstrate that when socioeconomic status is controlled for, disparities across race still exist in Latin America, as discussed in this chapter in relation to the labor market.

The Brazilian context also keenly establishes the independent influence of racial bias in the marginalization of Afro-descendants, because of the plethora of studies that control for class status. For this reason,

---

[54] Alonso Mata, "Epsy Campbell se Mantendrá en el PAC," Nacion.com, June 2, 2009, http://wvw.nacion.com/ln_ee/2009/junio/02/pais1983157.html.

[55] "Special Edition: 'Etnia Negra' in Panama," *Noticiero Popular Panameño*, May 2008.

[56] Mala Htun and Mark Jones, "Engendering the Right to Participate in Decisionmaking: Electoral Quotas and Women's Leadership in Latin America," in N. Craske and M. Molyneux (eds.), *Gender and the Politics of Rights and Democracy in Latin America* (London: Palgrave Macmillan, 2002).

it is useful to elaborate upon the Brazilian context as a case study. Brazil serves as a particularly useful case study because even though Afro-descendants constitute a majority (or at least a plurality) of the population, they remain relatively powerless today despite their numbers. Thus the situation for Afro-descendants in other countries, where their numbers are not as large, is often more dire. In short, the extent to which ongoing white privilege and racial bias influence the marginalization of the larger number of Afro-Brazilians strongly suggests that in all other countries where Afro-descendants are less numerous and often less politically powerful, the Afro-Brazilian pattern of racial exclusion can serve as a useful representation of how racial bias influences the socioeconomic status and exclusion of Afro-descendants.

THE BRAZILIAN CASE STUDY

As in the rest of Latin America, socioeconomic indicators in Brazil show considerable inequalities between black and white Brazilians, despite the fact that Afro-Brazilians were reported as 51.1 percent of the population in the Census Bureau data for 2009.[57] It should be noted that Brazilian social scientists collapse the *preto* /black and *pardo* /mulatto–mixed-race census categories into one Afro-Brazilian unit of analysis in order to obviate concerns about the ambiguity in how individuals choose to racially identify themselves with either the *preto* and *pardo* color categories, and because the data frequently suggest that the prevalent racial disparities exist between whites and nonwhites, rather than between *pretos* and *pardos*. Whites on average earn almost two times what nonwhites earn.[58] The Brazilian Ministry of Health data similarly suggest a nation of separate spheres for whites and Afro-descendants.[59] Specifically, the child mortality rate not only

[57] "Síntese de Indicadores Socias: Uma Análise das Condiçoes de Vida da População Brasileira," Instituto Brasiliero de Geografia e Estatística, 2010, table 8.1, http://www.ibge.gov.br/home/estatistica/populacao/condicaodevida/indicadoresminimos/sinteseindicsociais2010/default.shtm.
[58] Ibid. at table 8.6.
[59] "Entidades Criticam 'Racismo Institucional'," *Correio de Sergipe*, November 20, 2008, http://correiodesergipe.com/lernoticia.php?noticia=30545 (describing ONG Crioula's study of Ministry of Health statistics by race); Carta Aberta ao Ministro,

is greater for Afro-Brazilian children, but has always historically been so, and even worsened in 2000.[60] Afro-Brazilian children have a 44 percent higher risk of dying from infectious diseases before their first birthday than do white children. Afro-Brazilian children also have 68 percent more chance of dying from tuberculosis than white children. Afro-Brazilian maternal mortality rates are 41 percent greater than those of white women. Racial disparities are also prevalent in life expectancy rates, housing situations, and access to durable goods and digital communications.[61]

Segregated residential patterns are also manifested in Brazil.[62] While Brazilian racial segregation is not statistically as severe as that documented in the United States, Afro-Brazilian public figures describe the de facto racial segregation of Brazil as having a comparable visceral effect to that of apartheid South Africa, where there are two Brazils – one in the exclusive white hotel areas, and another in the primarily nonwhite favelas and streets.[63]

> Brazilians in disproportionate numbers live in urban shantytowns called favelas, mocambos, or palafitas. To visit Rio de Janeiro's Central Station is to witness dangerously dilapidated trains taking hours to transport mostly black workers from the huge metropolitan area called the Baixada Fluminense to their jobs in the capital city, a scene that recalls black South Africans' commute from segregated townships. The racial contrast between a public school in

Secretarias Estaduais e Municipais de Saude, in Crioula, September 27, 2008, http://www.crioula.org.br/agenda_carta.htm.

[60] Charles H. Wood, José Alberto Magno de Caravalho, and Cláudia Júlia Guimarães Horta, "The Color of Child Mortality in Brazil, 1950–2000," *Latin American Research Review* 45 (2010), 114–39.

[61] *Fundo de Desenvolvimento das Nações Unidas para a Mulher, & Secretaria Especial de Políticas para as Mulheres, Retrato das desigualdades de gênero e raça*, 3rd ed. (Brazil: Instituto de Pesquisa Econômica Aplicada, September 2008); Peggy A. Lovell, "Race, Gender, and Work in São Paulo, Brazil, 1960–2000," *Latin American Research Review* 41 (October 2006), 63–87.

[62] Edward Telles, "Residential Segregation by Skin Color in Brazil," *American Sociological Review* 57 (1992), 186.

[63] Telma Marotto, "Brazilian Secret 93 Million Don't Want to Talk about Is Racism," Bloomberg.com News, June 26, 2008, http://www.bloomberg.com/apps/news?pid=20601109&refer=news&sid=aIezjRWRd5Tk; Antônio Pitanga, Larry Crook (ed.), and Randal Johnson (ed.), Where Are the Blacks? in *Black Brazil: Culture, Identity, and Social Mobilization* (Los Angeles: UCLA Latin American Center, 1999), pp. 31–2.

the Baixada – or in poor suburbs or favelas almost anywhere in
Brazil – and a university in a rich area like Rio de Janeiro's Zona
Sul suggests the difference between a township school and a uni-
versity in South Africa.[64]

While white middle-class neighborhoods in Brazil are in closer proximity to black-dominated favelas than the physical distance between
white middle-class neighborhoods and black neighborhoods in the
United States, the white middle-class neighborhoods in Brazil are
just as psychologically and symbolically segregated. The segregation
is effectuated by the installation of high-walled gated communities
that keep Afro-Brazilians hidden from view.[65] Moreover, those Afro-
Brazilians who do manage to integrate themselves into a residential
area often experience a high degree of social isolation and ostracism.[66]
Even the mythical notion of a racially integrated annual carnival celebration has been debunked by one Brazilian race relations scholar,
who observes:

> All join together in the world's greatest carnival – everyone par-
> ticipates, "each in his or her place." There is no social interaction
> among the groups, and ropes mark the physical limits of each. In
> view of blacks' affirmation in carnival, the middle and upper clas-
> ses, self-identified as whites, react by establishing rigid criteria
> of social and racial discrimination for participation in their own
> organizations.[67]

And the segregation of carnival is exacerbated by the huge numbers of
white Brazilians who flee their homes for the duration of carnival week

---

[64] Abdias do Nascimento and Elisa Larkin Nascimento, "Dance of Deception:
Reading of Race Relations in Brazil," in Charles V. Hamilton, Lynn Huntley, Neville
Alexander, Antonio Sérgio Alfredo Guimarães, and Wilmot James (eds.), *Beyond
Racism: Race and Inequality in Brazil, South Africa, and the United States* (Boulder,
CO: Lynne Rienner, 2001), p. 108.

[65] Robin E. Sheriff, *Dreaming Equality: Color, Race and Racism in Urban Brazil* (New
Brunswick, NJ: Rutgers University Press, 2001), p. 152.

[66] France Windance Twine, *Racism in a Racial Democracy: The Maintenance of White
Supremacy in Brazil* (New Brunswick, NJ: Rutgers University Press, 1998), p. 26.

[67] Jeferson Bacelar, "Black in Salvador: Racial Paths," in Larry Crook and Randal
Johnson (eds.), *Black Brazil: Culture, Identity, and Social Mobilization* (Los Angeles:
UCLA Latin American Center, 1999), pp. 85, 99.

in order to avoid the disorder attributed to Afro-Brazilian revelers. This segregation exceeds the concern about the presumed criminality of nearby favelas, given how extensively whites organize themselves into insular worlds with extremely limited interaction with Afro-Brazilians outside the hierarchical employer-servant relationships.[68] "The reality is that they [blacks] are not normally incorporated into your life, they are not in your social circles."[69] The vigilance of protecting whites from blackness is apparent in white parental directives to avoid interactions with blacks and anyone who could even be perceived as black simply from time in the sun. "She [my mother] wanted me to stay very white, to characterize my Aryan race, right? To stay white. I didn't go to the beach so that I wouldn't get dark like other people."[70]

Nor are low-income residential settings sites of multiracial inclusion. For instance, ethnographic studies of Brazilian favelas (slum dwellings) have demonstrated that many whites who live in favelas among Afro-Brazilian neighbors retain a sense of white superiority as reflected in one white resident's remarking, "They are gross. They are badly brought up. I don't like pretos [blacks]."[71] The disdain for Afro-Brazilian neighbors is also evident in the outrage of white parents when their children date Afro-Brazilian neighbors in the favelas – "You're going to dirty the family."[72] Consequently, favela residents firmly believe that having lighter skin and European features, increases the potential for success and a better life.[73] Surveys in favelas indicate that Afro-Brazilians there experience relative disadvantage as compared to white residents, who consistently have higher incomes and shorter average rates of residence in a favela.[74] This is mirrored by the racial disparities in living conditions whereby lack of Afro-Brazilian

---

[68] Sheriff, *Dreaming Equality*, pp. 151, 161.

[69] Ibid. at p. 169.

[70] Ibid. at p. 163.

[71] Ibid. at p. 132.

[72] Ibid. at pp. 138–9.

[73] Donna M. Goldstein, *Laughter Out of Place: Race, Class, Violence, and Sexuality in a Rio Shantytown* (Berkeley: University of California Press, 2003), p. 108.

[74] João H. Costa Vargas, "When a Favela Dared to Become a Gated Community: The Politics of Race and Urban Space in Rio de Janeiro," *Latin American Perspectives* 33 (July 2006), 49–81, 64.

access to sanitation, garbage collection, and running water is greater than can be accounted for by regional differences.[75]

Examining Brazilian racial disparity in the educational context reveals startling patterns. In Brazil, illiteracy among the nonwhite population is more than double than that of whites.[76] A study holding per capita family income constant showed that (1) nonwhites have a lower rate of schooling than whites, (2) nonwhite students have a higher likelihood of falling behind in school than white students, and (3) nonwhite students attend schools that are likely to offer fewer classroom hours than schools attended by white students.[77] Students of African descent achieve educational levels consistently inferior to those achieved by whites from the same socioeconomic level, and African-descended students' returns to education are disproportionately lower.[78] Whites have a vastly disproportionately greater likelihood of completing college than nonwhites. In the 1990s there was a sevenfold greater likelihood of completing college among whites.[79] Even with the advent of university affirmative action policies in the 1990s, today Brazilian whites are still admitted to universities at twice the rate of nonwhites.[80]

Moreover, as family income decreases, the differential disadvantage in access to schooling between students of European and African ancestry increases.[81] Clearly, the unsatisfactory life circumstances of Afro-Brazilians cannot be attributed solely to an issue of class status. Despite expectations to the contrary, economic development has not corrected racial disparities in the educational system.[82] Some

---

[75] Elisa Larkin Nascimento, *The Sorcery of Color: Identity, Race, and Gender in Brazil* (Philadelphia: Temple University Press, 2007), p. 47.

[76] Ibid. at table 8.2.

[77] Silva and Hasenbalg, "Race and Educational Opportunity in Brazil," pp. 53, 54 (research conducted by the Carlos Chagas Foundation in São Paulo, Brazil).

[78] Ibid. at 54 (citing C. Hasenbalg and N. V. Silva (eds.), *Estrutura Social, Mobilidade e Raça* (São Paulo: Vertice, 1988)).

[79] Silva and Hasenbalg, "Race and Educational Opportunity in Brazil," pp. 54–5.

[80] Ibid. at table 8.12.

[81] Nelson do Valle Silva and Carlos A. Hasenbalg, "Race and Educational Opportunity in Brazil," in Rebecca Reichmann (ed.), *Race in Contemporary Brazil: From Indifference to Inequality* (University Park: Penn State University Press, 1999), pp. 53, 58.

[82] Diana DeG. Brown, "Power, Invention, and the Politics of Race: Umbanda Past and Future," in Larry Crook and Randal Johnson (eds.), *Black Brazil: Culture, Identity, and Social Mobilization* (Los Angeles: UCLA Latin American Center, 1999), pp. 213–14.

commentators even suggest that periods of socioeconomic national development have increased rather than decreased racial inequality, especially for those at the higher end of the social structure.[83] This matter is only made worse by the racial disparities in university enrollment rates.[84]

The deficiencies of the public primary and secondary school content are magnified by the racialized treatment Afro-Brazilian children receive in school.[85] For example, social scientists have documented that the majority of Brazilian teachers view Afro-Brazilian students as lacking the potential to learn.[86] Schoolteachers' assessments of student potential and performance are directly influenced by race.[87] As one such teacher states, "They can't learn, they're not disciplined, they're lazy and they give up too soon. All they want is soccer and samba. It's in the blood."[88] Even studies of the predominantly Afro-descended northeastern state of Bahia, demonstrate that school officials there view children of Afro-descent as deficient in their capacity to learn.[89]

Racialized attitudes are also manifested in the textbooks children are assigned, in which black people are consistently depicted as animallike, as socially subordinate, and in other stereotyped manners.[90] When black children are targeted with racist behavior by classmates who have internalized the societal bias against those with dark skin,

[83] Lovell, *Race, Gender, and Work in São Paulo*, p. 81.

[84] "Síntese de Indicadores Socias 2008, Estudos & Pesquisas: Informação Demográfica e Socioeconômica num. 23," Instituto Brasiliero de Geografia e Estatística, 2008, http://www.ibge.gov.br/home/estatistica/populacao/condicaodevida/indicadoresminimos/sinteseindicsociais2008/default.shtm.

[85] Cleusa Simão, "Mulher Negra: Identidade e Exclusão Social," unpublished master's dissertation, Universidade São Marcos (2004), pp. 85, 104.

[86] Rosana Aparecida Peronti Chiarello, "Preconceitos E Discriminações Racias: Um Olhar de Professoras Sobre Seus (Suas) Alunos (as) Negros (as)," master's thesis, Federal University of São Carlos (2003), pp. 50–3.

[87] Cesar Rossato, Verônica Gesser, and Eliane Cavalleiro (ed.), "A Experiencia da Branquitude Diante de Conflitos Racias: Estudos de Realidades Brasileiras e Estadunidenses," in *Racismo E Anti-Racismo Na Educaçao: Repensando nossa Escola* (São Paulo: Selo Negro, 2001), pp. 11, 19.

[88] Elisa Larkin Nascimento, "It's in the Blood: Notes on Race Attitudes in Brazil from a Different Perspective," in Hamilton (ed.), *Beyond Racism*, pp. 509, 518.

[89] Bernd Reiter, "Inequality and School Reform in Bahia, Brazil," *International Review of Education* 55 (2009), 345–56.

[90] Hédio Silva, Jr., *Discriminação Racial nas Escolas: Entre a Lei e as Práticas Socias* (Brasília: UNESCO, 2002), pp. 34–8.

school authorities condone the behavior by characterizing it as harmless teasing and joking.[91] These racialized attitudes may in turn help explain the reasons for the neglect of public primary and secondary education by the government[92] and may also help explain why educational specialists observe that in Brazil, the "benefits of 'universally' designed programs to improve educational outcomes do not reach the poor adequately."[93]

Yet, children of African descent encounter in Brazil not only an environment inhospitable for learning, but also a racialized access to schooling.[94] For instance, even though it is compulsory for children aged seven to fourteen to attend school,[95] it is common for Brazilian families who informally adopt children of color, in an unstated exchange for their unpaid labor, to prevent them from attending primary school,[96] and for school officials not to enforce compulsory school attendance.[97] The Afro-Brazilian students who do manage to stay in school often encounter a substandard quality of instruction.[98] For example, in the rural Northeast, where the majority of residents are Afro-Brazilian, less than half of the primary school teachers have themselves completed primary schooling.[99] Furthermore, even middle-class Afro-Brazilian children encounter barriers in enrolling in the private schools their parents are able to afford. For instance, a 2008 report notes that when an Afro-Brazilian college-educated

---

[91] Ibid.

[92] David N. Plank, *The Means of Our Salvation: Public Education in Brazil, 1930–1995* (Boulder, CO: Westview Press, 1996), p. 6.

[93] Laurence Wolff and Claudio de Moura Castro, *Secondary Education in Latin America and the Caribbean: The Challenge of Growth and Reform* (Washington, DC: Inter-American Development Bank, 2000), p. 45, annex. 1.

[94] "Brazil's Unfinished Battle for Racial Democracy," *The Economist*, April 22, 2000, p. 31.

[95] Silva and Hasenbalg, "Race and Educational Opportunity in Brazil," p. 55.

[96] Twine, *Racism in a Racial Democracy*, p. 37.

[97] Plank, *Means of Our Salvation*, p. 6; Abraham Lama, "Market Reforms Come at a Cost to Education," Inter Press Service, October 9, 1997, p. 1.

[98] Linda Larach, *Secondary Education Profile: A Summary of "Secondary Education: Time to Move Forward,"* Human Development Network Secondary Education Series Brazil (Washington, DC: World Bank, 2001), p. 7, http://www.wds.worldbank.org/servlet/WDSContentServer/WDSP/IB/ 2002/09/07/000094946_02082104033872/Rendered/PDF/multi0page.pdf.

[99] Plank, *Means of Our Salvation*, p. 7.

professional woman sought to enroll her six-year-old in an exclusive São Paulo neighborhood school, another mother said, "Do you see any other black child here?" as an explanation as to why the child had been rejected.[100]

The racial disparity in basic schooling results in a racially segregated public university setting as well because the public primary and secondary schools fail to prepare their students for the public university entrance examination.[101] In contrast, the white children whose parents are better able to pay the fees for the racially exclusive private primary and secondary schools are then better trained for the public university entrance examination. As a result, the free, elite, and well-funded public universities of Brazil are disproportionately attended by white students. In turn, the major companies who recruit heavily from the elite public universities for their trainees have a racially exclusive white trainee pool.[102]

In Brazil, there is a consistent pattern whereby Afro-Brazilian investments in education provide less of an improvement in labor market opportunities than they do for white Brazilians.[103] To be specific, with just two additional years in the average rate of schooling for whites (8.5 years as compared to 6.4 years for Afro-Brazilians), white Brazilians average a monthly salary 3.6 times the minimum wage as compared to Afro-Brazilians, who only average a monthly salary of 1.9 times the minimum wage.[104] When Afro-Brazilians and white Brazilians have the same years of schooling, whites earn 40 percent more.[105] Wage inequality exists even among Afro-Brazilians with the highest level of education, and the disparity is more accentuated in the higher-income brackets.[106] In fact, Brazil's own Census Bureau, IBGE

[100] Marotto, "Brazilian Secret."
[101] Nascimento and Nascimento, "Dance of Deception," p. 117.
[102] Marotto, "Brazilian Secret."
[103] Samuel Kilsztajn et al., "Concentração e Distribuição do Rendimento por Raça No Brasil," *Revista de Economia Contemporânea* 9 (May/August 2005), 367–84.
[104] "Síntese de Indicadores Socias 2006, Estudos & Pesquisas: Informação Demográfica e Socioeconômica num. 19," Instituto Brasiliero de Geografia e Estatística, 2006, Table 9.7, http://www.ibge.gov.br/home/estatistica/populacao/condicaodevida/indicadoresminimos/sinteseindicsociais2006/default.shtm.
[105] Ibid.
[106] Nascimento, *Sorcery of Color*, p. 46.

(Instituto Brasileiro de Geografia e Estatística), specifically states that "education cannot be characterized as a sufficient factor for overcoming racial inequalities in income in Brazil."[107]

Racial disparity is so prevalent in the Brazilian labor market that it is consistent across different sectors.[108] Indeed, even the hiring practices for television actors reflect racial exclusion and hierarchy whereby the few Afro-Brazilians who are hired portray stereotyped and negative images of Afro-Brazilians.[109] Similarly, few Afro-Brazilian models are hired to represent "Brazilian" beauty despite the prevalence of persons of African descent in the population.[110] Even the context of Catholic appointment of priests and bishops is characterized by racial stratification, whereby only 6.3 percent of Catholic priests in Brazil are Afro-Brazilians, and only 2.5 percent of Catholic bishops are Afro-Brazilian.[111] As a result of the labor market disparities, Afro-Brazilians represent 73 percent of the most indigent sector of society and only 12 percent of the most rich. In contrast, white Brazilians represent only 12 percent of the indigent population and 86 percent of the higher-income population.[112] It is thus not surprising that Afro-Brazilian children have higher rates of labor market involvement than white children.[113]

The systemic racial discrimination suggested by the preceding quantitative data is also underscored by the numerous accounts of racialized treatment in the workplace, schools, and other social settings. For example, interviews of Afro-Brazilian workers consistently reveal racial discrimination as a set of daily practices manifested in all types of

[107] "Síntese de Indicadores Socias 2006," table 9.7.

[108] Fernando Lobo Braga, "Discriminação No Mercado de Trabalho: Diferenças Racias e Por Sexo No Ano de 2003," master's dissertation, Universidade Católica de Brasília (2005), p. 30.

[109] Joel Zito Araújo, *A Negação do Brasil: O Negro na Telenovela Brasileira* (Documentary 2000).

[110] Marcelo Sabino Luiz, "A Mulher Negra No Mercado de Trabalho: A Pseudoequidade Marcada Pela Discriminação da Sociedade E a Mídia No Seculo," *Partes* 21 (September 9, 2010), http://www.partes.com.br/politicas/mulhernegranotrabalho. asp.

[111] Wagner Gomes, "Negros São Minoria Na Igreja," *O Globo*, May 14, 2007, p. 3.

[112] "Síntese de Indicadores Socias 2008," table 9.10.

[113] Patricia Duarte, "Negros São Maiores Vítimas do Trabalho Infantil no País," *O Globo*, November 18, 2006.

jobs from domestic servants to professional workers.[114] Afro-Brazilians whose job applicant test scores qualify them for white-collar positions are routinely denied such positions and instead directed to lower-ranked positions.[115] As one Afro-Brazilian relates, after having qualified for a store sales position by virtue of his test score, he was then told "that there were no openings at the front counter but that there was an opening in the stockroom, in back. But she didn't even know my name; later she asked me, 'What is your name?' So she didn't even look [at my test score]."[116] Afro-Brazilians are only welcomed as front counter cashiers in large grocery stores that are not the purveyors of status, in addition to being welcomed to the low-status position of domestic servant.[117] Indeed, when exceptional Afro-Brazilians manage to obtain access to well-regarded job positions with job mobility within a firm, the racial discrimination escalates. Because many white colleagues are uncomfortable with Afro-Brazilians' rising to positions of power, working professionals of African descent report that coworkers seek to avoid working under black authority by instead dealing with other superiors and looking for minuscule errors in Afro-Brazilians' work.[118] It is thus unsurprising that the workplace has been observed to be the context in which racism is most often experienced by Afro-Brazilians.[119]

Nonetheless, the pain of racism asserts itself in other social contexts as well. In the public sphere, Afro-Brazilian professionals commonly report that despite their higher incomes, they are often treated with disdain. Poor or no service at restaurants and retail establishments in particular is a "constant reminder that they do not belong in a public space ... because they are out of place."[120] While there may be no

---

[114] Maria Aparecida Silva Bento, "Silent Conflict: Discriminatory Practices and Black Responses in the Workplace," in Reichmann (ed.), *From Indifference to Inequality*, pp. 109–22.

[115] Sheriff, *Dreaming Equality*, pp. 208–9.

[116] Ibid. at p. 208.

[117] John Burdick, *Blessed Anastácia: Women, Race, and Popular Christianity in Brazil* (New York: Routledge, 1998), pp. 46–7.

[118] Bento, "Silent Conflict," pp. 115–16.

[119] Sheriff, *Dreaming Equality*, p. 86.

[120] Graziella Moraes da Silva and Elisa P. Reis, "Perceptions of Racial Discrimination among Black Professionals in Rio de Janeiro," *Latin American Research Review* 46 (2011), pp. 55–78; Angela Figueiredo, "'Out of Place:'The Experience of the Black Middle Class," in Bernd Reiter and Gladys L. Mitchell (eds.), *Brazil's New Racial Politics* (Boulder, CO: Lynne Rienner, 2010), pp. 51–3.

written policy of exclusion, it is systematically imposed. For example, one Afro-Brazilian athlete was excluded from the swimming pool of a Rio athletic club in the 1980s, and a friend explained that he had unfortunately arrived "at an hour during which negros are not permitted to swim in the pool."[121] More commonly, Afro-Brazilians are under suspicion when entering stores. "People stare at you, give you the mau olhado [nasty looks]. It's not even that they always think you'll steal something, although that sometimes happens. It's like they find us ugly or something like that, like you shouldn't be there."[122]

The white hypervigilance of blackness also occurs in social gatherings. For instance, "when a dark person arrives at a party people keep staring. A party that you were invited to by another person, full of whites, where there are more whites. The pretinho [little black] who arrives always feels that they're being a little mistreated."[123] Similarly, when Brazilians date across color lines, the interracial relationships not only raise a few eyebrows but may also provoke censure and harassment.[124]

Nor are family structures free from racial bias in Brazil and the rest of Latin America. The darkest children in many families are often the subject of racialized joking and commentary, while the lightest family member is viewed as the most attractive and intelligent.[125] Ethnographers report that narratives about parents' giving preferential treatment to lighter-skinned children are not hard to find. For example, in a family with twin daughters, the dark-skinned girl was treated like a servant in the house while the lighter-skinned girl was pampered and allowed various privileges.[126]

Unfortunately, such racial bias is not confined to the private sphere. Indeed, police violence is riddled with racial bias. For example, the police harassment of Afro-Brazilians is manifested in an explicitly racial manner, whereby racial slurs are uttered while the abuse occurs.[127] One typical police practice includes entering city buses and

---

[121] Sheriff, *Dreaming Equality*, p. 207.
[122] Ibid. at p. 91.
[123] Ibid. at p. 92.
[124] Ibid. at p. 40.
[125] Ibid. at pp. 143–4.
[126] Burdick, *Blessed Anastácia*, p. 43.
[127] Ibid. at p. 94.

ordering young black men to get off for a *revista* (review) to be frisked and interrogated simply on the suspicion of being black. Moreover, the most extreme police violence is targeted against Afro-Brazilians with the seeming sanction of the general population.[128] For instance, it has been documented that the Rio de Janeiro police alone kill more than 2.5 times as many persons in a month as the New York City Police Department kills in a year, and that the majority of the victims are Afro-Brazilians.[129] Systematic interviews and focus group research in Rio de Janeiro favelas indicate that the police so closely align blackness with criminality that they make no effort to distinguish law abiding favela residents from the lawbreakers when raiding the favelas with violent police tactics.[130]

These racialized attitudes are infused throughout the law enforcement context of Brazil. In a seminal study of all criminal actions for robbery in the city of São Paulo that were initially processed in 1993, it was shown that almost twice as many whites as Afro-Brazilians (27% versus 15%) were released on bail.[131] The study also found racial disparity in conviction rates with a conviction rate of 59.4 percent for white defendants and 68.8 percent for blacks. One study published in 2003 confirms this tendency toward the greater punishment of Afro-Brazilians, in terms of their disproportionate rates of arrest and conviction.[132]

Experiences of racism are prevalent even among the emerging black middle class. In an ethnographic study of persons self-identifying as *negro*/black in the middle-class neighborhood of Pituba, Salvador, in the predominantly black Northeast of Brazil, 71

---

[128] Michael J. Mitchell and Charles H. Wood, "Ironies of Citizenship: Skin Color, Police Brutality, and the Challenge to Democracy in Brazil," *Social Forces* 77 (March 1999), 1001–20.

[129] Vargas, "When a Favela Dared to Become a Gated Community," p. 56.

[130] "Rompendo o Cerceamento da Palavra: A Voz dos Favelados em Busca de Reconhecimento," Instituto Brasileiro de Análises Socias e Econômicas, November 11, 2007, http://www.ibase.br/modules.php?name=Conteudo&pid=2077&print=1.

[131] Sérgio Adorno, "Discriminação Racial e Justiça Criminal em São Paulo," *Novos Estudos CEBRAP* 43 (November 1995), 45–63.

[132] Renato Sêrgio de Lima, Alessandra Teixeira, and Jacqueline Signoretto, "Mulheres Negras: As Mais Punidas Nos Crimes de Roubo," *Boletín del Núcleo de Pesquisas IBCCRIM* 125 (April 2003), 3.

percent indicated that they had experienced racial discrimination.[133] Indeed, the only Afro-Brazilian justice on the Federal Supreme Court, Justice Joaquim Barbosa, has stated that in comparison to his travels abroad to Europe and the United States, Brazil was the location where he had actual experiences of racial discrimination.[134] In fact, not only is middle-class standing not a shield from racial discrimination, it can aggravate matters when middle-class Afro-descendants attempt to enter social spaces understood as only for white elites.[135] For instance, an Afro-Brazilian who worked in the financial market of São Paulo for twenty-six years as an economic planning manager dressed in the professional attire of a suit and tie reported in 2008 that every single day he observed white women "tighten the grip on their handbags as he passed."[136]

An examination of the intersectional gendered and racialized position of Afro-descended women further highlights the role of race in Latin America.[137] The social indicators for Afro-descended women across the region paint a devastating picture of intersectional racial exclusion and bias.[138] In Brazil, for example, Afro-Brazilian women have the worst socioeconomic indicators given the more intensive social barriers at the intersection of race and gender.[139] The most recent government statistics reveal that Afro-Brazilian women are worse off in the labor market than white women and than men of all races, because

---

[133] Santos Silva, "Negros Com Renda Média No Bairro da Pituba," master's thesis, Universidade Salvador-UNIFACS (2007), p. 75.

[134] Frederico Vasconcelos, "Situações de Discriminação Só Tive No Brasil, Diz Ministro do STF," Folha de São Paulo Online, November 23, 2008, http://www1.folha.uol.com.br/folha/brasil/ult96u470662.shtml.

[135] Kia Lilly Caldwell, *Negras in Brazil: Re-envisioning Black Women, Citizenship, and the Politics of Identity* (New Brunswick, NJ: Rutgers University Press 2007), p. 69.

[136] Marotto, "Brazilian Secret."

[137] Peter Wade, Fernando Urrea Giraldo and Mara Viveros Vigoya (eds.), *Raza, Etnicidad y Sexualidades: Ciudadanía y Multiculturalismo en América Latina* (Bogotá: Universidad Nacional de Colombia, 2008).

[138] Helen I. Safa, "Racial and Gender Inequality in Latin America: Afro-descendant Women Respond," *Feminist Africa Diaspora Voices* (2007), http://www.feminista-frica.org.

[139] Peggy A. Lovell, "Gender, Race, and the Struggle for Social Justice in Brazil," *Latin American Perspectives.* 27 (November 2000), 85–102; Rosana Heringer, "Diversidade Racial e Relações de Gênero no Brasil Contemporâneo," in *CEPIA* (ed.), *O Progresso Das Mulheres No Brasil* (Brazil: UNIFEM, 2006), p. 142.

they disproportionately work in the informal labor market without rights to unemployment insurance and maternity leave.[140] Indeed, they are the most indigent group of the entire population.[141] The median salary for Afro-Brazilian women is half that of white women.[142] Even when Afro-Brazilian women have the same years of schooling as white women, white women still earn 40 percent more than they do.[143] Moreover, Afro-Brazilian women have the highest unemployment rate in the nation, despite the fact that they enter the labor market earlier than all other groups and retire the latest.[144] Analyses of labor market changes during periods of rapid industrialization demonstrate that white women still gain access to higher education and better-paying occupations in much greater numbers than Afro-Brazilian women.[145] In addition, white women continue to be paid higher wages in every occupation. In fact, when sociodemographic differences such as educational level and occupational placement are controlled for in statistical studies, Afro-Brazilian women are still shown to be paid less than similarly qualified white women.[146] Furthermore, Afro-Brazilian women who rise to the top of the occupational hierarchy actually experience increased wage inequality.[147]

Even in São Paulo, the most economically dynamic region of the country, Afro-Brazilian women remain overwhelmingly concentrated as domestic workers in the labor market and are paid less

[140] "Síntese de Indicadores Socias: Uma Análise das Condiçoes de Vida da População Brasileira," Instituto Brasiliero de Geografia e Estatística, table 9.4, http://www.ibge.gov.br/home/estatistica/populacao/condicaodevida/indicadoresminimos/sinteseindicsociais2010/default.shtm.

[141] Luiz Marcelo Sabino, "A Mulher Negra No Mercado de Trabalho: A Pseudoequidade, Marcada Pela Discriminação da Socidedade E a Mídia No Século 21," *Partes* 21 (September 9, 2010), http://www.partes.com.br/politica/mulhernegranotrabalho.asp.

[142] Maria Aparecida Silva Bento, "A Mulher Negra No Mercado de Trabalho," *Observatório Social*, March 2004, p. 29.

[143] Ibid.

[144] Ibid.

[145] Peggy A. Lovell, "Women and Racial Inequality at Work in Brazil," in Michael Hanchard (ed.), *Racial Politics in Contemporary Brazil* (Durham, NC: Duke University Press, 1999), pp. 138, 149.

[146] Ibid. at p. 150.

[147] Ibid.

than white women and Afro-Brazilian men in all educational categories.[148] Furthermore, the occupational mobility of Afro-Brazilian women in São Paulo is significantly stagnant in contrast to that of white women and Afro-Brazilian men.[149]

For Afro-Brazilian women, racial discrimination often takes the form of being sexually objectified as prostitutes or directed to service entrances as presumed domestic servants despite their apparel and trappings of middle-class status.[150] They also experience exclusion from job positions explicitly and implicitly requiring *boa aparência* (a good appearance), widely understood as a white appearance.[151] Even in the context of the Afro-Brazilian-dominated domestic service sector, Afro-Brazilian applicants find that "they prefer white maids [*empregadas*] over black maids (pretas)."[152] And those Afro-Brazilians who are hired as domestic servants observe a pattern of white employers' designating separate plates, utensils, and foods, seemingly motivated by a fear of racial contamination.[153] In fact, the racial motivation of the employers is often quite explicit, as demonstrated by such employer comments as "No, you can't [work here]. No, my husband doesn't like black people. Oh, I don't want you [here], no, because my children don't get along with negras."[154]

Rather than hire black women as maids, many white employers in Brazil and Latin America prefer to informally adopt young black girls who can attend to the domestic chores. In this practice of *criação* (which I translate as "informal paperless adoption"), upper- and middle-class Brazilian families take in Afro-Brazilian girls and care for them in an unstated exchange for their unpaid labor. As one such woman explains:

> I needed an extra maid. I asked Jose Costa ... to find me a young girl
> from the rural area near Alianca. And so he drove to the villa during

[148] *See* Lovell, "Gender, Race, and the Struggle for Social Justice in Brazil."
[149] Edward E. Telles, *Race in Another America: The Significance of Skin Color in Brazil* (Princeton, NJ: Princeton University Press, 2004), pp. 143–4.
[150] Caldwell, *Negras in Brazil*, pp. xviii–xix.
[151] Ibid. at pp. 66–7.
[152] Sheriff, *Dreaming Equality*, p. 101.
[153] Ibid. at p. 102.
[154] Ibid. at p. 103.

his lunch hour and he knocked on the door of a woman to whom
he had been referred. ... I have not made her into a slave the way
some of the wealthy treat their foster children or the way our grandmothers and great grandmothers treated their adoptive children....
My own mother kept a black girl as a kind of slave, and when my
mother died, I inherited her as a middle-aged woman, a childlike
adult who had never married and didn't know anything other than
taking care of my mother. ... I kept her until she died.[155]

In contrast, formal adoption leaves most Afro-Brazilian children lan-
guishing in institutional care facilities because they are not wanted by
white adoptive parents in much the same way that African- American
babies in the United States are treated as the least desired subjects of
adoption.[156] With the informal adoption system of *criação*, the unpaid
workload of cleaning, cooking, and caring for children that the adoptive families impose upon their Afro-Brazilian charges does not permit
them to attend school. When one such girl was asked whether she had
chosen to stop attending primary school, she responded:

No. I left because I was obliged to leave, understand? I had to work.
I used to have to cook [for my adoptive family]. And this didn't
leave me the time to go to school and to do the same things [as my
adoptive sister].[157]

It is thus not surprising that Afro-Brazilian women have the lowest
literacy rates in the population and are not well served by the underre-
sourced public school systems primarily populated by Afro-Brazilian
children.[158] Even the health care context reveals the intersectional
discrimination against Afro-Brazilian women. When hospitalized for
childbirth, Afro-Brazilian women have much higher rates of not receiving anesthesia when compared to white pregnant women (21.8% and

---

[155] Twine, *Racism in a Racial Democracy*, p. 35 (quoting Nancy Scheper-Hughes)
(alteration in original).
[156] Elizabeth Cezar Nunes, "Discriminação da Criança Negra no Processo de Adoção,"
J.D. dissertation, Centro Universitário de Brasilia (2008); Patricia J. Williams, "Spare
Parts, Family Values, Old Children, Cheap," *New England Law Review* 28 (1994),
913–27.
[157] Twine, *Racism in a Racial Democracy*, p. 43.
[158] Telles, *Race in Another America*, pp. 129–30.

13.5%, respectively).[159] It is also believed that Afro-Brazilian women are disproportionately sterilized.[160]

Thus, a wealth of qualitative and quantitative research confirms that Brazil like the rest of Latin America is a racially stratified society in which Afro-Brazilians experience both explicit and subtle discrimination, and Afro-Brazilian women experience intersectional discrimination. Indeed, the Organization of American States (OAS) has stated that the pervasive existence of racial discrimination in Brazil will hinder its ability to meet the goals of the United Nations Millennium Development Goals for 2015, which it committed to do as a precise and measurable manner of decreasing social exclusion in the nation.[161]

In short, a growing number of qualitative and quantitative studies of race in Latin America challenge the culturally embedded notion that race has no social or economic relevance.[162] Yet, Latin American elites have long indulged in the practice of presenting Latin America as morally superior to the United States vis-à-vis its lack of state-mandated segregation and presumably any other indicator of racial discrimination. The legacy of the postemancipation customary law of race regulation in Latin America has socially and economically marginalized Afro-descendants. At the same time, the state's strategic comparisons to the United States have long hindered the ability to challenge racial subordination. Nevertheless, in the attempt to address the pervasive racial inequality, Afro-descendant social justice movements have turned to the law as an arena for change in Latin America – a topic that shall be explored in the next chapter.

---

[159] "Negras Recembem Menos Anesthesia do Que Brancas," *O Globo*, November 26, 2006.

[160] Caldwell, *Negras in Brazil*, p. 163; Burdick, *Blessed Anastácia*, p. 2; Jurema Werneck, "The Beautiful and the Pure? Racism, Eugenics and New (Bio)technologies," in Alejandra Rotania and Jurema Werneck (eds.), *Under the Sign of Biopolitics: Critical Voices from Civil Society Reflections in Brazil* (Rio de Janeiro: E-papers, 2004), vol. I, pp. 51–63.

[161] Roberta Lopes, "Discriminação Racial Pode Fazer Com Que Brasil Não Cumpra Metas do Milênio," Agência Brasil, November 23, 2006, http://www.agenciabrasil. gov.br/noticias/2006/11/23/materia.2006–11–23.6429391562/view.

[162] Ariel E. Dulitzky, "A Region in Denial: Racial Discrimination and Racism in Latin America," in Dzidzienyo and Oboler (eds.), *Neither Enemies nor Friends*, pp. 39–59.

5 AFRO-DESCENDANT SOCIAL JUSTICE MOVEMENTS AND THE NEW ANTIDISCRIMINATION LAWS

THE DEVELOPMENT OF RACIAL DISCRIMINATION LEGISLATION IN THE REGION

With the growth of democratically elected governments in the 1990s, Afro-descendants faced less state opposition to organizing into nongovernmental organizations (NGOs) and community-based organizations. This in turn provided greater space for articulating the plight of Afro-descendants, and therefore many race-specific NGOs began to proliferate throughout the region. For instance, in Venezuela Afro-descendant activists organized the 1994 Congress of Afro-Venezuelan Communities.[1] Even in Cuba, despite government strictures on political mobilization outside the Communist Party, a new black organization, the Cofradía de la Negritud, formed in Havana in 1999. In Peru alone there are at least fifteen independent Afro-Peruvian social movement organizations.[2] Appendix A provides a list of many of the Afro-descendant organizations throughout the region.

With this growing activism, Afro-descendant organizations were able to garner important political and financial support from U.S. and European foundations committed to racial justice, in addition to support from the social inclusion programs of the Inter-American Development Bank, the Ford Foundation, and the International Human Rights Law Group. At the same time, the organizations have been able

---

[1] George Reid Andrews, *Afro-Latin America, 1800–2000* (New York: Oxford University Press, 2004), p. 195.

[2] Tanya María Golash-Boza, *Yo Soy Negro: Blackness in Peru* (Gainesville: University of Florida Press, 2011), p. 5.

to communicate with other similar NGOs in the region through the formation of regional networks and conferences. As a result of their transnational collaborations, Afro-descendant organizations have been able to articulate their perspectives in the public discourse more forcefully.[3]

The United Nations 2001 World Conference against Racism and all the preparatory meetings that preceded it were particularly important in galvanizing large numbers of civil society organizations to call public attention to the plight of Afro-descendants in Latin America. More than seventeen hundred activists attended the preparatory conference in Santiago, Chile, in 2000 alone. With the greater political participation of Afro-descendant civil society organizations, a more realistic picture of the status of racial hierarchy in the region has begun to develop. As a result of the African Diaspora–wide organizing and resulting media attention, public pressure was brought to bear on the nation-states, and antidiscrimination legislative activity began.

While it is possible to legislate a broad array of antidiscrimination measures to address discrimination in employment, housing, voting, and public accommodations (including consumer transactions, banking, education, health care, and government contracting), most Latin American countries have tended to focus on just a few areas. Appendix B, Typology of Latin American Racial Antidiscrimination Measures, illustrates the array of antidiscrimination laws. To begin with, most countries in the region have traditionally relied upon broadly worded constitutional equality provisions as the confirmation that racial inequality has been adequately addressed. An example of the generally worded constitutional provisions that all Latin American countries have with some variation (with the exception of Uruguay) can be seen in Nicaragua's equality provision, which states:

> All people are equal before the law and have the right to equal protection. There will be no discrimination on account of birth,

[3] Kwame Dixon, "Transnational Black Social Justice Movements in Latin America: Afro-Colombians and the Struggle for Human Rights," in Richard Stahler-Sholk, Harry E. Vanden, and Glen David Kuecker (eds.), *Latin American Social Justice Movements in the Twenty-First Century: Resistance, Power, and Democracy* (Lanham: Rowman & Littlefield, 2008), pp. 181–96.

nationality, political belief, race, sex, language, opinion, economic status or social position.[4]

Beyond the general constitutional equality provisions, antidiscrimination measures have ranged from constitutionally recognizing the multiracial and multiethnic status of the population, providing collective land title rights for blacks as a distinctive cultural group with-long-standing ties to particular parcels of land often originally settled as fugitive slave maroon societies, imposing sanctions for racial discrimination in the denial of access to places of public accommodation, prohibiting discrimination in the workplace, legislating the inclusion of Afro-descendant material in the national educational curriculums, prohibiting the dissemination of ideas based on racial superiority, and criminally prohibiting discrimination generally. Appendix B provides a listing by country of where these various antidiscrimination measures have been adopted.

CRIMINAL LAW FOCUS OF ANTIDISCRIMINATION LAW

Yet despite this variation in the type of antidiscrimination measures, the vast majority of countries in the region have focused upon criminal law as the vehicle for addressing racial discrimination. The reason for that focus is deeply rooted in the Latin American image of racial innocence. In reliance upon the notion that Latin American nation-states have been innocent of racial wrongdoing given the absence of state-mandated Jim Crow segregation in the region, the legal stance toward racism has been to view it as an aberration rather than a systemic part of a national culture. As a result, the legal response has been to treat racism as the work of isolated individuals, who are presumably abnormal in their prejudices. In short, racists are criminals rather than representatives of long-standing racist cultural norms. This also helps to explain why the large majority of hate speech laws in Latin America are part of the criminal codes in the region. Unfortunately, limiting the idea of racism to biased words uttered by those labeled as aberrant racists overlooks the structural and institutional aspects

---

[4] Constitución Política de la República de Nicaragua, art. 27.

of discrimination that operate in the absence of racist commentary. For instance, the scholar Carlos de la Torre notes with respect to the plight of Afro-Ecuadorians, "Reducing racism to the hostile words and actions of ignorant, ethnocentric, and parochial individuals, a view that was dominant in American sociology until recently, does not take into account power relations."[5]

Moreover, some countries in Latin America maintain a singular criminal approach to discrimination. For example, in the Dominican Republic, the 1997 Ley contra la Violencia Intrafamiliar (Law against Interfamily Violence) makes it a crime to inflict unequal or humiliating treatment based on race or ethnicity. Persons found guilty of the crime of discrimination can be imprisoned for a year and one month and fined two to three times the minimum wage.[6] In Nicaragua, the Criminal Code penalizes the obstruction of a constitutional right because of race or ethnicity.[7] The penalty is six months to one year of imprisonment. If the racially motivated obstruction of a constitutional right is found to have been publicly promoted, an additional fine can be imposed. The Criminal Code also authorizes the augmentation of a penalty for other crimes when they are racially motivated.[8]

Even though the criminalization of racial discrimination suggests a strong normative commitment to the eradication of discrimination, it may, as a practical matter, have had the ironic effect of making the legal system less capable of dealing with the problems of inequality and discrimination. Criminal cases require stronger evidence and a higher burden of proof than civil cases. For instance, in an analysis of Peruvian grievances regarding the experience of filing a criminal complaint of discrimination, it was found that the evidentiary standard for discrimination cases was high and that it is often difficult for a victim to prove that he/she has experienced discrimination.[9] An illustrative

---

[5] Carlos de la Torre, "Afro-Ecuadorian Responses to Racism: Between Citizenship and Corporatism," in Anani Dzidzienyo and Suzanne Oboler (eds.), *Neither Enemies nor Friends: Latinos, Blacks, Afro-Latinos* (New York: Palgrave Macmillan, 2005).

[6] Ley No. 24–97, Párrafo III, Art. 9 (Dominican Republic), http://www.iin.oea.org/badaj/docs/l24-97do.htm#Texto (modifies prior articulos 336, 337 and 339).

[7] Law No. 641, Criminal Code, Art. 427, 428 (Nicaragua).

[8] Criminal Code, Art. 36.5 (Nicaragua).

[9] *La Discriminación en el Perú: Problemática, Normatividad y Tareas Pendientes* (Perú: Defensoría del Pueblo, República Del Perú, 2007), p. 119.

case described in the report is that of an individual who lodged a complaint against the police department alleging discrimination for the inappropriate issuance of a traffic ticket because of his race. The public prosecutor indicated that this complaint did not merit a criminal investigation or action because the evidence presented was not enough: the complainant had submitted an affidavit and that of a family member who witnessed the incident. It is difficult to fathom what more the complainant could have submitted to support his allegations. The demand for more is thus emblematic of the Latin American resistance to considering racial discrimination a viable criminal complaint.

In addition to the reluctance of prosecutors to proceed with racial discrimination cases, judges are reluctant to impose criminal sanctions. Latin American criminal justice systems are overloaded with traditional crimes of violence and property crimes. In a system plagued with such problems and systemic inefficiencies, the crimes of racism and racial discrimination have and are likely to continue to have a low priority.

Moreover, entrusting the enforcement of the criminal law to public authorities risks having the law undermined by the complacent inaction of public officials who may harbor the same racial bias as the agents of discrimination. Indeed, commentators have noted that Latin American police officers are often the perpetrators of racial violence against persons of African descent because they see their role as protecting society from "marginal elements" by any means necessary without regard to the rule of law.[10] This is a particular danger in Latin America, where police officers are consistently found to discourage Afro-descendants from filing racial discrimination complaints and are often the perpetrators of discrimination and violence themselves.[11]

---

[10] Paulo Sérgio Pinheiro, "The Rule of Law and the Underprivileged in Latin America: Introduction," in Juan E. Méndez, Guillermo O'Donnell, and Paulo Sérgio Pinheiro (eds.), *The (Un)Rule of Law and the Underprivileged in Latin America* (Notre Dame, IN: University of Notre Dame Press, 1999), pp. 1–16.

[11] Daniel M. Brinks, *The Judicial Response to Police Killings in Latin America: Inequality and the Rule of Law* (Cambridge: Cambridge University Press, 2008), pp. 49–54; Michael J. Mitchell and Charles H. Wood, "Ironies of Citizenship: Skin Color, Police Brutality, and the Challenge to Democracy in Brazil," *Social Forces* 77 (1999), 1001–20.

The contrast between the civil and criminal contexts is best exemplified by the Brazilian case of *Tiririca*, in which the same fact pattern of hate speech yielded success for the plaintiffs in the civil court but not in the criminal court. Francisco Everado Oliveira Silva, whose stage name is Tiririca, is a Brazilian entertainer who released a song with the Sony Music company entitled "Veja os Cabelos Dela" ("Look at Her Hair") in 1996. The song was in essence a long tirade against the inherent distasteful animal smell of black women and the ugliness of their natural hair. The lyrics stated in significant part,

> When she passes she calls my attention, but her hair, there's no way no. Her *catinga* [African] (body odor) almost caused me to faint. Look, I cannot stand her odor. Look, look, look at her hair! It looks like a scouring pad for cleaning pans. I already told her to wash herself. But she insisted and didn't want to listen to me. This smelly *negra* (Black woman) ... Stinking animal that smells worse than a skunk.[12]

The black feminist NGO Criola, in conjunction with the NGO CEAP (Centro de Articulação de Populações Marginalizadas), and a number of other social justice organizations filed lawsuits against the singer and Sony Music company in both criminal and civil courts. In the criminal court action, the plaintiff filed a complaint of racism. The plaintiff lost because the judge found that there was no criminal intent to offend black women.[13] The criminal law standard was too high to overcome given the infrequency with which individuals overtly state their intent to discriminate before nonparty witnesses. As a result, the song remained in circulation for commercial sale.

In contrast, the civil court action was successful. The civil public action was filed pursuant to Article 3 of the Constitution, which states that the national objective is "to promote the well-being of all without prejudice as to origin, race, sex, color, age, and any other form of

---

[12] Kia Lilly Caldwell, "Look at Her Hair": The Body Politics of Black Womanhood in Brazil," *Transforming Anthropology* 11 (2004), 18 (translating Portuguese lyrics).
[13] Juiz Carlos Flores da Cunha, 23 Vara Criminal do Rio de Janeiro, February 18, 1998, http://estudoodireito.spaceblog.com.br/58156/QUESTOES-DE-DIREITO-CONSTITUCIONAL.

discrimination."[14] The case sought to protect the diffuse and collective rights of black women to be free of discrimination. Diffuse rights are a category of legal rights that provide guarantees to a group of individuals who have common legal interests despite being dispersed within the political community.[15] Free of the criminal context, which requires a finding of intent to discriminate, the civil court held that the defendant's authorship of the lyrics was discriminatory itself because the words inherently provoke feelings of humiliation in black women.[16] The court took note that because the singer, Tiririca, was also a popular entertainer for children (who was often nationally televised in a clown costume), the insulting and injurious content of the song was also prejudicial to the formation of black youth.

As compensation for the moral damages of collective emotional harm to dignity, in 2008, the court ordered payment of 300,000 reais (approximately US $162,000) in addition to attorney's fees and costs.[17] In 2012, the court revised the monetary judgment to include sums retroactive to the date the case was filed in 1997, thereby raising the judgment to 1.2 million reais (approximately US $678,736,870). In civil law legal systems like Brazil's, moral damages are nonpecuniary damages that compensate for the injury of emotional distress from harm to one's honor or reputation.[18] Often, moral damages are not available for every sort of tort action, but only for those that create dignitary harm. The monetary payment for the damage to the collective equality interest of black women was paid to the Federal Ministry of Justice's Fund

---

[14] Constituição Federal [C.F.] [Constitution] art. 3, para. IV (Braz.). Authorization to litigate a public civil action is obtained pursuant to Lei No. 7.347, de 24 de Julho de 1985 (Brazil).

[15] Law No. 7.347, de 24 Julho 1985, D.O.U. of 25 Julho 1985, as amended by Law Nos. 8.078 of September 11, 1990; 8.884 de June 11, 1994; 9.494 de September 10, 1997 (Brazil); Provisional Measure No. 2.102–28 de February 23, 2001 (Brazil).

[16] T.J.R.J., Embargos Infringentes No. 2005.005.00060, *CEAP v. Sony Music Entertainment Brasil*, 11 Câmara Cível do Tribunal de Justiça do Estado do Rio De Janeiro, Acórdão 14.12.2005 (Brazil).

[17] "10 Year Currency Converter," Bank of Canada, http://www.bankofcanada.ca/en/rates/exchform.html (indicating a 0.54 U.S. dollar exchange rate for the Brazilian real on September 28, 2008 [the date of the *Tiririca* civil damages award judgment]).

[18] Saul Litvinoff, "Moral Damages," *Louisiana Law Review* 38 (1977), 1–30; Jorge A. Vargas, "Moral Damages under the Civil Law of Mexico: Are These Damages Equivalent to U.S. Punitive Damages?" *University of Miami Inter-American Law Review* 35 (2004), 183, 208–11.

for the Defense of Diffuse Rights, for the creation of educational anti-racism youth programs disseminated through radio, television, film, and printed materials for elementary schools in the state.

What the *Tiririca* case demonstrates is that in the civil context, the absence of the imprisonment feature enables a judge to consider modern perspectives about racial equality when deciding whether the discrimination that has been historically prevalent in Latin America but invisible as "culture" should be actionable. A civil framework can provide broader theories of discrimination and less burdensome evidentiary standards.[19] In addition, the civil context carries less risk of selective enforcement whereby vulnerable populations are disproportionately targeted for prosecution. This is because, unlike in criminal prosecutions, the state need not be the primary enforcer of the legislation. Yet because of the prevalent notion that criminal laws against discrimination show how serious the state is about racism, the development of civil law measures has been slow and their reach has been modest.

THE PERUVIAN EXAMPLE OF CONSUMER AND EMPLOYMENT LAWS

In Peru, apart from its criminal law against discrimination,[20] there are several civil laws that prohibit racial discrimination. The first civil law was passed in 1997; it prohibits discriminatory requirements in offers of employment and educational access.[21] Thereafter, the media started to publicize the discriminatory practices of dance clubs in Lima that consistently denied entry to Afro-Peruvians.[22] INDECOPI,

[19] Seth Racusen, "A Mulato Cannot Be Prejudiced: The Legal Construction of Racial Discrimination in Contemporary Brazil," PhD dissertation, Massachusetts Institute of Technology (2002), pp. 87–8.

[20] Ley Contra Actos de Discriminación, Ley No. 27270 (2000), http://www.ilo.org/dyn/natlex/docs/WEBTEXT/56275/65196/S00PER02.htm (Peru).

[21] Ley No. 26772 (1997) *modified by* Ley No. 27270 (2000) http://www.congreso.gob.pe/comisiones/2002/discapacidad/leyes/26772.htm (Peru).

[22] "Examples of Cases Studied by the Project (Peru, 1995–2000)," International Development Research Centre, http://www.idrc.ca/en/ev-112282-201-1-DO_TOPIC.html.

a government agency created to ensure open and honest economic competition and protect citizens' intellectual property rights,[23] investigated and later launched a lobbying campaign against the dance clubs on behalf of consumers.[24] Television footage was used in this case to prove that racial discrimination was the sole reason some consumers were denied entry. In response to the public outcry over the incidents, Congress passed a second law, Ley No. 27049, which prohibits any form of racial discrimination by owners of establishments open to the public. While the law is clear that discrimination in business establishments is prohibited, Congress rejected creating an individual cause of action before the courts for persons aggrieved. Instead, the provisions of Ley No. 27270 are regulated by Supreme Decree No. 002–98-TR, which authorizes the Administrative Labor Authority to investigate acts of discrimination but only after a request to investigate or complaint has been made.[25]

While individual consumers can file complaints with either INDECOPI, Instituto de la Libre Competencia y la Propiedad Intelectual (Institute for Free Competition and Intellectual Property), or SAC, La Oficina de Servicio de Atencíon Ciudadano (the Office for Citizenship Care Service), the complaint process presents obstacles of its own. First, INDECOPI charges a processing fee for every complaint filed.[26] The fee is a problem for members of the Afro-Peruvian community, who are overwhelmingly poor. Second, the majority of citizens do not know how to follow through with the complaint, and many complain of rudeness and poor service by agency staff.[27] Third, INDECOPI does not have offices throughout the country, making both the initial filing and subsequent follow-up difficult.

[23] Decreto Ley No. 25868, Ley De Organización y Funciones Del Instituto Nacional De Defensa De La Competencia y De La Protección De La Propiedad Intelectual (INDECOPI) (November 6, 1992), http://www.concytec.gob.pe/infocyt/25868.html.

[24] "Examples of Cases Studied," http://www.idrc.ca/en/ev-112282–201–1-DO_TOPIC.html.

[25] "Annual Report: Peru (2000)," Inter-American Commission on Human Rights, http://www.cidh.oas.org/annualrep/2000eng/annex.htm.

[26] "Denuncias Por Discriminación," Instituto Nacional de Defensa de la Competencia Y de la Protección de la Propiedad Intellecutal, http://www.indecopi.gob.pe/denunciasDiscriminacion.jsp.

[27] Wilfredo Ardito Vega, "Discriminación en los servicios turísticos," *La Insignia*, December 5, 2006, http://www.lainsignia.org/2006/diciembre/ibe_011.htm.

For a claim to be successful under the consumer protection law, the consumer has the burden of proof in showing differential treatment; the owner then has to show that his actions were objective and justified; if this is proven, the consumer then has the burden of proving that the owner's justification is a pretext to engage in discriminatory practices. This process parallels the U.S. model for proving discrimination under Title VII of the Civil Rights Act of 1964. Therefore, it is very difficult for a person to prove to the consumer protection agency that he or she has been discriminated against as a consumer. While this is a popular claim, it has been pointed out that there are requirements that are applied arbitrarily by officials of the consumer protection agency that prevent parties who experience discrimination from placing a complaint. One such requirement is to show a receipt of the place where the person experienced discrimination. This requirement is particularly puzzling since the crux of the complaint is that the person was denied access to an establishment and, therefore, could not consume anything for which to obtain a receipt. Another weakness of the consumer protection legal enforcement is its focus on consumer access to places of entertainment, rather than on nondiscriminatory treatment within health care facilities. This is a significant omission given the fact that discrimination within health care services was listed as the most prevalent area of racial discrimination, in a 2009 study of racism in Peru.[28]

There is also a growing trend among business owners to circumvent antidiscrimination laws by claiming to be operating businesses that cater exclusively to North American and European tourists, who presumably prefer a whites-only service sector.[29] Particularly in large cities like Lima, owners operating "tourists only" businesses have been successful in not only excluding Afro-Peruvians but also avoiding detection of their discriminatory practices.[30]

The employment context presents similar enforcement challenges. The Ministry of Labor and Employment Promotion (MTPE) is in

---

[28] María Elena Planas and Néstor Valdivia, "Discriminación y Racismo en el Perú: Un Estudio Sobre Modalidades, Motivos, y Lugares de Discriminación en Lima y Cusco," typescript, May 2009, 35 www.grade.org.pe.

[29] Vega, "Discriminación en los servicios turísticos."

[30] "Aprodeh Señala Que Hay Más Discriminación Racial en Lima, Cusco y Arequipa," *El Comercio*, March 10, 2005.

charge of investigating discrimination allegations.[31] To start this process, a claimant may bring an action to the attention of the MTPE; if the accused party is found to have published a discriminatory advertisement, then he or she is fined. This law also obligates media outlets to call these discriminatory advertisements to the attention of the Peruvian labor administration and to collaborate in the investigation of the cases. A business that violates the law can be closed for a period of less than a year. A victim of discrimination can also bring a suit against an employer as a violation of Law 26772, through a Labor Court of First Instance or through the Constitutional Tribunal for cases involving constitutionally defined rights.[32]

In employment offer cases, the MTPE's regulations allow employers to ask for certain requirements that could be seen as discriminatory if they can show an "objective and reasonable justification," that is, if these requirements relate to the necessary qualifications of the job.[33] So, for example, a race requirement could presumably be allowed when hiring an actor to play a racially specific role in much the same way that the U.S. Title VII law technically permits national origin specific job requirements (while barring race-specific job requirements).[34]

This law, however, has not adequately addressed the problem of discriminatory advertisement; it is still common to see employers mandate the racially coded *buena apariencia* (good appearance) requirement that is a well known euphemism for a white phenotype. Yet, MTPE reported that between 1998 and 2006 only fourteen complaints were filed and six of them were resolved.[35] In 2010, MTPE received twenty-eight complaints and fined three violating companies. Thereafter, the Ministry of Labor relaunched an effort to combat these kinds of discriminatory employment advertisements and has proposed

[31] "Labor Rights Report 31 (September 2007)," Bureau of International Labor Affairs, Department of Labor, Peru, http://www.dol.gov/ilab/media/reports/usfta/PLRReport.pdf.

[32] Ibid.

[33] Wilfredo Ardito Vega, "Las ordenanzas contra la discriminación," Working Paper No. 13, Pontificia Universidad Católica del Perú (2009), http://departamento.pucp.edu.pe/derecho/images/documentos/Cuaderno%2013.pdf.

[34] George Rutherglen, *Employment Discrimination Law: Visions of Equality in Theory and Doctrine* (New York: Foundation Press, 2010), p. 129.

[35] *La Discriminación en el Perú*, p. 205.

to strengthen its enforcement.[36] Specifically, MTPE announced that it will implement a comprehensive system to manage complaints from job applicants who think they have experienced discrimination. This new system would allow individuals to place their complaints in writing, by phone, or through the Internet.

The law also prohibits discrimination that happens at the workplace, in the course of the employment relation, both under the Peruvian Constitution and through the Labor Productivity Law.[37] Under this law a judge can enjoin the discrimination and fine the employer. If the employee wants to terminate the employment contract because of discriminatory practices, the employee can collect severance pay. This law also invalidates discriminatory terminations of employment. Under this law, if the court finds that the claim is well founded, a worker can be reinstated to his or her job or can opt for severance pay.

Yet, the ability of the revamped employment laws to address racial discrimination fully will likely be hindered by the government's continued ambivalence with respect to engaging the needs of Afro-Peruvians directly. For instance, the government issued an apology in 2009, in the form of a state resolution expressing "historic regret to the Afro-Peruvian people for the abuses, exclusion and discrimination committed against them from the colonial period until the present."[38] Yet at the official state ceremony in which the president announced the state apology, he asserted that the apology would "cleanse the state and history of blame."[39] It would appear that President García views the Peruvian harms against its Afro-descendants as minor enough to be addressed with the declaration of an apology. As such, it is yet another example of how the Latin American implicit comparison to the "real racism" of the United States still situates Peru as a racial innocent whose passive inheritance of Spain's colonial racism and absence of

---

[36] "Listo Proyecto Para Prohibir Discriminación Laboral en las Ofertas de Empleo," Jóvenes a la Obra, Programa Nacional de Empleo Juvenil (2010), http://www.projoven.gob.pe/noticia.php?id=32.

[37] Decreto Supremo No. 003–97-TR (Peru), www.mpfn.gob.pe/descargas/texto_unico_ordenado_ds_03–97-tr.pdf.

[38] Resolución Suprema No. 010–2009-MIMDES, November 27, 2009 (Peru).

[39] "Alan García pidió perdón a pueblo afroperuano en ceremonia oficial," El Comercio, December 7, 2009, http://elcomercio.pe/politica/378597/noticia-presidente-garcia-pidio-perdon-pueblo-afroperuano-ceremonia-oficial.

Jim Crow segregation absolves the state of any direct action for remediation. It will therefore be difficult to promote more effective legal reforms against discrimination, with a state government confident that a formal apology is sufficient for addressing the harms. At the same time, given the Afro-Peruvian struggle against invisibility within their own country, the apology's recognition of their existence and discrimination against them can continue to propel the efforts of the Afro-Peruvian civil rights community.

THE COLOMBIAN EXAMPLE OF MULTICULTURAL CONSTITUTIONS, LAND RIGHTS, AND CURRICULUM REFORM

The 1991 Colombian Constitution provides for the recognition and protection of the ethnic and cultural diversity of the nation.[40] In this manner, Colombia joined several other Latin American countries such as Bolivia, Ecuador, Guatemala, Mexico, Nicaragua, Paraguay, and Venezuela in their constitutional recognition of the multicultural and multiethnic character of their nations. There are many different definitions of what makes a constitution "multicultural." Political theorists discuss it as differentiated citizenship, while legal theorists generally discuss it as the constitutionalism of a multicultural state.[41] Here I characterize constitutions as multicultural to the extent their text explicitly refers to the importance of state protection of the ethnic or cultural diversity of the nation, or it recognizes the nation as multiethnic and seeks to facilitate inclusionary politics.[42]

Yet not all multicultural constitutions similarly situate Afro-descended communities. Juliet Hooker aptly notes that because Latin American states have primarily envisioned multicultural rights as pertaining to indigenous peoples, who are viewed as deserving "ethnic" group members, Afro-descendants have often been excluded as distinct "racial" subjects without an ethnic identity

---

[40] Constitución Política de Colombia, art. 7.
[41] Kirsten Matoy Carlson, "Notice: Premature Predictions of Multiculturalism?" *Michigan Law Review* 100 (May 2002), 1470–87.
[42] Daniel Bonilla Maldonado, *La Constitución Multicultural* (Bogotá: Siglo del Hombre Editores, 2006).

needing constitutional protection.[43] The dichotomy drawn between deserving "ethnic" indigenous persons and the undeserving "racial" Afro-descendants overlooks both the racialization of indigenous peoples as well as the cultural identities of Afro-descended communities. For this reason, Colombia stands out as a jurisdiction that has included Afro-descendants while also exemplifying the limitations of a nation equating multicultural rights with ethnic group status. Colombia thus makes a illustrative contrast to countries like Mexico and Venezuela that completely exclude Afro-descendants from their multicultural rights landscape. Colombia also contrasts with those countries that have accorded Afro-descendants the same collective rights to land and culture, such as Guatemala, Honduras, and Nicaragua. Juliet Hooker characterizes Colombia, Brazil, Ecuador, and Peru as those jurisdictions where Afro-descendants have obtained some multicultural constitutional rights but not to the same extent as indigenous communities.

The Colombian Constitution states that it "recognizes and protects the ethnic and cultural diversity of the Colombian nation."[44] Transitory Article 55 of the 1991 Constitution mandated that laws recognizing the Afro-descendant right to collective property be enacted. The constitutional provisions have thus been augmented by specific legislation. In order to implement Article 55's mandate, in 1993 Ley 70 (Law 70) was enacted to protect the rights of Afro-Colombians to traditional landholdings. The law provides for the election of community representatives to represent community concerns over land and other issues in a system of prior consultation. Article 7 of Ley 70 provides that collective titles are inalienable, protected from seizure, and exempt from statutes of limitations. However, this law is limited to the Pacific Coast area and other specifically articulated zones.[45] Other areas explicitly not within the law's land provisions are urban

---

[43] Juliet Hooker, *Race and the Politics of Solidarity* (Oxford: Oxford University Press, 2009), pp. 80–2.

[44] Constitución Política de Colombia, art. 7.

[45] "A Report on the Development of Ley 70 of 1993 Submitted to the Inter-American Commission on Human Rights," The Bernard and Audre Center for Human Rights and Justice (2007), p. 8, http://www.utexas.edu/law/academics/centers/humanrights/students/FINAL%20REPORT.pdf.

areas, indigenous territories, national park areas, and areas reserved
for national security and defense. What this effectively means is that
the vast numbers of urban Afro-descendants outside the Pacific Coast
are excluded because they are not viewed as having firmly rooted ties
to specific parcels of land as indigenous communities have with collective land titles. Ley 70 then only addresses the needs of one segment of
the Afro-Colombian populace.

And even those Afro-Colombians who are eligible to apply for a
Ley 70 land title have only garnered modest results. This is because the
claims are often delayed by land studies. In addition, Ley 70 requires
that only lands deemed to be *tierras baldías* (state-owned vacant land)
can be passed on to collective ownership. Because Afro-Colombians
are regionally and ethnically diverse, they do not all live on such land.
(Indeed, some Afro-Colombians are not even primarily Spanish speak-
ers. The Raizales are an English Creole-speaking Afro-Caribbean ethnic group within Colombia.) Furthermore, the land title process is
particularly demanding in that it requires the production of historical,
demographic, economic, and cartographic studies of the community
claiming collective ownership.

Moreover, many Afro-Colombians have been dissuaded from pursuing the land title process by the violence of paramilitary groups and
the Colombian Army.[46] Afro-Colombian community organizers seeking collective ownership have seen themselves labeled as guerrillas or
terrorists and then targeted for violence by a government interested in
controlling resource-rich Afro-Colombian areas for corporate development.[47] In addition, right-wing paramilitary squads long enmeshed
in drug trafficking are similarly involved in seizing the land.[48] Indeed,
at least one study found that 33 percent of all Afro-Colombians have

---

[46] Jaime Arocha, "Inclusion of Afro-Colombians: Unreachable National Goal?" *Latin
American Perspectives* 25 (May 1998), 70–89.
[47] Kiran Asher, *Black and Green: Afro-Colombians, Development, and Nature in the Pacific
Lowlands* (Durham, NC: Duke University Press, 2009).
[48] Carlos Rosero, "Los Afrodescendientes y el Conflicto Armado en Colombia: La
Insistencia en lo Propio Como Alternativa," in Claudia Mosquera, Mauricio Pardo,
and Odile Hoffman (eds.), *Afrodescendientes en las Américas: Trayectorias Sociales e
Identitarias, 150 Años de la Abolición de la Esclavitud en Colombia* (Bogotá: Universidad
Nacional de Colombia, 2002), pp. 547–59.

been expelled from their own land by armed groups.[49] Of the people displaced from their land because of the ongoing civil war, the largest percentage have been Afro-Colombian.[50] Moreover, an Afro-Colombian is 84 percent more likely to be displaced than a mestizo. Of the Afro-Colombian population with registered collective property titles in 2007 alone, 79 percent had been forcibly dispossessed from their lands.[51] So significant has been the displacement of Afro-Colombians (and indigenous communities as well) that in 1999, the United Nations officially put the Colombian government on notice to address it as a form of racial discrimination.[52] Thereafter, Colombia's Constitutional Court evaluated the government's policy for dealing with the plight of the many dispossessed and held that the policy was inadequate and unconstitutional in its violation of the fundamental rights of Colombian citizens.[53] Since that court order, the government has been obligated to design policies to prevent the forced removal of landowners, in addition to ameliorating the poor living conditions of the dispossessed. Unfortunately, the government's deliberations regarding the needs of the dispossessed have not focused upon the particular impact on Afro-Colombians as a targeted group.[54]

---

[49] "Latin America: Promoting the Rights of Colombia's Afro-Descendants," Global Rights Partners for Justice, www.globalrights.org.

[50] "Afrocolombianos Desplazados, Un Drama Sin Tregua," Consultoría Para los Derechos Humanos y el Dezplazamiento, May 22, 2008, http://www.codhes.org/index.php?option=com_content@task=view@id=157; "Desplazamiento Forzado y Enfoques Diferenciales," Doc. No. 9, Consultoría Para los Derechos Humanos y el Dezplazamiento, http://www.codhes.org/images/stories/publicaciones/enfoque%20dif_thumb.JPG.

[51] César Augusto Rodríguez Garavito, Tatiana Andrea Alfonso Sierra, and Isabel Cavelier Adarve, *El Derecho a no Ser Discriminado: Primer Informe Sobre Discriminación Racial y Derechos de la Población Afrocolombiana (Versión Resumida)* (Bogotá: Universidad de Los Andes, 2008), pp. 34–5.

[52] "Concluding Observations of the Committee on the Elimination of Racial Discrimination: Colombia," United Nations, August 20, 1999, http://www.unhchr.ch/tbs/doc.nsf/(Symbol)/c318bd791cc8a6ea8025686b0043560f?Opendocument.

[53] Corte Constitucional, Sentencia T-025 (2004).

[54] Luis Gerardo Martínez Miranda, "Desde Adentro: una aproximación al tema de Verdad, Justicia y Reparación a partir de las víctimas afrocolombianas," in Claudia Mosquera Rosero-Labbé and Luiz Claudio Barcelos (eds.), *Afro-reparacions: Memorias de la Esclavitud y Justicia Reparativa para negros, afrocolombianos y raizales* (Bogotá: Universidad Nacional de Colombia, 2006), pp. 42–7.

In contrast, the government has been willing to focus upon Afro-Colombians as a group with respect to educational reform. In 1998, President Álvaro Uribe passed a presidential decree mandating that schools teach Afro-Colombian history and culture.[55] Article 160 of Ley 115 provides that the board of each education district must include a member representing the local Afro-Colombian community, if such a local community exists.[56] It is to be hoped that with the greater educational exposure to the contributions of Afro-Colombians to Colombian society, true racial equality will become desirable to the entire populace.

Yet, the promise of multicultural constitutions will need to confront the long embedded history of racially exclusionary politics in Latin America. For example, even though the implementing legislation for the "multicultural protection" of the Constitution requires that government authorities consult Afro-descended communities before making decisions that affect their communal lands, Afro-Colombians confront barriers to the consultation process because the government must first officially recognize a preestablished "community council" of Afro-descendants before those Afro-descendants are entitled to be consulted. The official recognition process has been perceived as overly bureaucratic and restrictive. Nonetheless, after so many years of marginalization, even the symbolic constitutional recognition of the importance of Afro-descendants is indeed some measure of progress.[57] One alternative to multicultural constitutions has been Brazil's attempt to legislate comprehensive antidiscrimination laws.

THE BRAZILIAN EXAMPLE OF STRIVING FOR A COMPREHENSIVE ANTIDISCRIMINATION LEGAL SYSTEM

Because Brazil has made significant strides with regard to creating and enforcing antidiscrimination laws, its context warrants closer

---

[55] Decree No. 1122, June 18, 1998 (Colombia).
[56] Ley 115 de Febrero 8 de 1994, Art. 160, §10 (Colombia).
[57] Donna Lee Van Cott, *The Friendly Liquidation of the Past: The Politics of Diversity in Latin America* (Pittsburgh: University of Pittsburgh Press, 2000).

examination. The concerted effort to use the law as a vehicle for social change in Brazil is particularly significant because of its long-standing literacy requirement for voting.[58] Because the literacy voting requirement, which effectively disenfranchised a majority of the Afro-Brazilian population, was not abolished until 1985, the political arena was not the most promising venue for social change. Thus, modern Brazilian civil rights legislation did not begin until 1951 with the enactment of the civil rights statute Lei Afonso Arinos.[59] The statute criminalized racial discrimination in employment, commerce, public accommodations, public office, and education. Discrimination in these fields was declared a crime punishable by a jail sentence or fines.

The statute began what has become a pattern in Brazilian civil rights legislation – treating racial discrimination as a criminal offense. As a result, antidiscrimination legislation has traditionally been under-enforced and thus ineffective. In fact, Lei Afonso Arinos is widely discussed as merely a public relations gesture designed to mitigate the bad publicity generated when the African-American dancer Katherine Dunham was barred from a prestigious Brazilian hotel purportedly because of the racist influence of U.S. industrialism and commercialism in Brazil (not Brazil's own racism).[60] Consequently, Lei Afonso Arinos did not acknowledge native Brazilian racism nor seek to address it, despite the fact that it was Afro-Brazilian social justice activists who caused the Katherine Dunham incident and others to be called to the attention of the public and media outlets. Indeed, the law that was passed was a diluted version of a 1946 antidiscrimination bill that Afro-Brazilian activists themselves had tried to introduce.[61]

Only nine defendants were convicted under the statute in the forty-six-year period following the statute's enactment in 1951.[62]

---

[58] Anthony W. Marx, *Making Race and Nation: A Comparison of South Africa, the United States, and Brazil* (Cambridge: Cambridge University Press, 1998), p. 258.

[59] Lei Número 1.390, de 3 Julho 1951.

[60] Edward E. Telles, *Race in Another America: The Significance of Skin Color in Brazil* (Princeton, NJ: Princeton University Press, 2004), p. 38.

[61] Elisa Larkin Nascimento, *The Sorcery of Color: Identity, Race, and Gender in Brazil* (Philadelphia: Temple University Press 2007), pp. 148–9.

[62] Raquel Coelho Lenz Cesar, "Acesso A Justiça Para Minorias Racias no Brasil: É a Açao Afirmativa o Melhor Caminho? Riscos e Açertos no Caso da UERJ," PhD dissertation, State University of Rio de Janeiro (2003), pp. 212–13.

During Brazil's military dictatorship (1964–86), antidiscrimination laws continued to be unenforced and were not taken seriously by governmental actors. Consequently, the current endeavors to use the legal arena for the social transformation of the nation have occurred against a backdrop of preexisting civil rights laws that were long ineffective.

Each of Brazil's Federal Constitutions has consistently enshrined the principle of formal equal treatment under the law. With the return to democracy, the present Federal Constitution was adopted in 1988 and included a variety of different clauses related to racial discrimination that social justice advocates were successful in having included as part of the broad-based reform following the end of the military dictatorship in 1986.[63] In Title 1, entitled "Of Fundamental Principles," the Constitution establishes that one of the bases of the rule of democratic law in Brazil is "to promote the well-being of all, without prejudice as to the origin, race, sex, color, age, and any other forms of discrimination" (Art. 3.IV). The same title establishes that international relationships of the government of Brazil are governed by, among other principles, the rejection of racism (Art. 4.VIII).

For its part, Title II of the Federal Constitution, which refers to fundamental rights and guarantees, establishes in Article 5, Section 1, the equality of all persons before the law. Number XLII of the same article states, "The practice of racism is a non-bailable crime with no limitation, subject to the penalty of confinement under the terms of the law."

Further on, Art. 215, paragraph 1, of the Constitution establishes that "the State shall protect the expressions of popular, indigenous, and Afro-Brazilian cultures, as well as those of other groups participating in the national civilization process." Article 216, paragraph 5, gives protection to all documents and places with historic meaning for the *quilombos* (communities created by escaped slaves during the period of slavery). Last, Transitory Disposition 68 recognizes all remaining *quilombo* residents as the definitive owners of the communal land that they occupy. Yet by May 2008, only 87 of the 3,550 *quilombos* currently recognized by the Brazilian government had received land titles.[64]

---

[63] Constituição da Republica Federativa do Brasil 5 de Octubro de 1988, Art. 5, Section XLII.

[64] "Between the Law and Their Land: Afro-Brazilian Quilombo Communities' Struggle for Land Rights" (Austin, TX: Bernard and Audre Rapoport Center for Human

The 1988 Constitution was quickly followed by the passage of additional civil rights legislation. One year after the enactment of the 1988 Constitution, Congress passed Lei 7716 criminalizing discrimination based on race or color in public accommodations, in employment, and in the private sector.[65] The statute, known as Lei Caó, was lengthy, and many critics charged that it was too vague and allowed for too many loopholes.[66] In its original text, the law criminalized a series of actions that are the result of racial or color-based bias, including acts such as impeding access to public administration or public service agencies; denying or blocking employment in a private company; refusing or impeding access to commercial establishments in general; failing to serve a client, or similar behavior in access to hotels, restaurants, public transportation, sports arenas, hair salons; impeding entrance to buildings or to elevators; and impeding access to the armed forces, educational establishments; impeding or blocking, in any manner, marriage or family and social life. Lei Caó is thus more extensive and specific than the 1951 Lei Afonso Arinos law. Punishments for these offenses range from imprisonment for one to five years.

In 1990, Law 8081 modified Law 7716, passed the year before, adding a new crime, which consisted of "practicing, inducing or inciting, by means of public communication or publications of any nature, discrimination or prejudice on the basis of race, religion, ethnicity, or national origin."[67] A penalty of two to five years in prison was the punishment for this behavior.

Lei Paim revised Law 7716 in 1997, with its specification that any crimes on the basis of race, ethnicity, religion, color, or national origin could be punishable for one to three years imprisonment as well as with a fine.[68] The modifications were mostly procedural changes that reduced the sentence for the crime of racist expressions to a range

Rights and Justice, September 22, 2008), http://www.utexas.edu/law/centers/human-rights/projects_and_publications/brazil-report.pdf.

[65] Lei Número 7.716 de 5 de Janeiro de 1989.

[66] Eliezer Gomes da Silva and Ivonei Sfoggia, "O Crime de Raçismo na Legislação Penal Brasileira: Passado, Presente e Futuro," *Igualdade: Revista Trimestral do Centro de Apoio Operacional das Promotorias da Criança e do Adolescente* 5 (January/March 1997), 11–28.

[67] Lei Número 8.081, de 21 de Setembro de 1990.

[68] Lei Número 9.459 de 1997.

of one to three years in prison and reformed the Criminal Procedure Code's definition of crimes against honor to include the crime of "racial insult" (*injúria racial*).[69] Racial insult differs from the crime of racism, because it penalizes the harm to the dignity of an individual. In contrast, the crime of racism targets an undetermined number of persons in its exclusion of an entire race or color. For that reason, unlike the individualized crime of racial insult, the group-based crime of racism is not subject to a prescription period and is a nonbailable offense. With racial insult, a judge has discretion to suspend the one- to three-year jail sentence, and the claim is subject to an eight-year prescription period.[70]

In the civil sphere, general civil laws of responsibility for moral damages may be applied in cases of racial discrimination. ("Moral damages" compensate the injury of pain and suffering or emotional distress from harm to one's honor or reputation.) Article 5 of the Federal Constitution guarantees compensation for material damage, moral damages, or damage to one's image. In addition, Article 159 of the Civil Code states that "whoever, by act or voluntary omission, negligence or malpractice, violates the rights or causes injury to others, is obliged to repair the damage."

Despite the wide array of antidiscrimination laws, very few complaints are litigated. This is the case, notwithstanding the existence of specialty police units for investigating and enforcing those laws.[71] Studies have shown that only a small percentage of discrimination complaints get to the higher courts and that complaints are often dismissed by police officials. One thesis by a Brazilian commentator has suggested that the legal system tends to treat racism and discrimination as isolated and rare cases, and not as part of larger societal patterns.[72]

---

[69] Código Penal [Penal Code] art. 140, § 3 (Brazil).
[70] Samantha Ribeiro Meyer-Pflug, *Liberdade de Expressão e Discurso do ódio* (São Paulo: Editora Revista dos Tribunais, 2009), pp. 102–3.
[71] "Report on the Situation of Human Rights in Brazil," Inter-American Commission on Human Rights, http://www.cidh.oas.org/countryrep/brazil-eng/Chaper%209%20. htm.
[72] Cláudia Margarida Ribas Marinho, "O Racismo no Brasil – Uma análise do desenvolvimento histórico do tema e da eficácia da lei como instrumento de combate à discriminação racial," Undergraduate thesis in Law, Universidade Federal de Santa Catarina (July 1999), http://infojur.ccj.ufsc.br/arquivos/ccj/ monoMarinho-RacismoBADHTELICDR.PDF.

As such, many lawyers and civil rights advocates have complained about the ambiguities of the laws and the refusal of the higher courts to try such cases.

In his examination of Brazilian antidiscrimination law, before being appointed the first black justice to the Federal Supreme Court, Justice Joaquim B. Barbosa Gomes critiqued the Federal Public Ministry's (Ministério Público Federal's prosecution office) lack of effective enforcement. He attributed the ministry's ineffectiveness to lack of organization, fiscal chaos, and even internal ideological battles.[73] For Barbosa, the public prosecutor's office's lack of involvement has been encouraged by the courts and the Brazilian judicial system in general and is reflected in "the exacerbated individualism, extreme formalism, lack of rationality or practicality in the great majority of instruments for action, etc." He adds that "it is not surprising given this context that the overall situation of public civil suits is so squalid that there is nothing to analyze in the column referring to protection of minorities' rights by the public prosecutor's office!"[74] Since becoming a Federal Supreme Court judge, Justice Barbosa has observed that "the racial democracy myth impedes people from bringing cases. The few people who might approach a state prosecutor encounter prosecutors who would conclude that they don't have a valid case."[75]

In light of the perceived ineffectiveness of Brazilian antidiscrimination law, many NGOs have dedicated their efforts to reforming civil rights legislation. A conference in Brasília organized by the lawyer Sérgio Martins of the Escritório Nacional Zumbi in March 2000 aimed at developing mechanisms to combat racism and discrimination. Other NGOs in Brazil such as CEAP – Centro de Articulação de Populações Marginalizadas (Center for the Connection of

---

[73] Joaquim B. Barbosa Gomes, "Discriminação Racial: Um Grande Desafio Para o Direito Brasileiro," Adami Advogados Associado, http://www.adami.adv.br/raciais/19.asp.

[74] Joaquim B. Barbosa Gomes, "O Ministério Público e os efeitos da discriminaçao racial no Brasil: Da Indiferença à Inércia; in: *Boletim dos Procuradores da República*, Ano II No. 15 (July 1999) 21, 15–25.

[75] Interview with Joaquim Barbosa (May 14, 2007), transcript, p. 2 (transcript in Tanya K. Hernández's possession).

Marginalized Populations) have served as advocacy groups for reforming antidiscrimination legislation.[76]

There are indications that aside from civil rights activists, many
in the legal profession regard antidiscrimination law as somewhat
peripheral. Few attorneys see great benefit in bringing such cases,
fearing that they are likely to meet with quick dismissal. The combination of a general lack of awareness of rights against discrimination
with the reticence of the legal profession to take on cases of alleged
discrimination and the scarcity of access to legal aid probably lead
to thousands of cases of racial discrimination that are simply not
reported every year.[77]

Yet, the last few years have seen judicial decisions on cases of discrimination against the Afro-descendant population in a variety of
areas, including criminal and civilian complaints and judicial reviews
of affirmative action norms. In addition, for the first time exploratory
studies of the judicial treatment of defendants in criminal cases are
being carried out, as are investigations of the situation of black women
in the same context. As an example, the Instituto do Negro Padre
Batista (the Father Batista Institute for Blacks) in the state of São
Paulo was created through an agreement with the Procurador Geral
do Estado (Attorney General's Office) to bring actions of racism in
the criminal courts. Under the agreement, the Procurador will hand
over to this body all cases of racism and racial insult occurring in the
state of São Paulo. In 2004, the institute had only approximately 100
cases then pending, quite a low number considering the size of the
Afro-Brazilian population in that state. Only a few other nongovernmental organizations that represent Afro-descendants process judicial
cases, one of which is the Instituto da Mulher Negra Geledés.

Factors that contribute to this situation include the lack of public awareness that would allow these problems to be addressed and
the scant confidence in the judicial system's ability to resolve them
adequately. Another factor is that police precincts – where victims must

---

[76] CEAP, http://www.alternex.com.br/ceap/home.html.
[77] "The Judicial System and Racism against People of African Descent: The Cases of
Brazil, Colombia, The Dominican Republic and Peru" (Justice Studies Center of the
Americas, March 2004), http://www.cejamericas.org/portal/index.php/es/biblioteca/
biblioteca-virtual/cat_view/43-documentos/66-informes-comparativos.

initially turn to in reporting crimes – frequently fail to take reports of racism seriously or inform victims adequately of how to proceed. The actions of police precincts show that the application of antiracist laws has encountered serious problems since enactment. One empirical study demonstrates serious deficiencies in delegations' response to complaints of racism, which they tend to view as simple questions of honor, even though these may involve prohibiting access to transportation, labor rights, and consumer protection.[78] The author of the study stated that "as a result, black attorneys rightly complain about the real swelling of cases of crimes against honor reported against the police."[79]

In Rio de Janeiro state, judicial cases have been handled by the public agency Programa Disque Racismo. Many of the situations observed in São Paulo are also seen in Rio de Janeiro. For example, members of Disque Racismo highlight the difficulty associated with obtaining favorable outcomes in criminal racism cases. In the first four years since the program was launched in 1999, the organization obtained only three convictions.[80] In a Latin American civil context like Brazil where judges rather than juries resolve legal cases, the low conviction rate reflects the judicial skepticism toward discrimination claims.

Nevertheless, public awareness of the antidiscrimination legal tools is increasing, as evidenced by the rising number of cases filed. In Bahia (a northeastern state with a large majority of Afro-Brazilian residents) alone, 220 persons filed complaints of racial discrimination from January to October 2008. This is a sharp contrast to the 308 total of cases from the past ten years of processing claims at the Public Ministry of Bahia.[81] Yet, a vast majority of the complaints lodged are not successful. A study of cases on file for 2005–6 found that only 32.9 percent were successful for the plaintiff.[82] Similarly, a study of cases

---

[78] Antonio Sérgio Guimarães, *Preconceito e Discriminação: Queixas de Ofensas e Tratamento Desigual dos Negros no Brasil* (Salvador: Novos Toques, 1998), p. 47.

[79] Ibid. at p. 47.

[80] "Judicial System and Racism," p. 18.

[81] "Racismo: mais de 200 pessoas procuram o MP/BA esse ano," *Jornal Írohin*, November 19, 2008, www.irohin.org.br/onl/new.php?sec=news&id=3856.

[82] Maiá Menezes, "Vitimas de racismo perdem 57.7% das ações," *O Globo*, November 20, 2008, http://oglobo.globo.com/pais/noblat/post.asp?t=vitimas_de _racismo_perdem_57_7_das_acoes&cod_Post=141465&a=111.

decided in 2007–8 again found that only 30 percent were successful for the plaintiff.[83] This parallels the difficulty that employment discrimination plaintiffs in the United States encounter in winning their cases, where 94 percent of filed cases never even reach trial. More than 40 percent of employment discrimination cases in the United States are dismissed before trial, and another 54 percent of plaintiffs often receive only token amounts to settle their cases out of court. Of the 6 percent that progress to trial in the United States, only one in three has a chance of winning.[84]

Another factor that impedes the effective enforcement of antidiscrimination laws is the demand for direct evidence of racial bias rather than indirect evidence such as statistical showings of patterns of racial disparity. A 2004 Justice Studies Center of the Americas report on the judicial system of Brazil indicates that the majority of Brazilian judicial decisions demand evidence of direct discrimination.[85] This criterion requires a higher standard of proof, which makes it more difficult to win the case. In effect, under direct discrimination the plaintiff must basically demonstrate the existence of three separate elements: the discriminatory act, prejudice by the accused toward the plaintiff, and a causal relationship between the racial prejudice and the discriminatory act. This therefore requires that the accused make explicit his or her intention to discriminate. This requirement is extremely difficult to satisfy in a society that identifies itself as a racial democracy and thus does not attribute racism to the commonplace expressions of antiblack attitudes.

The restrictive or formalist interpretation of the law also impedes the presentation of direct discrimination actions in court. On occasion, judges have required that a certain behavior or expression may only be directed toward a person of African descent in order for it to qualify as criminally admissible. In this sense, for example, one court found that

---

[83] Marcelo Paixão, Irene Rossetto, Fabiana Montovanele, and Luiz M. Carvano, *Relatório Anual das Desigualdades Raciais no Brasil; 2009–2010* (Rio de Janeiro: Editora Garamond, 2010), p. 264.

[84] Laura Beth Nielsen, Robert L. Nelson, and Roy Lancaster, "Individual Justice or Collective Legal Mobilization? Employment Discrimination Litigation in the Post Civil Rights United States," *Journal of Empirical Legal Studies* 7 (June 2010), 175–201.

[85] "Judicial System and Racism."

characterizing someone as a prostitute, as a bum, or as monkeylike did not constitute racism given that white people could also be described in this manner. The court thus ignores the cultural stereotypes that specifically associate blackness with prostitution, laziness, and animal qualities. Furthermore, the ruling manifests the myth of "racial democracy" by stating that

> [in Brazil] people with darker skin can even be the idols of people with lighter skin in sports and music, and women who are popularly referred to as "*mulatas*" would seem to be proud of that condition and are exhibited with great success in many famous and popular places. In Brazil "white" people normally marry "black" people and have children.... We do not have the rigorous and cruel racism observed in other countries, where non-"whites" are segregated, separated and do not have the same rights. That is racism.[86]

In some cases involving an action or expression directed at a specific person of African descent, the courts have ruled that this does not represent behavior consistent with racism, because it does not prove that the prejudice or discriminatory intent was directed against the Afro-descendant population as a whole. For example, in the state of São Paulo the existence of the crime of racism was not accepted by a court in one case in which the accused, a mayor, said to an employee upon his dismissal from the municipality, "Marginal people and dirty blacks won't work here anymore during my tenure." The opinion states that "saying that a particular person is a 'dirty black' or that the municipal administration will not allow them any more does not represent the crime [of racism]." The court adds that

> discriminating, according to the meaning of the verb itself, involves prohibiting certain races or persons from certain religions or of certain colors from making use of some rights or opportunities that are conferred on some segment of the population. It does not involve removing someone from their job (in a place in which many other blacks most certainly continue to work) under the rude statement that he or she is a "dirty black," at least in order to satisfy the crime established in Article 20 of the special law in question [Law 7716 against racism].

---

[86] Guimarães, *Preconceito e Discriminação*, p. 35.

The finding also states that "as a result, there is no evidence of general opposition to the black race in the statement of the accused, but instead a verbal attack that was exclusive to the victim, and nothing more because, it is important to note, many blacks continue to serve in the municipality [in question]." The court concludes that at most there may have been slander involved; this, however, was ruled out in the case in question, as a result of which the case was closed.[87]

Brazilian courts have made little use of the criterion of indirect discrimination, under which the discriminatory character of a behavior can be determined from the presence of circumstantial evidence. In such a case, the prosecution must prove that the victim is part of a certain group (racial in this case) and that he or she receives different (inferior) treatment than that received by a person outside that group, independently of the existence of explicit manifestations of racist intent. The principle of indirect discrimination seems to be applied only to racism linked to consumers' rights. This criterion has been used to sanction discrimination in access to social clubs or treatment received by Afro-descendants in banks. In an example of the first case, a court ruled that discrimination had occurred in a nightclub: the locale had two lines, one supposedly for members and one for nonmembers, though in effect the whites from the first line were admitted to the locale while Afro-descendants from the other were not allowed to purchase tickets. The case concluded that there had been discriminatory treatment against members of that group despite the absence of direct discriminatory intent.[88] In the area of consumer rights, a well-known case involved a black client who, when he attempted to transfer a small amount of money from his bank account to his wife's, was subjected to long and complex interrogations that far exceeded normal banking practices for white clients. The court also found this behavior to be racially motivated.[89]

Because Brazilian law has traditionally sought to criminalize racism and racial discrimination,[90] there has been an attempt to amplify the

---

[87] Tribunal de Justiça do Estado de São Paulo, 2ª Câmara Criminal, Proceso No. 272.907, September 20, 1999.

[88] Apelação Criminal No. 294.08, 4ª Câmara Criminal do Tribunal da Alzada, Rio Grande do Sul.

[89] Racusen, "Mulato Cannot Be Prejudiced."

[90] Fabiana Augusto Martins Silveira, *Da criminalização do racismo: aspectos jurídicos e sociocriminológicos* (Belo Horizonte: Del Rey, 2006).

mechanisms for addressing discrimination. In July 2010, Brazil enacted a Statute of Racial Equality (Estatuto da Igualdade Racial). The statute issues a federal government mandate to administer programs and specific measures for reducing racial inequality.[91] Article 1 states that it is the goal of the statute "to assure to the Afro-Brazilian population the achievement of equal opportunities, the support of individual collective and diffuse ethnic rights and the struggle against discrimination and other forms of ethnic intolerance." It is noteworthy as the first comprehensive racial equality legislation in the region, with the articulation of government goals for promoting racial inclusion and developing affirmative action policies for addressing inequalities in "education, culture, sport and leisure, health, safety, work, housing, means of mass communication, public funding, access to land, justice and others."[92] Article 51 of the law also establishes a Permanent Ombudsman for the Defense of Racial Equality to receive and forward complaints of discrimination and monitor the implementation of measures promoting equality. Yet the statute has been criticized by Afro-Brazilian activists as being purely aspirational and failing to provide concrete rights to enforce equality such as mandated affirmative action policies.[93]

Throughout the rest of Latin America, victims of racial discrimination can draw upon only broad constitutional principles of equality. While few attorneys have attempted to litigate a racial discrimination claim pursuant to the general constitutional equality provision, the judicial feature of *amparo* provides the possibility for the development of a social justice litigation strategy.

AMPARO CONSTITUTIONAL ENFORCEMENT IN LATIN AMERICA

One consistent source of enforcement power that exists in the region is the judicial remedy of *amparo* (and its alternative name of *tutela*).

---

[91] Law No. 12.288, de 20 Julio 2010, http://www.portaldaigualdade.gov.br/.arquivos/Estatuto%20em%20ingles.pdf.
[92] Law No. 12.288, de 20 Julio 2010, art. 4 (VII).
[93] Jaime Alves, "Ouro de Tolos: O Estatuto da Igualdade e a Submissão Política Negra II," *Ìrohìn*, June 21, 2010, http://www.irohin.org.br/onl/new.php?sec=news&id=8090.

Amparo is a judicial proceeding that enables petitioners to protect their constitutional and human rights with a panoply of equitable remedies (including injunctions, declaratory judgments, and mandamus orders). In all Latin American countries, except the Dominican Republic, the *amparo* provision is set forth in the national constitutions.[94] *Amparo* is considered an extraordinary remedy that should only be used when no other effective judicial means is available for the immediate protection of human rights. Yet, more importantly, it is a personal right of action that any individual who has suffered harm is entitled to bring. There is also a growing trend to use the *amparo* proceeding to protect group-based collective rights through the petition of an injured party. Five countries specifically exclude the *amparo* proceeding from being used in cases against private individuals rather than public authorities: Brazil, El Salvador, Guatemala, Mexico, and Panama. In contrast, ten countries, Argentina, Bolivia, Chile, Costa Rica, Dominican Republic, Nicaragua, Paraguay, Peru, Uruguay, and Venezuela, all specifically authorize *amparo* actions against persons in their individual capacities. Because *amparo* is fundamentally a personal right of action to protect constitutional rights, a court decision only binds the parties to the suit with respect to the litigated controversy. It has no formal precedential value and is thus limited by its inability to make a generally applicable declaration regarding a challenged statute. Nevertheless, *amparo* decisions can informally create a precedential effect whereby a succession of *amparo* decisions before the same judges, challenging the application of the same law and based on largely similar facts, increases the likelihood of relative uniformity.

One example of a successful use of *amparo* to advance racial equality occurred in the seminal case of Liliana Cuellar Sinisterra, a Colombian citizen of African descent, who was in Cartagena on a business trip from the Houston office of Deloitte and Touche.[95] On July 2, 2005, Ms. Sinisterra was denied entry to a disco allegedly for the color of

---

[94] Allan R. Brewer-Carías, *Constitutional Protection of Human Rights in Latin America: A Comparative Study of Amparo Proceedings* (Cambridge: Cambridge University Press, 2009).

[95] Tutela T-1250871, Sentencia T-131/06 (February 23, 2006) Lilliana Cuellar Sinisterra contra los establecimientos comerciales la Carbonera LTDA y la Discoteca QKA-YITO.

her skin. The plaintiff used Colombia's *tutela* (*amparo* equivalent) to file a complaint against the discotheque that had denied her admission while admitting whites. With the *tutela* she filed a claim pursuant to the Constitution's Article 13 guarantee of equality, human dignity, and honor. After losing in the Cartagena municipal court, Ms. Sinisterra appealed to the Colombian Constitutional Court, and the court exercised its discretion in favor of accepting a review of the *tutela* decision. The Constitutional Court of Colombia vindicated her claim of a right to be free of racial discrimination in admission to places of public accommodation and enjoined the disco from denying anyone entry for illegal reasons. Yet despite the existence of the *amparo/tutela* judicial remedy and the development of more domestic antidiscrimination legislation, there are several barriers to their effective enforcement across Latin America, as discussed in the following section.

Census Racial Data Enforcement Challenge

The legacy of and continued support for the myth of racial democracy in Latin America have interfered with the acknowledgment that collecting data by race can be a useful aid to pursuing racial equality. A census inquiry into racial identity has been viewed as an act of racial discrimination itself. Racial justice activists in Latin America have begun to challenge that presumption because of their urgent need to demonstrate concretely with statistics how racialized social attitudes have subordinated Afro-descendants.

While countries may vary in the extent to which judges will admit social science data of racial disparities in individual cases of racial discrimination, the consistent collection of the data is nevertheless useful. This is because individual claims of discrimination can be more readily appreciated as discrimination when judges are already exposed to the public discourse regarding widespread racial disparities that contradict the myth of racial democracy. In addition, the availability of racial data facilitates the lobbying for racial equality government policies.

For example, because Brazil has been one of the few countries in the region that have most consistently included a racial identification question on their decennial census, its racial justice organizations have been able to utilize the data to support their claims of unacceptable racial disparities in the country. It is in large part for this reason that Brazil has also been one of the few countries in the region to implement affirmative action policies in the public sector hiring and educational contexts.

In contrast, as discussed in Chapter 2, most of Spanish America and the Caribbean has refused consistently to collect racial data on the census. Yet even this is slowly beginning to change. Even though Venezuela has refused to collect racial data on its census forms since 1873 (twenty years after the abolition of slavery in 1854), in 2008 the government announced that it would include a new race question on the 2010 census. This was the result of much lobbying by various Afro-Venezuelan organizations with the support of the Inter-American Development Bank and the World Bank. With their funding of an international conference in 2000 focused on the regional need for census racial data, the Inter-American Development Bank and World Bank helped many Latin American countries apply political pressure to their governments.[96]

In addition, the Inter-American Development Bank has provided a small but growing number of pipeline loans to national statistics institutes to conduct national censuses to improve data collection on race and ethnicity. It has also provided some technical support to finance specialized studies and surveys on race and ethnicity. Now the census forms of Colombia, Cuba, Ecuador, El Salvador, Costa Rica, Puerto Rico, and Venezuela explicitly count Afro-descendants. Guatemala, Honduras, and Nicaragua partially count Afro-descendants by including a question regarding Garífuna ethnic ancestry. Unfortunately, a 2002 follow-up Inter-American Development Bank conference found that while advances had been made on the collection of indigenous data, only limited progress had been made on the data collection regarding Afro-descendants.[97] Until more countries in the region commit

---

[96] "Political Feasibility Assessment: Country Potential for New Research on Race in Latin America," presentation at "International Conference, Todos Contamos: Los Grupos Étnicos en los Censos," Inter-American Development Bank, Cartagena de Indias (November 8–10, 2000).

[97] Jacqueline Mazza, "Todos Contamos II: National Censuses and Social Inclusion – A Back to Office Report," Inter-American Development Bank (November 15, 2002), pp. 3–5, http:www.bid.org.uy/sds/doc/soc-BacktoOfficeTCII.pdf.

themselves to soliciting racial data on the census, Afro-descendants will continue to struggle to make their plight visible in the public discourse and tangible in courts of law.

While some countries have yielded to the demand for racial data on the census, other governments have deflected the demand with the claim that the fluidity of racial identities in Latin America subverts the ability to collect racial data. The government assertion is tantamount to saying, "How can we truly figure out who is black?" It is certainly true that the demography and racial ideology of Latin America have dissuaded many persons of African ancestry from identifying as black. Yet the growth of black social justice movements in Latin America demonstrates that racial fluidity in personal racial identity need not conflict with a political understanding of racial hierarchy and disparity. Certainly, the ability of multiracial Brazil to conduct a racial census decade after decade speaks to the ability of other multiracial Latin American nations to do so as well. For instance, despite the fact that Ecuador only reinstituted a race question on its census in 2001, almost 5 percent of the population identified themselves as *negro* (black) or *mulato* (mulatto). Moreover, when the census bureau conducted a 2004 employment survey with a question about racism, most Afro-Ecuadorians stated they understood what racism was in contrast to the small percentage of indigenous respondents who asserted the same.[98] This accords with a 2002 study of Afro-Ecuadorians in Quito who were both race conscious and keenly aware of racism and prejudice in their communities and daily lives.[99] Similarly, in contemporary Cuba despite the unifying rhetoric of socialist patriotism and racial democracy, racial categories are understood as coherent and salient to an understanding of social stratification.[100] In other words, the legacy of racial democracy need not continue obstructing the recognition of racial difference and disparity as long as the legal system is provided with the appropriate support for effective processing of claims.

[98] Scott H. Beck, Kenneth J. Mijeski, and Meagan M. Stark, "¿Qué es Racismo? Awareness of Racism and Discrimination in Ecuador," *Latin American Research Review* 46 (2011), 102–25.

[99] Carlos de la Torre, *Afroquiteños: Cidadania y Racismo* (Quito: Centro Andino de Acción Popular, 2002).

[100] Mark Q. Sawyer, *Racial Politics in Post-Revolutionary Cuba* (Cambridge: Cambridge University Press, 2006), pp. 134–8.

Rule of Law Enforcement Challenge

Reform of the legal system to enhance its stability has long been an issue of concern in Latin America. In particular, the 1980s began an intensive period of judicial reform.[101] Reform projects attempted to increase judicial personnel training, increase judicial sector budgets, and improve judicial career standards. The judicial reform priorities were set in response to country assessments that indicated that judges in the hemisphere were routinely denied resources such as training, staff, basic legal materials, updated codes, sound court buildings, and decent salaries. Furthermore, the assessments stated that judges were often subject to political influence, conflicts of interest, and outright corruption.

Since that time, the judiciary in Latin America is still perceived by many of its users to be in a state of crisis,[102] and the countries of the region consider justice reform to be a priority.[103] Opinion polls routinely demonstrate that citizens have little expectation of fair treatment by the Latin American judicial systems and that these institutions are the least respected in the public or private sectors.[104] Corruption continues to run rampant because funding for the judiciary is contingent upon the political will. Furthermore, while the general public perceives the judicial appointment process to be political, secretive, and thus without public accountability, low-income citizens have a particularly low level of confidence in the judicial system. Accordingly, growing numbers of Latin American countries have begun to institute life tenure and other security measures to insulate judges from political influence.[105]

[101] José E. Álvarez, "Promoting the 'Rule of Law' in Latin America: Problems and Prospects," *George Washington Journal of International Law & Economics* 25 (1991).

[102] María Dakolias, *The Judicial Sector in Latin America and the Caribbean: Elements of Reform* (Washington, DC: International Bank of Reconstruction and Development, 1996), p. 1.

[103] Christina Biebesheimer, "Justice Reform in Latin America and the Caribbean: The IDB Perspective," in Pilar Domingo and Rachel Sieder (eds.), *Rule of Law in Latin America: The International Promotion of Judicial Reform* (2001) (London: Institute of Latin American Studies, 2001), p. 99.

[104] Linn A. Hammergren, *The Politics of Justice and Justice Reform in Latin America* (Boulder, CO: Westview Press, 1998), p. 4.

[105] Jorge Correa Sutil, "Judicial Reforms in Latin America: Good News for the Underprivileged?" in Juan E. Méndez, Guillermo O'Donnell, and Paulo Sérgio

Recently, however, scholars have begun to question the pervasive image of Latin America as a region of "failed law" when the characterizations of undue formalism, inefficiency, and corruption also apply to all legal systems to varying degrees. In particular, Jorge Esquirol identifies the promulgation of an image of Latin American law as failed as a mechanism for justifying neoliberal development policy changes without further reflection on the effects of such changes on marginalized populations.[106] For example, under the banner of failed law discourse, much of the historical protections that Latin American labor codes have accorded to workers have been eroded. With the trope of failed law, wide-scale privatization is favored and the power of governments to further social justice is undermined. As a result, Esquirol cautions subordinated populations against discounting the value of Latin American law as a venue for promoting social justice.

Nevertheless, for civil rights reforms to be most effective, the unconscious racial bias of judges will need to be addressed.[107] In fact, the existence of rampant antiblack and antiindigenous sentiment in Latin America and Caribbean social contexts may very well lead jurists unconsciously to misperceive civil rights laws as being merely symbolic and not being "real law" that must be rigorously enforced.[108] Commentators note that social discrimination and class bias are still strong in the Latin American legal system.[109] In order for civil rights to be meaningful in Latin America, judicial training on the existence of discrimination and contours of civil rights law will also be needed. Furthermore, the larger context of judicial reform must address the fact that historically "constitutional guarantees have often provided little or no protection in practice for weak and vulnerable groups" and that "powerful elites tend to operate 'above' or 'outside' the law; impunity is widespread and powerful wrongdoers are rarely made accountable

Pinheiro (eds.), *The (Un)Rule of Law and the Underprivileged in Latin America* (Notre Dame, IN: University of Notre Dame Press, 1999), pp. 255–77.

[106] Jorge L. Esquirol, "The Failed Law of Latin America," *American Journal of Comparative Law* 56 (Winter 2008), 75–124.

[107] Hammergren, *Politics of Justice*, p. 31.

[108] John Valery White, "The Activist Insecurity and the Demise of Civil Rights Law," *Louisiana Law Review* 63 (2003), 785–873.

[109] Alison Brysk, *From Tribal Village to Global Village: Indian Rights and International Relations in Latin America* (Stanford, CA: Stanford University Press, 2000), p. 258.

through legal means."[110] Because the text of civil rights laws alone is
not able to mitigate the undermining influence of judicial bias, perhaps the primary way to counteract its effects is by directly addressing
it in the form of judicial training sessions. This could be implemented
through the vehicle of judicial schools that have flourished in Latin
America as the initial initiatives of modern judicial reform efforts.

Furthermore, the judicial training sessions could also address the
importance of considering social science data in the assessment of discrimination claims,[111] given the fact that judges are not yet accustomed
to hearing arguments based on such data.[112] This stems in part from
the fact that Latin American law training is a specialized course of
undergraduate study that is separate from the social science depart-
ments in the rest of the university.[113] Furthermore, because many
Latin American law professors are full-time practitioners who only
teach part time, they generally do not publish research or engage in
interdisciplinary study. This is in marked contrast to the U.S. educational context, where graduate legal studies are preceded by four years
of undergraduate university studies that can encompass social science courses among others selected by the student. The U.S. graduate
course of legal studies is supervised by law professors employed not
only for their skill in teaching but for their dedication to research and
scholarly publication that can be interdisciplinary in nature.

Fortunately, the emergence of a Latin American community of
public interest litigators has begun to broaden the landscape of appropriate evidence in court.[114] Law schools in the region have slowly
begun to include public interest lawyering courses in their curricular

---

[110] Rachel Sieder, "Conclusions: Promoting the Rule of Law in Latin America,"
in Pilar Domingo and Rachel Sieder (eds.), *Rule of Law in Latin America: The
International Promotion of Judicial Reform* (London: Brookings Institution Press,
2001), pp. 142, 151.
[111] Joseph L. Gastwirth, "Issues Arising in the Use of Statistical Evidence in
Discrimination Cases," in Joseph L. Gastwirth (ed.), *Statistical Science in the
Courtroom* (New York: Springer, 2000).
[112] Rebecca J. Cook, "Overcoming Discrimination: Introduction," in Méndez,
O'Donnell, and Pinheiro (eds.), *The (Un)Rule of Law and the Underprivileged in
Latin America*, pp. 109–15.
[113] Rogelio Pérez-Perdomo, *Latin American Lawyers: A Historical Introduction*
(Stanford, CA: Stanford University Press, 2006), p. 1049.
[114] Sutil, "Judicial Reforms in Latin America," pp. 255–77.

offerings. For instance, courses on racial discrimination are offered at law schools in Argentina, Chile, Colombia, Ecuador, Peru, and Puerto Rico.[115] More generalized courses on discrimination are offered at various law schools in Argentina and Ecuador.[116] Mexican and Venezuelan law schools offer courses on social rights and equality.[117] Furthermore, virtually all Latin American law schools offer courses on human rights and their international law sources.

[115] These courses include Universidad Nacional de Córdoba (Argentina), Human Rights UNIT III – Civil and Political Rights (including Anti-Discrimination), and Human Rights UNIT VII.2 International Anti-Discrimination Sources, http://www.uncu.edu.ar/contenido/index.php?Opcion=titulos&tid=16&filter_id_facultad=122&filter_id_carrera=276&filter_id_titulo=72; Universidad la República Law School (Chile): Damages for Discrimination, http://www.fder.edu.uy/contenido/post/derecho-de-danos.pdf; Universidad del Cauca – Facultad de Derecho y Ciencias Politicas y Sociales Law School (Colombia), Rights of Ethnic Groups, http://www.unicauca.edu.co/contenidos.php?seccion=programapre_plan&CatSub=1.1.0&Idprogpre=27&Idfac=5; Pontificia Universidad Católica del Perú Law School, Equality in Employment and Anti-Discrimination, http://www.pucp.edu.pe/facultad/derecho/images/documentos/3.cursosadictarseenell y-2semestre2009–1.pdf; Eugenio María De Hostos School of Law (Puerto Rico): Discrimination in Employment, www.hostos.edu/index.php?option=com_content&task=view&id=328&Itemid=257; and Universidad Interamericana de Puerto Rico School of Law, Employment Discrimination, http://www.derecho.inter.edu/catalogo08–10.pdf.

[116] These courses include Universidad de Mendoza Law School (Argentina), Human Rights and Social Work (including affirmative action), http://fade.uncoma.edu.ar/posgrados/humanos.htm;

Universidad de Palermo Law School (Argentina), Social Rights (including social exclusion and inequality), http://www.palermo.edu/derecho/posgrados/p_constitucional.html; Universidad Nacional de Córdoba Law School (Argentina), Social Inequality and Access to Justice, http://www.derecho.unc.edu.ar/modules.php?name=Content&pa=showpage&pid=56; Pontificia Universidad Católica del Ecuador Law School, Theory and Practice of Human Rights (including antidiscrimination and affirmative action), http://www.puce.edu.ec/sitios/documentos_DGA/13_9_0901_2008–02_15470_1706303144_S_1.pdf.

[117] These courses include Universidad La Salle Pachua, Law School (Mexico), Social and Individual Guarantees and Rights of Vulnerable Groups, http://www.lasallep.edu.mx/OFERTA/licDerecho.asp; Universidad Nacional Autónoma de México Law School, Ethics and Human Rights (including equality law), https://www.dgae.unam.mx/planes/f_derecho/DERECHO.pdf; Universidad Panamericana – Law School (Mexico), Human Rights Seminar: Equality and Antidiscrimination (Igualdad y no discriminación), http://www.mixcoac.upmx.mx/Default.aspx?doc=14672; Universidad Católica Andrés Bello Law School (Venezuela), Social, Economic, and Political Conditions to the Access of Justice, http://www.ucab.edu.ve/tl_files/CDH/recursos/info_web_ucab_de_acceso.doc.

One constraint that continues to impair access to the courts is the concentration of legal service agencies within urban areas. Public Ministry offices and other government provided lawyers are primarily located in urban areas. This system prevents much of the rural population of color from accessing legal providers.[118] Mexico and Guatemala are among the very few countries that have instituted Agrarian Government Attorney Offices.[119]

The alternative of using a private lawyer is similarly constrained by their limited numbers in rural locations, in addition to the obligation of legally demonstrating a sufficient prospect of success to obtain the privilege to litigate without administrative costs. Without an initial threshold showing of probable success, private attorneys are less inclined to take on what are now novel discrimination claims. Furthermore, only those plaintiffs who qualify for this assistance are able to be exempted from the civil law practice of requiring a losing party to pay the attorney's fees and costs of the winning party. This is in contrast to the U.S. legal system, in which losing parties are not automatically obligated to pay the attorney's fees and costs of the winning party, except where authorized by statutes. For instance, while Title VII of the Civil Rights Act of 1964 permits a prevailing plaintiff to seek attorney's fees in an employment discrimination lawsuit, prevailing defendants are only entitled to an award of attorney's fees if the plaintiff's case was "unreasonable, frivolous, meritless or vexatious."[120] Thus, while there are structural features that are designed to facilitate the access of the underprivileged to Latin American courts, the constraints on their implementation limits their efficacy. With all these constraints on the domestic enforcement of antidiscrimination legislation, social justice activists in the region have also focused on the international law arena as a venue for litigating claims and for advancing domestic law reform.

---

[118] Alejandro M. Garro, "Access to Justice for the Poor in Latin America," in Méndez, O'Donnell, and Pinheiro (eds.), *The (Un)Rule of Law and the Underprivileged in Latin America*, pp. 278–301.

[119] Roger Plant, "The Rule of Law and the Underprivileged in Latin America: A Rural Perspective," in Méndez, O'Donnell, and Pinheiro (eds.), *The (Un)Rule of Law and the Underprivileged in Latin America*, pp. 87–105.

[120] *Christiansburg Garment Co. v. EEOC*, 434 U.S. 412, 420 (1978).

The International Human Rights Context

Most Latin American countries are signatories to the International Convention on the Elimination of All Forms of Racial Discrimination (ICERD).[121] This is in marked contrast to the United States, which has claimed a reservation to the application of the convention. Article 6 of the convention states that "member states will ensure all people under their jurisdiction protection and effective recourse in competent national courts and other State institutions against any act of racial discrimination contemplated in this Convention, (...) the right to request that those [national] courts satisfy or compensate all damages to which they may be subjected as a result of that discrimination in a just and adequate manner." The convention is enforced by the United Nations Committee on the Elimination of Racial Discrimination.

All nations that are signatories to the convention are obliged to submit reports every two years to the United Nations Committee on the Elimination of Racial Discrimination (CERD) detailing how the rights are being implemented. The UN evaluates the reports and provides written recommendations to the state party.[122] Every four years the UN Human Rights Council also reviews the human rights records of each member state.

Article 14 of the convention establishes an individual complaints mechanism for individual persons and groups to allege harms inflicted by a member state. Complainants must have exhausted all domestic remedies and complaints. Upon receipt of the complaint, the committee can request information from and make recommendations to a party. The UN committee meets twice a year at its headquarters in Geneva to review the written documentation of the complaints and then issue

---

[121] The list of Latin American signatories includes Bolivia, Brazil, Chile, Colombia, Costa Rica, Cuba, Dominican Republic, Ecuador, El Salvador, Guatemala, Honduras, Mexico, Nicaragua, Panama, Paraguay, Peru, Uruguay, and Venezuela. International Convention on the Elimination of All Forms of Racial Discrimination, March 7, 1966, in force January 4, 1969, http://treaties.un.org/Pages/ViewDetails. aspx?src=TREATY&mtdsg_no=IV-2&chapter=4&lang=en#EndDec.

[122] "Compilation of Final Observations of the Committee for the Elimination of Racial Discrimination Regarding the Countries of Latin America and the Caribbean: 1970–2006 (June 2006)," United Nations High Commission for Human Rights, Latin America and The Caribbean Regional Representation, http://www2.ohchr. org/english/bodies/cerd/index.htm.

recommendations to the nation-states. Even though complainants are not required to travel to Geneva for the hearings, Latin American victims of racial discrimination have not generally availed themselves of the ICERD complaint process. This is because an ICERD complaint cannot be considered if the same situation is being investigated under another international procedure. The international venue of choice has instead been the Inter-American Commission on Human Rights.

Like the UN committee, the Inter-American Commission on Human Rights prepares reports on human rights conditions in the Western Hemisphere, in addition to receiving complaints from individuals or organizations regarding human rights abuses that violate the 1969 American Convention on Human Rights. The convention supports the right to equal protection of the law and the right to judicial protection against violations of fundamental rights. But before a complaint can be filed, the petitioner must have exhausted all available legal remedies in the state where the alleged violation occurred.

The commission reports with their conclusions and recommendations are binding upon the member state investigated to the extent that the member state is obligated to respond to the report with clarifications and plans for amelioration. The commission then decides which complaints it shall bring before the Inter-American Court of Human Rights (located in Costa Rica). The court is authorized to order nation-states to reform their laws or adopt other measures to address the complaints. Once a judgment is issued, the Organization of American States (OAS) has the mandate to monitor effective compliance.

Unfortunately, it has been noted that the OAS has limited itself to complying with only the formality of receiving reports without itself conducting effective follow-up investigations of compliance.[123] Moreover, the Inter-American court as well as the Inter-American commission lack means of direct coercion through which they can enforce their respective decisions or recommendations when they declare a state responsible for the violation of human rights and order

---

[123] "Using the Inter-American System for Human Rights: A Practical Guide for NGOs," *Global Rights Partners for Justice* (2004), 14–15.

certain measures of reparation for the victim. However, ignoring the legal pronouncements that emanate from the Inter-American system risks reputational harm to a nation and thereby carries political costs. In short, the value of the Inter-American system stems from its ability to provide leverage in the venue of public influence.

To be specific, what has been viewed as especially useful about the Inter-American system are the media attention and related influence nongovernmental organizations can garner. When the Inter-American commission conducts an on-site visit to investigate a claim or prepare a country report, the commission holds meetings with public officials, the armed forces, detention center officials, the police, churches, and civil society organizations. As such, the mere presence of the commission in a country generates public debate about human rights. Civil society organizations are better positioned to exert demands upon their governments when the Inter-American commission and court obligate a state to investigate a violation and punish those responsible; order a state to pay monetary or symbolic reparations; order the implementation of appropriate legislative, administrative, or other reforms to eradicate a practice that has been found to violate human rights. In particular, the Inter-American demand for legislative reform is especially helpful in those nations without effective internal legislation for addressing racial discrimination.

As a complement to the Inter-American system, in 2004 the Inter-American commission created a Rapporteurship on the Rights of Afro-Descendants and against Racial Discrimination. The core objective of the rapporteurship is to have a special rapporteur work with OAS member states to generate awareness of the states' duty to respect the human rights of Afro-descendants and work toward the elimination of all forms of racial discrimination, analyze the current challenges that confront countries of the region regarding race, formulate recommendations designed to overcome the obstacles and identify and share best practices in the region, and monitor and provide any technical assistance requested by member states in the implementation of the recommendations in national law and practice. The work of the rapporteur can provide NGOs with targeted data regarding the existence of racial discrimination rather than having such data folded within a general report on human rights.

Consequently, the rapporteur provides the opportunity for greater political leverage for racial reform. A useful example is that of the 2009 country report the rapporteur produced regarding racial discrimination in Colombia.[124] The rapporteur's report unequivocally states that Colombia's laws sanctioning racial discrimination are insufficient to eradicate the vast racial disparities that currently exist. Instead, the report urges the government to be actively engaged in and supportive of legal policies designed to decrease social exclusion and racial disparities. In short, the specialized focus of the rapporteur facilitates a more profound assessment of racial discrimination issues. With the advent of the special rapporteur, NGOs and individual victims of discrimination may be better positioned to utilize the international law venues for addressing issues of racial discrimination.

Nevertheless, the Inter-American system has been difficult for racial discrimination victims and their advocates to access for a number of reasons.[125] The Inter-American commission requirement that petitioners exhaust the internal legal remedies available in the state where the alleged violation occurred may inadvertently dissuade individuals from filing. It may very well appear a daunting proposition to expend resources exhausting internal remedies that inadequately address the harms of racial discrimination in order to then expend even more resources filing an international law complaint.

Yet the Inter-American commission does not require exhaustion of internal remedies if the victim has been denied access to those remedies, if the local laws do not afford due process of law for the protection of his or her rights, when the state has caused unwarranted delay, when a person does not have the financial means to pay for an attorney and the state does not provide one free of charge, or when the lawyers in the country in question are afraid to represent the petitioner. But each of these exceptions will require the petitioner to expend resources in demonstrating the applicability of the exception and thus also presents a disincentive to filing a complaint. Furthermore, litigating the

---

[124] "Inter-American Commission on Human Rights Release Report on Afro-Descendants in Colombia," Inter-American Commission on Human Rights (May 15, 2009), http://www.cidh.org/Comunicados/English/2009/28–09eng.htm.

[125] Claudio Grossman, "The Inter-American System of Human Rights: Challenges for the Future," *Indiana Law Journal* 83 (2008), 1267–82.

international claim itself is challenging given the fact that the petitioner carries the burden of proof and must therefore compile significant evidence about the issue or situation. Because the complaints can be sent in the mail and the proceedings are primarily based upon the written documents, petitioners are not obligated to travel to Washington, DC (the seat of the Inter-American commission) or Costa Rica (the seat of the Inter-American court). Nevertheless, because the Inter-American process can last for several years, the petitioner must be prepared to sustain the litigation over a prolonged period. This is a particularly significant constraint, given the Inter-American court's option to retry a case that has already been heard before the Inter-American commission, if in the court's judgment the commission's proceedings did not meet their standards.[126] The potential need to fly witnesses to two separate international locations to provide testimony increases the cost of litigating.

Despite the constraints on the Inter-American system for human rights, it remains a promising alternative venue for addressing issues of racial discrimination in the hemisphere. It is encouraging that the Inter-American court has explicitly stated that a narrow conception of rights in domestic law does not trump a nation's broader obligations under international law.[127] Indeed, there has been a dramatic increase in cases administered by the Inter-American system. While the Inter-American commission only received 517 petitions in 1998, in 2005 it received 1,330 petitions.[128] Even more significant has been the Inter-American system's recent decisions indicating that it is receptive to assessing complex issues involving racial bias in the region.

For instance, in 2006, the commission concluded that the state of Brazil breached its obligations to assure racial equality and the right to a fair trial in the case of Simone André Diniz.[129] In that case, Ms. Diniz applied for a domestic service work position advertised in a newspaper

---

[126] Rules of Procedure of the Inter-American Court of Human Rights, reprinted in Basic Documents Pertaining to Human Rights in the Inter-American System, OEA/Ser.L/V/I.rev.9 (2003).

[127] Case of the *Mayagna (Sumo) Awas Tingni Community v. Nicaragua*, 2001 Inter-Am. Ct. H.R. (ser. C) No. 79 (August 31, 2001).

[128] Inter-Am. C.H.R., Annual Report, OEA/Ser.L/V/II.124, doc. 5, ch. 3 at ¶ 8 (2006).

[129] *Diniz v. Brazil*, Case 12.001, Inter-Am. Comm'n Report No. 83/04 (2004).

that indicated that "whites" were preferred. When Ms. Diniz, who is black, called to inquire about the position, she was asked the color of her skin, and when she identified herself as a black woman, she was promptly told she did not meet the job requirements.

Yet when Ms. Diniz reported this violation of the Brazilian law against racism to the police, the Public Ministry in charge of prosecuting such crimes refused to proceed, claiming there was no basis in the record of a crime of racism. When this prosecutorial recommendation for dismissal went before a judge, the judge authorized the dismissal of the complaint despite the evidence of a legitimate allegation of racism. In reviewing the actions of the Brazilian state, the commission noted that the 2004 ICERD report observed that the Brazilian judiciary tended to be permissive with the practice of racial discrimination in its pattern of immediately dismissing racial discrimination complaints and that such was also the case with Ms. Diniz. The commission accordingly concluded that the Brazilian state had violated Article 24 of the American Convention on Human Rights' equality provision. The recommendations that the commission issued included fully compensating Ms. Diniz for the human rights violations, granting Ms. Diniz financial assistance so that she could further her education, reforming the antiracism law to make it more effective, initiating a complete investigation of her criminal allegation, and educating court and police officials in how to proceed properly in the enforcement of racism claims.

While the commission's recommendations are not legal mandates on a nation-state, the public attention that the commission's reports garner did have an influence in the Diniz case. By the time of the commission's 2010 Annual Report, they indicated that the Brazilian state had partially carried out the recommendations inasmuch as they had compensated Ms. Diniz for the human rights violations and had publicly acknowledged the state's responsibility for violating her human rights. To be sure, the Inter-American system is a lengthy process with ambiguous outcomes, but the Diniz case does show that it can bring pressure to bear in ways that further the cause of racial equality in Latin America.

Less successful, though, was the later case of Wallace De Almeida, a young soldier in the Brazilian army who was murdered by the Rio de Janeiro military police as he was walking to his home in Morro de Babilonia, a favela in Rio de Janeiro.[130] The commission concluded that the Brazilian state violated Article 24 of the American Convention on Human Rights' obligation to treat all persons equally before the law and without discrimination. Importantly, the commission noted that the Brazilian police force use of racial profiling to engage in violent police tactics systematically with the presumption that all black favela dwellers are inherently criminal was a violation of human rights that the Brazilian state was obligated to investigate without bias. This is because a state's obligation under the convention extends not only to its own direct actions but also to those of other public authorities like police officers, prosecutors, and judges. Consequently the commission recommended that the relatives of Wallace de Almeida be compensated for his murder, that a complete and impartial investigation of the murder commence with the aim of prosecuting the murderers, and that the state adopt measures to educate court and police officials to avoid racial discrimination in police operations, investigations, proceedings, and criminal convictions. The willingness of the commission to identify racial discrimination as a causal factor in the police murder of de Almeida was a significant victory for the petitioners. Unfortunately, more than ten years have elapsed since de Almeida's murder, the Brazilian state has yet to comply with any of the recommendations, and the commission is still monitoring the case.

In short, while Afro–Latin Americans have found some utility in availing themselves of the international law framework, weak enforcement structures, lengthy time frames, and the limited access that is available underscore the necessity to continue reforming the domestic legal frameworks for enforcing racial equality. Indeed, the General Assembly of the Organization of American States has itself noted the difficulties of addressing issues of racial discrimination under the more general category of human rights. As a result, the OAS in 2000 initiated a project for the development of an Inter-American Convention against Racism and All Forms of Discrimination and Intolerance.[131]

---

[130] De Almeida v. Brazil, Case No. 12.440, Inter-Am. Comm'n Report No. 73/06 (2006).

[131] "Brief Summary of the Status of the Negotiations of the Working Group Organized to Elaborate a Draft of an Inter-American Convention against Racism and All Forms

Since then a draft convention has been produced and special sessions conducted for the purposes of promoting its adoption by the OAS member states. If widely adopted, the convention could support research to promote awareness of racial discrimination in the region, in addition to monitoring state patterns of racial disparity. By identifying people of African)" descent in the Americas as specific subjects of rights, the convention would help facilitate the important struggle to have nation-states understand and respond to racial inequality.

Yet, there has been resistance to the adoption of the Inter-American Convention against Racism and All Forms of Discrimination and Intolerance.[132] A number of member states have opposed its focus on the issue of racism and have proposed that the convention be reworded and expanded to address other sources of bias and marginalization more broadly such as ageism, xenophobia, and many others. Underlying this resistance is the view that racial discrimination is not the most salient lens with which to address social problems in Latin America and thus does not warrant a single-issue convention. This perspective is in marked contrast to the international law framework of the last two decades, which has moved toward the use of conventions on single issues. For instance, the single focus on gender exists with the Inter-American Convention on the Prevention, Punishment and Eradication of Violence against Women, and a single focus on disabilities exists with the Inter-American Convention on the Elimination of All Forms of Discrimination against Persons with Disabilities. It is also a huge shift from the way the Inter-American Convention against Racism and All Forms of Discrimination and Intolerance was conceived in 2000, as a mechanism for making the antiracism focus of the International Convention on the Elimination of All Forms of Racial Discrimination (ICERD) more relevant to the needs of the Americas, since ICERD's initial focus forty years ago on matters of apartheid and colonialism. Over time, the input from the various nation-states

of Discrimination and Intolerance," Organization of American States International Law Department (May 28, 2009), http://scm.oas.org/doc_public/SPANISH/HIST_09/CP22305S04.doc.

[132] "The Need for a Narrow-Focused Inter-American Convention against Racial Discrimination," Position Paper No. 1, University of Texas School of Law Human Rights Clinic (May 2009).

has sought to dilute the single focus on racism in ways that reflect the conception of Latin America as racially innocent. In reliance upon the notion that Latin American nation-states have been innocent of racial wrongdoing given the absence of state-mandated Jim Crow segregation in the region, Latin American nation-state delegations view racism as an aberration rather than a systemic part of each national culture. This book's account of the role of the customary law of race regulation within Latin America severely contradicts such a perspective and could perhaps be helpful in the efforts to oppose the resistance to a single-issue race-focused convention. Invoking the history of customary law of race regulation can accord social justice movement actors the rhetorical power needed to dispel the notion of state racial innocence that hinders the consideration of targeted and effective measures for addressing racism with a race-focused convention.

Latin America is slowly emerging from its veil of presumed racial democracy and is beginning to establish mechanisms for recognizing the harms of racial discrimination. But for a population that has long been viewed as free of the harshness of U.S. discrimination, Afro–Latin Americans continue to be disproportionately poor, unemployed, and poorly educated. The development of antidiscrimination structures in Latin America will surely be a helpful tool in assisting Afro-descendants to strive for racial equality. Yet much more remains to be done. Afro-descendant movements are cognizant that broader legal protections are still needed against racial discrimination. As a result, in addition to lobbying for more effective civil rights enforcement, the social justice movements have also argued forcefully for the implementation of affirmative action policies, as will be discussed in the next chapter.

6   BRAZIL: AT THE FOREFRONT OF LATIN AMERICAN RACE-BASED AFFIRMATIVE ACTION POLICIES AND CENSUS RACIAL DATA COLLECTION

The absence of census racial data in many Latin American countries impedes not only the ability to systematically gather group-based statistics demonstrating racial exclusion, but also the capacity to lobby effectively for race-based affirmative action policies to ameliorate that racial exclusion. Thus far, the creation of affirmative action programs and policies in Spanish America has been quite modest.

Colombia is unique in allocating legislative seats to Afro-Colombians in the Chamber of Deputies (rather than solely to women, as in many Latin American countries such as Argentina, Bolivia, Colombia, Costa Rica, Dominican Republic, Ecuador, Mexico, Panama, Paraguay, and Peru).[1] Specifically, the Colombian Constitution provides for the political representation of Afro-descendants and indigenous populations in the Colombian house of representatives and senate.[2] In addition, in 1996, Colombia created an Afro-Colombian Educational Credits Program (Programa de Créditos Educativos para Comunidades Afro-Colombianas).[3] This program consists of the allocation of university credits to Afro-Colombians for service work "by means of community work, social or academic, in agreement with a project of work presented when applying for the credit, which is guaranteed by a base organization." The requirements to be a beneficiary of the program are

---

[1] Mala N. Htun, *Dimensions of Political Inclusion and Exclusion in Brazil: Gender and Race*, Technical Papers (Washington, DC: Inter-American Development Bank, December 2003), appendix A, table A (Statutory Gender Quotas and Reservations).

[2] Constitución Política de Colombia, Tit. VI, art. 171, 176.

[3] "Instituto Colombiano de Crédito Educativo y Estudios Técnicos en el Exterior," ICETEX, http://www.icetex.gov.co/portal/Default.aspx?tabid=275.

certified participation in an Afro-Colombian community, academic excellence, limited socioeconomic resources, and presentation of a directed project to solve problems or needs of the origin community.[4]

Moreover, several Colombian universities, both public and private, have created special admissions programs for ethnic minorities, including Afro-Colombians.[5] The reserved seats range from two to five per course.[6] The affirmative action programs began admitting indigenous students first and then expanded to include Afro-Colombians.[7]

Similarly, in Ecuador, the government has made plans to establish a 10 percent Afro-Ecuadorian and indigenous student quota for public and private secondary education institutions. This is because Article 11.2 of the Ecuadorian Constitution states, "The state will adopt affirmative action measures that promote equality in favor of those who find themselves in a situation of inequality."[8] The government also plans to set quotas for faculty and research staff at higher education institutions.[9] In a more limited fashion, the government in conjunction with the Universidad Andina Simón Bolívar created a program in which fifteen Afro-Ecuadorian attorneys will be awarded

[4] Magdalena León and Jimena Holguín, "La Acción Afirmativa en La Universidad de los Andes: El caso del programa 'Oportunidades para talentos nacionales,'" *Revista de Estudios Sociales* 19 (December 2004), http://res.uniandes.edu.co/view.php/405/indexar.php? c=Revista+No+18.

[5] Magdalena León and Jimena Holguín, *Acción Afirmativa Hacia Democracias Inclusivas: Colombia* (Chile: Fundación Equitas, March 2005), pp. 208–11, http://www.fundacionequitas.org/archivo.aspx?cod_idioma=ES&id=29 (chart 9 describes all the affirmative action programs, including admissions); León and Holguín, "La Acción Afirmativa en la Universidad de los Andes," p. 60.

[6] *Actualidad Afrodescendiente en Iberoamérica: Estudio Sobre Organizaciones Civiles y Políticas de Acción Afirmativa* (Madrid: Secretaria General Iberoamericana, July 2010), p. 42, http://segib.org/publicaciones/files/2010/07/Actualidad-Afrodescendiente-Iberoamerica.pdf.

[7] Castro Heredia et al., "Un breve acercamiento a las políticas de Acción Afirmativa: orígenes, aplicación y experiencia para grupos étnico-raciales en Colombia y Cali," *Revista Sociedad y Economía* 169 (January 2009), http://redalyc.uaemex.mx/redalyc/pdf/996/99612491009.pdf.

[8] *Constitución Del Ecuador*, http://www.asambleanacional.gov.ec/documentos/constitucion_de_bolsillo.pdf

[9] *Plan Plurinacional Para Eliminar la Discriminación Racial y la Exclusión Étnica y Cultural* (Quito: CODAE, September 2009), p. 35, http://www.codae.gob.ec/index.php?option=com_content&view=article&id=188%3Aplan-plurinacional-para-eliminar-la-discriminacion-racial-y-la-exclusion-etnica-y-cultural&catid=27&Itemid=63.

scholarships for specialization in human rights, particularly as it refers to Afro-descendant communities.[10] Another program by the government awards ten scholarships for Afro-Ecuadorian students who want to pursue master's degrees.[11] In public sector employment, the Ecuadorian government has also planned an affirmative action policy for hiring in various government agencies.[12]

The Ecuadorian government has also made agreements with six different local governments to build housing specifically targeted to Afro-Ecuadorians.[13] For example, in an agreement with the Municipality of Cantón Ibarra, the government pledged to provide $700,000 for the implementation of a program that would create 250 housing units for Afro-descendants of that municipality, and the municipality would be responsible for implementing the program.[14] While $700,000 may seem to be a modest sum, it should be noted that on average it costs an individual $36,000 to build a 1,200-square-foot house in Ecuador.

In Honduras, the government created a scholarship program for Afro-Honduran students who want to continue their secondary education and attend university.[15] In Uruguay, the Ministry of Education and Culture has a fund that promotes scholarships for Afro-Uruguayan students. There are also postgraduate scholarships, such as the Beca Carlos Quijano, which targets Afro-Uruguayan students.[16]

In short, the availability of race-based affirmative action programs in Latin America is quite limited as compared to the United States, where countless numbers of employers, universities, and government entities have affirmative action policies. The initial steps to consideration of

---

[10] "15 Abogados Afroecuatorianos se Especializan," CODAE, May 13, 2011, http://www.codae.gob.ec/index.php?option=com_k2&view=item&id=137:15-abogados-afroecuatorianos-se-especializan.

[11] "Becas y Maestrías," CODAE, May 2011, http://www.codae.gob.ec/index.php?option=com_content&view=article&id=194:becas-y-maestrias&catid=1.

[12] *Plan Plurinacional Para Eliminar*, p. 39.

[13] "Proyectos de Viviendas," CODAE, http://www.codae.gob.ec/index.php?option=com_content&view=article&id=202&Itemid=74.

[14] *Convenio de Cooperación Interinstitucional Entre La Corporación de Desarrollo Afroecuatoriano-CODAE y El Ilustre Municipio Del Cantón Ibarra* (Quito: CODAE, 2010), http://www.codae.gob.ec/images/stories/transparencia/proyectos /convenio%20ibarra.pdf.

[15] Executive Decree 09–2007 (Honduras).

[16] *Actualidad Afrodescendiente en Iberoamérica*, p. 44.

affirmative action in Latin America more broadly have instead taken the form of government agencies created to assist in the equality of Afro-descendants. Special government ombudsmen dealing with racism now operate in every Latin American country except El Salvador, Chile, and Paraguay. For instance, in Venezuela, the Presidential Commission for the Prevention and Elimination of All Forms of Racial Discrimination and Other Distinctions in the Venezuelan Educational System is responsible for promulgating antidiscrimination- related policies. Yet the only legislation that has been put into effect is the decree declaring May 10 Afro-Venezuelan Day.[17]

While such symbolic legislation is certainly worthwhile for engaging in endeavors that focus public attention on the existence and plight of Afro-descendants, there is a dearth in Latin America of programs that directly address the issue of providing access to institutions that bar Afro-descendants on the basis of racial bias and stereotype. Venezuela is thus emblematic of the nascent development of affirmative action in Latin America. In contrast, Brazil stands out as the Latin American nation with the greatest number of race-based affirmative action policies that target Afro-descendants.

BRAZIL'S AFFIRMATIVE ACTION DEBATE

There are several reasons for Brazil's more intense focus on race-based affirmative action. Afro-Brazilian social justice movements were active participants in the United Nations World Conference against Racism in 2001. The public attention that the UN conference provided for issues of racial equality, enabled the NGOs to exert pressure upon the Brazilian government. In addition, the conference's emphasis upon the International Convention on the Elimination of All Forms of Racial Discrimination's support for affirmative action provided a legal justification for executive action. Article 1, Section 4, of the convention (to which Brazil is a signatory) establishes that

> special measures taken for the sole purpose of securing adequate advancement of certain racial or ethnic groups or individuals

[17] Decreto No. 428 (2005) (Venezuela).

requiring such protection as may be necessary in order to ensure
such groups or individuals equal enjoyment or exercise of human
rights and fundamental freedoms shall not be deemed racial discrimination, provided, however, that such measures do not, as a
consequence, lead to the maintenance of separate rights for different racial groups and that they shall not be continued after the
objectives for which they were taken have been achieved.

The then-president Fernando Henrique Cardoso was especially receptive to the lobbying for affirmative action because of his own intellectual
work as a prominent sociologist addressing racial inequality in Brazil.[18]
For instance, as a sociologist, President Cardoso coauthored with
Octavio Ianni the book *Côr e mobilidade social em Florianópolis:Aspectos
das relaçoes entre negros e brancos numa comunidade do Brasil meridional*
(Color and Social Mobility in Florianopolis: Aspects of the Relations
between Blacks and Whites in a Southern Brazil Community).[19]

Accordingly, Brazil began instituting affirmative action policies in
2001, when the minister of agriculture issued an executive order mandating that 20 percent of his staff be black, that 20 percent of the
staff of firms contracting with the agency be of African descent, and
that another 20 percent of the firms' staff be women.[20] Thereafter, the
Federal Supreme Court and all other cabinet agencies instituted affirmative action policies as well.[21] The Federal Supreme Court's affirmative action program set a quota of 20 percent for Afro-descendants
for third-party contractors.[22] The Ministry of Justice's affirmative
action program set out that 20 percent of supervisory and upper-level
advisory positions should go to Afro-Brazilians. The Federal Public
Administration established the National Affirmative Action Program,

---

[18] Mala Htun, "From 'Racial Democracy' to Affirmative Action: Changing State Policy
on Race in Brazil," *Latin American Research Review* 39 (February 2004), 60–89.

[19] Fernando Henrique Cardoso and Octavio Ianni, *Côr e mobilidade social em
Florianópolis: Aspectos das relaçoes entre negros e brancos numa comunidade do Brasil
meridional* (São Paulo: Companhia Ed. Nac., 1960).

[20] Seth Racusen, "Making the 'Impossible' Determination: Flexible Identity and
Targeted Opportunity in Contemporary Brazil," *Connecticut Law Review* 36 (2004),
811–12.

[21] Ibid. at 812–13.

[22] Raquel Coelho Lenz Cesar, "Acesso A Justiça Para Minorias Racias no Brasil: É
a Açao Afirmativa o Melhor Caminho? Riscos e Açertos no Caso da UERJ," PhD
dissertation, State University of Rio de Janeiro (2003), p. 28.

providing percentage-based goals for Afro-descendants' participation on professional teams. A Rio Branco Institute program aimed at educating diplomats provided scholarships for black applicants to study for the public service entrance examination. In addition, in 2002, Law 10.558 was passed creating the University Diversity Program under the Ministry of Education. This program aims to "implement and evaluate strategies for promoting access to higher education to people who belong to socially disadvantaged groups, particularly Afro-descendants and members of Brazilian indigenous communities." The program includes funding for public and private nonprofit entities working toward the program goals.

Like the Brazilian federal government, local governments have begun to institute affirmative action programs. For example, in June 2011, the state of Rio de Janeiro issued a decree instituting a 20 percent set-aside of vacancies for blacks and persons of indigenous descent in the public examinations for civil service positions in the state government.[23] It should be noted that while much of the public discourse in Brazil conflates the concept of affirmative action with outright quotas, in point of fact the affirmative action programs that exist vary in their content and structure.[24] In other words, not all the affirmative action programs in Brazil contain outright quotas.

Most controversial, though, has been the direct implementation of race-based affirmative action programs in higher education, which most ministers of education are on record as opposing.[25] In 2000, the State University of Rio de Janeiro (Universidade Estadual do Río de Janeiro – UERJ) inaugurated an outright quota of 40 percent for top-scoring black/*negra* or brown/*parda* students and a 10 percent quota for students with disabilities.[26] The affirmative action policy was

[23] Decreto No. 43007, de 6 de Junho de 2011 (Brazil).
[24] Rosana Heringer, "Ação Afirmativa e Promoção da Igualdade Racial no Brasil: O Desafio da Prática," in Angela Randolpho Paiva (ed.), *Ação Afirmativa na Universidade: Reflexão Sobre Experiências Concretas Brasil-Estados Unidos* (Rio de Janeiro: Editora-PUC Rio, 2004), pp. 55–86.
[25] Anani Dzidzienyo, "The Changing World of Brazilian Race Relations?" in Anani Dzidzienyo and Suzanne Oboler (eds.), *Neither Enemies nor Friends: Latinos, Blacks, Afro-Latinos* (New York: Palgrave Macmillan, 2005), pp. 137–55, 147.
[26] Public Law 3708/2001, State of Rio de Janeiro, http://www.alerj.rj.gov/top_leis_ordinairas.htm; Public Law 3524/2000, State of Rio de Janeiro, http://www.alerj.rj.gov/top_leis_ordinairas.htm.

initially challenged before the Federal Supreme Court of Brazil by a state legislator and an association of private schools (CONFENEN) as a violation of the Brazilian constitutional provision for proportionality in the exercise of legislative discretion (*razãoabilidade*).[27] This lawsuit was ruled moot when the state legislature revised the policy in September 2003, to establish the more limited quotas of 20 percent for self-declared blacks/*Negros*, 20 percent for public school students, and 5 percent for other disabled students and indigenous Brazilians in total.[28] In addition, all students admitted under the new policy had to meet financial eligibility requirements.[29] This revised affirmative action policy was then challenged in court once again along with challenges to the Federal University of Brasilia, Federal University of Rio Grande do Sul, and the State University of North Fluminense affirmative action policies.[30] More than three hundred disgruntled applicants brought challenges to the affirmative action policies of the two state universities in Rio de Janeiro alone.[31]

Furthermore, 114 academics signed a 2006 "manifesto" opposing race-based affirmative action as unconstitutional and an engine for conflict and intolerance.[32] A few days later 330 intellectuals and social justice movement representatives signed a response entitled "Manifesto in Favor of the Laws." The documents were widely discussed in the Brazilian media and the debate has continued, as indicated by the 2008 national survey suggesting that 62 percent of Brazilians believe that the policies are essential, while another 53 percent believe that the programs are humiliating, and 62 percent think that the policies can themselves cause racism.[33] The overlapping survey results thus suggest that

[27] Racusen, "Making the 'Impossible' Determination," p. 816.
[28] Public Law 4151/2003, State of Rio de Janeiro, http://www.alerj.rj.gov.br/processo2.htm.
[29] Racusen, "Making the 'Impossible' Determination," 816–17.
[30] Supremo Tribunal Federal, Detalhes Da Ação Direta de Inconstitucionalidade http://gemini.stf.gov.br/cgi-bin/nph-brs?d=ADIN&s1=3197&u=http://www.stf.gov.br/Proc.
[31] Racusen, "Making the 'Impossible' Determination," p. 815.
[32] Mario Osava, "Brazil: Race Quotas – Accused of Racism," Inter Press Service News, July 26, 2006, http://ipsnews.net/news.asp?idnews=34111.
[33] Antônio Gois, "Brasileiros Vêem Cota Como Essencial e Humilhante, Revela Datafolha," Folha de São Paulo Online, November 23, 2008, http://www1.folha.uol.com.br/folha/brasil/ult96u470649.shtml.

many Brazilians are conflicted about the use of race-based affirmative action. Anti–affirmative action discourse has been so virulent that even some of the early beneficiaries of the policies articulated ambivalence about their advisability.[34] As a result, the Federal Supreme Court held a public hearing in March 2010 to gather information from people with experience and expertise in the area of affirmative action.

The legal challenge before the Federal Supreme Court alleged that the affirmative action quota system violated the constitutional principle of equality before the law, pursuant to Article 5 of the Brazilian Constitution of 1988. Article 5 of the Brazilian Constitution of 1988 states in relevant part, "All are equal before the law, without distinction of any nature, guaranteeing to Brazilians and to foreigners resident in Brazil, the inviolability of the right to life, liberty, equality, and property." The argument is that white students who were denied admission but scored more points on the entrance exam than candidates who were accepted under the quota system were thus treated unequally.[35] It is also important to note that the legal briefs of the challengers to affirmative action all assert that the absence of governmentally imposed institutionalized racism in Brazil (like U.S. Jim Crow segregation) undermines the need for affirmative action in Brazil such that the implementation of affirmative action would be an imposition of racism. For instance, in the legal challenge to the University of Brasilia affirmative action program, the plaintiff states that he challenges the legality of "whether the implementation of a racialized state or institutionalized racism, as practiced in the United States, South Africa or in Rwanda, would be suitable for Brazil."[36] The legal briefs as a whole further assert that the ideal of racial democracy should be upheld in such a racially mixed country where racial designations are too difficult to administer.[37] Completely missing from this narrative is the

---

[34] Mónica Treviño González, "Opportunities and Challenges for the Afro-Brazilian Movement," in Bernd Reiter and Gladys L. Mitchell (eds.), *Brazil's New Racial Politics* (Boulder, CO: Lynne Rienner, 2010), pp. 123–38.

[35] S.T.F., RE No. 597285, Relator: Min. Ricardo Lewandowski, 09.10.2009, 191 DJe 1479 (Brazil).

[36] ADPF 186, Petição Inicial 20/07/2009 (Initial Petition July 20, 2009).

[37] Marina Jacob Lopes da Silva, "Igualdade e Ações Afirmativas Sociais e Raciais no Ensino Superior: O Que se Discute no STF?" Research Monograph, Sociedade Brasileira de Direito Público (2009).

historic role of the state in facilitating racial exclusion and its customary law of race regulation.

Part of the appellate record before the Federal Supreme Court was
a May 2009 court opinion from the Rio de Janeiro State Appellate
Court declaring the Rio de Janeiro affirmative action law unconstitutional with a justification firmly entrenched in the dated notion of
Brazil as a racial democracy. Specifically, the court opinion states that
the affirmative action quota system

> creates privileges for part of the Brazilian population, which con-
> sists of people of irreversible racial mixing, and creates this priv-
> ilege at the highest point of our country's educational process,
> which are our universities. The possibility opens up of a country
> where racial mixing is the rule producing, by law, an apartheid that
> does not currently exist in Brazil.[38]

For this judge, as for much of the Brazilian white elite, the outright
rejection of affirmative action is firmly rooted in the premise that racial
exclusion is not part of Brazilian culture and that affirmative action will
create the segregation that currently exists in nations like the United
States that employ affirmative action.

But it is not clear that such dated perspectives will carry the day.
When the Rio de Janeiro state university affirmative action policy was
later appealed before a special panel of the Rio State Court of Appeals,
the court voted fifteen to six in favor of the constitutionality of the policy.[39] On March 19, 2012, the Federal Supreme Court dismissed the
federal appeal to the policy because the challenged 2003 law had been
superseded by a new state affirmative action law in 2008 that limited
its duration to ten years.[40]

More importantly, on April 26, 2012, the Federal Supreme
Court issued a momentous ruling with its decision that the Federal
University of Brasilia affirmative action policy is constitutionally

---

[38] T.J.R.J., Dir. Inc. No. 2009.007.00009, Relator: Des. José Carlos S. Murata Ribeiro,
25.05.2009 (Brazil).
[39] T.J.R.J. Representação Por Inconstitucionalidade No. 2009.007.00009, Relator: Des.
Sérgio Cavalieri Filho, 18.11.2009 (Brazil).
[40] Ação Direta De Inconstitucionalidade 3.197 Rio de Janeiro, Decisão de 19 de março
2012, Relator: Min. Celso de Mello (Brazil).

valid.[41] In a unanimous decision, the Court stated that in order for the state to effectuate the principle of equality, affirmative action policies are an important duty and social responsibility of the state because the Constitution requires reparation of past losses imposed on Afro-Brazilians. Furthermore, just one week later, the Court also confirmed the constitutionality of the University for All Program (ProUni), which provides scholarships for Afro-descended students from low-income families to attend private universities.[42] With this pair of decisions, the Brazilian Federal Supreme Court has affirmed the constitutional priority of reducing social inequalities and the use of affirmative action as an important tool of social integration.

Moreover with the passage of time growing numbers of Brazilians and program beneficiaries have come to view affirmative action as positive. Indeed, in the 2010 survey of applicants to the State University of Rio de Janeiro, 85.4 percent of the black and indigenous affirmative action candidates stated they were in agreement with the quota system.[43] In contrast, in 2005, only 66.8 percent of affirmative action candidates stated that the affirmative action policy was a positive thing.[44]

Especially revealing is a 2010 survey of attitudes toward affirmative action that more specifically identifies which portion of the Brazilian population opposes race-based affirmative action. In the Americas Barometer 2010 survey of Brazil, it was discovered that a high percentage of Brazilians believe that reserving slots in universities for Afro-descendants is fair. In fact, of the 66.2 percent who agree, 45.0 percent "strongly agree." Of the 27.4 percent who disagree, only 18 percent "strongly disagree." The remaining 6.5 percent neither agree nor disagree. However, the minority that strongly disagree are primarily

[41] "STF declared the constitutionality of the quota system at the University of Brasilia," STF Internacional (Federal Supreme Court of Brazil news portal), April 26, 2012, http://www2.stf.jus.br/portalStfInternacional/cms/destaquesClipping. php?sigla=portalStfDestaque_en_us&idConteudo=207138.

[42] "Supremo declara constitucionalidade do ProUni," Secretaria de Políticas de Promoção da Igualdade Racial, Últimas Notícias, May 4, 2012, http://www.seppir. gov.br/noticias/ultimas_noticias/2012/05/supremo-declara-constitucionalidade-do-prouni.

[43] "Dados Socioculturais 2010," Vestibular UERJ, www.vestibular.uerj.br (tabulation of UERJ sociocultural survey question data).

[44] González, "Opportunities and Challenges for the Afro-Brazilian Movement," p. 127.

white, university educated, and very vocal in the media and public discourse.[45] Thus while the Brazilian media have accorded significant space to the oppositional voices of the white and university educated critics of affirmative action, in actuality they are a small minority of the population. In fact, more than two-thirds of Brazilians in the Americas Barometer 2010 survey who support race-based affirmative action span all races and political affiliations.

This may account for why university affirmative action policies have continued to proliferate in various forms, despite the refusal of the federal legislature to mandate affirmative action policies in the 2010 Racial Equality Statute.[46] By August 2010, at least eighty public universities had adopted affirmative action policies. The structures of the current programs vary.[47] Some solely target Afro-Brazilian students from public secondary schools, as a way to reach the most needy of Afro-Brazilian students. Other programs set aside seats for public secondary school graduates of any race and then establish proportionate slots by race according to the census demographic percentages of the state. Another variation provides for separate quotas for Afro-Brazilian students (from public or private secondary schools), in addition to a quota for public school students of any race. Finally, a few universities award extra points to the *vestibular* entrance examination scores to Afro-Brazilian applicants and public secondary school graduates.

When considering the context of public university affirmative action programs, it is important to note that unlike in the United States, where many private colleges are considered more prestigious than all but a few state universities, Brazil's public institutions of higher learning are held in greater esteem than their private counterparts.[48] The tuition-free public colleges and the private colleges each administer

[45] Amy Erica Smith, "Who Supports Affirmative Action in Brazil," LAPOP Americas Barometer 2010 Insights No. 49 (Oct. 4, 2010), http://www.vanderbilt.edu/lapop/insights/I0849en.pdf.
[46] Law No. 12.288/10 (Brazil).
[47] Seth Racusen, "Fictions of Identity and Brazilian Affirmative Action," *National Black Law Journal* 21 (2009); "Cotas No Brasil: Um Panorama do Aplicação de Políticas Afirmativas Nas Universidades Públicas," *Revista Adusp* 43 (July 2008), 6–39.
[48] Edward E. Telles, *Race in Another America: The Significance of Skin Color in Brazil* (Princeton, NJ: Princeton University Press, 2004), pp. 124, 159.

their own admission test called the "vestibular."[49] University admission is based solely upon the entrance examination, and high school grades are completely disregarded. Because there is great competition for a very limited number of spaces, some students, usually those with greater financial resources, pay for a year-long enrollment in test preparatory courses called *cursinhos*.[50] The university entrance examinations aim to test substantive knowledge from all earlier years of study but are known to test on subjects not taught in the public primary and secondary schools.[51]

As a result, the elite public universities are attended disproportionately by white Brazilians whose parents paid for their superior private primary and secondary school educations.[52] The majority of Afro-Brazilians of limited means are excluded from the free elite public universities and are relegated to paying for private school tuition or not continuing their education at all.[53] As a result, in the year 2000, the Ministry of Education indicated that only 2 percent of all university students in the country were black.[54] Even worse, the representation of Afro-Brazilians was practically zero in the elite academic programs of medicine and law. While Afro-Brazilian social justice groups have created "prevestibular" courses to help prepare the excluded students for the university entrance exams, in addition to creating a black university – Unipalmares Universidade da Cidadania Zumbi dos Palmares – they cannot single-handedly make up for the deficiencies of the public primary school education and the resulting exclusion of the majority of Afro-Brazilians from higher education.[55] The politics of these

[49] Ibid. at 159; Zakiya Carr Johnson, "International Human Rights Law Group, Overview of Vestibular: The Brazilian College Entrance Exams" (May 2003), 2–3.
[50] Carr Johnson, "Overview of Vestibular," pp. 2–3.
[51] Ibid. at 3; César, "Acesso A Justiça," pp. 294–5.
[52] Telles, *Race in Another America*, p. 124.
[53] Ibid.; Antonio Sérgio Alfredo Guimarães, "Ações Afirmativas Para a População Negras Nas Universidades Brasileiras," in Renato Emerson dos Santos and Fatima Lobato (eds.), *Ações Afirmativas: Políticas Públicas Contra As Desigualdades Racias* (Brazil: Programa Políticas da Cor na Educação Brasileira, 2003), pp. 75, 76–7.
[54] José Jorge de Carvalho, "As Propostas de Cotas Para Negros e O Racismo Acadêmico No Brasil," *Sociedade e Cultura*, 4 (July/December 2001), 13–30, 17.
[55] Alexandre do Nascimento, "Movimentos Sociais, Educação E Cidadania: Um Estudo Sobre os Cursos Pré-Vestibulares Populares," master's thesis, State University of Rio de Janeiro (1999).

demographic patterns in university admissions is what prompted the movement for affirmative action policies in university admissions.[56]

Because the public debate regarding race-based affirmative action programs has been quite vociferous, it makes a remarkable contrast to the ease with which gender-based affirmative action programs were introduced previously.[57] To be specific, in 1995, Brazil adopted quotas for women in the electoral system. Article 11 of Federal Law 9.100 established that at least 20 percent of the candidates in municipal elections for legislative seats should be women. In 1997, Law 9.504 established a 25 percent quota of state and federal representatives in parliamentary elections. With more than a decade of experience with these gender-based affirmative policies, the public discourse has never characterized the policies as an unconstitutional form of discrimination. It is thus clear that the Brazilian elite objection to race-based affirmative action policies is not rooted in objections to affirmative action itself, but rather to the race-based nature of the policies.

This is also underscored by the fact that other non-race-based affirmative action policies have not caused public dissension. Affirmative action programs designed for farmers' children and the disabled preexisted the race-based policies. For instance, Law 5465 of 1968 established quotas for providing access to education to farmers' children.[58] For the disabled, the Federal Constitution of 1988, Article 37 § VIII, sets out that "the law reserves a percentage of public positions and jobs for people with disabilities and will define the criteria for their admission." The implementation of this clause has led to various laws that establish quotas for people who have disabilities in the public service (Law 8112 of 1990) and in the private sector (Law 8213 of 1991).

Even those who presumably favor race-based affirmative action programs in principle question whether they can be appropriately implemented within a nation of "mixed race" persons who have

---

[56] Telles, *Race in Another America*, pp. 59, 253.
[57] Mala N. Htun, *Dimensiones de la inclusión y exclusión política en Brasil: Género y raza*, Serie de informes técnicos del Departamento de Desarrollo Sostenible (Washington, DC: Banco Interamericano de Desarrollo, 2004), http://www.iadb.org/IDBDocs. cfm?docnum=361865.
[58] Raquel Cesar, "Açoes afirmativas no Brasil: e agora, doutor?" *Ciencia Hoje*, 33 (July 2003), 26–32.

ambiguous and fluid racial identities. The concern with fraudulent claims being made by white Brazilians has been addressed by structuring some affirmative action programs to target only those applicants who self-identify as *negro* (black), because "the category black tends to intimidate the opportunists."[59] The logic is that while the Brazilian racial democracy discourse romanticizes the notion of vague connections to African ancestry, it does not diminish the pejorative associations with an overt black identity. Nonetheless, the issue of fraudulent claims does arise and has been addressed programmatically in a variety of ways, which include requesting official documentation of racial identity, requesting photographs to verify racial identity, interviewing the candidate, and using the race proxy information of public elementary school attendance and family income verification.[60]

Nevertheless, critics of affirmative action challenge the efficacy of these programmatic endeavors and decry the presumed reduction in high-quality university graduates. The explicit subtext is that affirmative action is an ill-fitting U.S. imperialist import that cannot be applied effectively in a Latin American race context like Brazil's.[61] That is to say that the U.S. racial history of Jim Crow and its resulting rigid racial structure are so alien to the Latin American context that "U.S. affirmative action" has no place in Brazil or anywhere else in South America. This critique overlooks the state's historic complicity in the Latin American customary law of race regulation to such an extent that it situates Latin America as a racial innocent inappropriately burdened with the demand for racial justice.

Yet, not only have Brazilian officials developed their own mechanisms for administering race-based affirmative action programs, the studies of the student outcomes have shown the programs to be quite successful. For instance, a study of student outcomes at the State University of Campinas (Unicamp) found that students from socioeconomically and educationally disadvantaged backgrounds

---

[59] Joaze Bernardino-Costa, "Projeto Passagem do Meio: Qualificação de alunos negros de graduação para pesquisa acadêmica na UFG," *Sociedade e Cultura*, 10 (July/December 2007), 281–96, 283.
[60] Racusen, "Fictions of Identity and Brazilian Affirmative Action."
[61] Pierre Bourdieu and Loic Wacquant, "Sobre as Artimanhas de Razão Imperialista," *Estudos Afro-Asiáticos* 1 (2002), 15–33.

performed relatively better at the university than those from a higher socioeconomic and educational level.[62] The study concluded that the need for hard work when striving for greater opportunity (as in preparing for the university admission *vestibular* examination without the proper training from the public secondary schools) creates an "educational resilience" that furthers educational performance once a student is admitted to the university.[63] At Unicamp the affirmative action program allocates additional points to the entrance examination based on graduation from public secondary schools (where poor Afro-Brazilians predominate) and on the racial status of being black, brown, or indigenous. The "educational resilience" of the less privileged students was manifested directly in higher grade point averages of the affirmative action students after only one year of university study in thirty-one of the fifty-five possible undergraduate courses. Overall the relative performance of the affirmative action students was higher in forty-eight of the fifty-five courses.

Similarly, at the University of Brasilia (UnB), where 20 percent of admissions are reserved for black students, two-thirds or more of the courses of study showed no significant differences between the affirmative action students and other students.[64] In fact, in the class of 2005, the affirmative action students had higher grade point averages in 55 percent of thirty-three courses. In 2008, it was noted that black affirmative action students in twenty-seven different courses of study at UnB had higher grades than other enrolled UnB students.[65] The study of the University of Brasilia students also noted that this was a trend observed at other Brazilian universities as well. Indeed, the affirmative action students who in 2003 enrolled at the State University of North Fluminense (UENF) had grade point averages that were comparable to and in at least five courses of study exceeded the averages of

---

[62] Renato H.L. Pedrosa et al., "Academic Performance, Students' Background and Affirmative Action at a Brazilian University," *Higher Education Management and Policy* 19 (2007), 1–20.

[63] Ibid. at 13.

[64] Jacques Velloso, "Curso e Concurso: Rendimento No Universidade e Desempenho en um Vestibular Com Cotas da UnB," *Cadernos de Pesquisa* 39 (2009), 621–44.

[65] Claudete Batista Cardoso, "Efeitos da Política de Cotas na Universidade de Brasília: Uma Análise do Rendimento e da Evasão," master's dissertation, University of Brasilia (2008).

other students.[66] During the 2003 UENF admission cycle, the affirmative action program reserved slots for graduates of public secondary schools, black students, and brown students.

At the Federal University of Bahia (UFBA), the most competitive and prestigious courses of study (such as for medicine and law) yield similar average performances when comparing affirmative action students to other students.[67] The UFBA affirmative action program reserves slots for public secondary school graduates who are black, brown, and indigenous. In addition, slots are allocated to white public school secondary school graduates. When space is available, black and brown private secondary school graduates can also participate. In eleven of the eighteen most competitive courses of study at UFBA, 61 percent of the affirmative action students achieved equal or higher grade point averages than other students.

Similarly, in a study of the State University of Rio de Janeiro's (UERJ's) first class of medical students to graduate in 2010 that applied with an affirmative action program, there were no differences in the academic performance, retention, and success on the residency examinations of the program participants versus nonparticipants.[68] The UERJ affirmative action program reserves slots for low-income students, public secondary school graduates, black students, indigenous students, handicapped students, and children who have a deceased police officer parent.

Furthermore, a study of student retention rates at the Federal University of Espírito Santo found an overall lower dropout rate for affirmative action students as compared to other students.[69] Even

---

[66] André Brandão and Ludmila Gonçalves da Matta, "Avaliação da Política de Reserva de Vagas na Universidade Estadual do Norte Fluminense: Estudos dos Alunos Que Ingressarem em 2003," in André Augusto Brandão (ed.), *Cotas Raciais no Brasil: A Primeira Avaliação* (Rio de Janeiro: DP&A, 2007), pp. 46–80.

[67] Delcele Mascarenhas Queiroz and Jocelio Teles dos Santos, "Sistema de Cotas: Um Debate: Dos Dados a Manutençao de Privilegios e de Poder," *Educação e Sociedade* 27 (2006), 717–37.

[68] Márcia Vieira, "Médicos da Uerj Põem á Prova Sistema de Cotas," *O Estado de São Paulo*, May 8, 2011.

[69] Clara (Kaya) Ford, "The Impact of Socioeconomic Quotas on Student Retention: The Case of a Brazilian University," PhD dissertation, Capella University (2011), pp. 67–8.

private universities that have instituted affirmative action programs have seen very positive results. For instance, at the Pontifical Catholic University of Rio de Janeiro (PUC-Rio), the majority of the affirmative action students have been reported to be in the top 10 percent of their classes.[70] Moreover, in a study of the government's own scholarship program for private universities entitled ProUni, it was found that the retention rate for the scholarship students in the west zone of Rio de Janeiro was similar to the national average.[71]

In short, Brazil's successful use of race-based affirmative action policies can serve as an inspiration for other Latin American countries also seeking to ameliorate long-standing racial inequalities in the midst of oppositional racial democracy rhetoric. To be specific, like the rest of Latin America, Brazil has encountered resistance to affirmative action based upon the notion that the fluidity of racial identity and racial mixture will hinder an effective implementation of such policies. Here, an examination of Brazil's own racial mixture discourse and identity formation can provide additional guidance for other Latin American countries seeking to surmount the Latin American racial ideology obstacles to affirmative action. The assertion of racial identity on government census forms provides a useful analytic framework from which to discuss how Latin American presumptions about racial fluidity can coexist with a prescribed racial ordering in ways that affirmative action policies can respond to effectively.

CENSUS AND IDENTITY CHALLENGES TO ANTIDISCRIMNATION LAW IMPLEMENTATION

In view of how the state has historically shaped and deployed the census racial data to understate the presence of persons of African descent in the nation (detailed earlier in Chapters 2 and 3), racial justice organizations in Brazil have sought to address more directly the ways in

---

[70] González, "Opportunities and Challenges for the Afro-Brazilian Movement," p. 132.
[71] Daniela Patti do Amaral and Fátima Bayma de Oliveira, "O ProUni e a conclusão do ensino superior: questões introductórias sobre os egressos do programa na zona oeste do rio de janeiro," *Ensaio: Avaliação e Políticas Públicas em Educação* 19 (March 2011), 21–42.

which racial democracy rhetoric hinders accurate inquiry into racial demography. In Brazil, the last several census schedules used the color terms "white," "yellow," "brown," and "black." Although the Brazilian census schedules use the term "color" categories, the color categories utilized correspond directly with racial categories. The "yellow" color category corresponds to an Asian racial category, while "black" corresponds to African ancestry, and "brown" represents persons with mixed black and white ancestry. The only explicit "racial" category on the 1991 Brazilian census was the "indigenous" category for Brazil's native populations.

Demographers have noted that since the Brazilian census instituted self-classification for collecting racial data in 1950, a significant number of individuals have changed their color classification from one census enumeration to another. Yet the racial alterations fell into a specific pattern in which a large proportion of those who classified themselves as black (*preto*) on the 1950 census reclassified themselves as brown (*pardo*) on the 1980 census.[72] Similar reclassification patterns occurred with the census years that followed.

Sociological studies of other data collections in Brazil with racial data from both the respondent and an interviewer have more closely examined the practice of fluidity in racial classification and have noted that the "whitening effect" corresponds to a very specific pattern. In a study by Edward Telles, 79 percent of the time interviewers and respondents unambiguously chose the same color classification for the respondent.[73] While persons at the light end of the color continuum tend to be classified consistently, ambiguity is greater for those at the darker end. But even that ambiguity has limitations. Interviewers tended to whiten the classification of higher-educated self-identified brown (*pardo*) persons, particularly when they lived in nonwhite regions.

In contrast, there is much greater consistency in the classification of whites living in white-dominated regions. Furthermore, the

---

[72] José Alberto Magno de Carvalho et al., "Estimating the Stability of Census-Based Racial/Ethnic Classifications: The Case of Brazil," *Population Studies* 58 (2004), 331–43.

[73] Edward E. Telles, "Racial Ambiguity among the Brazilian Population," *Ethnic and Racial Studies* 25 (May 2002), 415–41.

whitening effect of higher educational status on racial classification is similarly constrained. In the case of the darkest males, education does not vary the color classification. It is people at the lighter end of the color spectrum living in predominantly nonwhite areas whose classification is more prone to be lightened. In short, racial democracy rhetoric theoretically enables anyone to whiten himself or herself, but in practice predetermined social norms circumscribe it. It would seem that only in regions (such as the Northeast) where few "actual whites" live are light-skinned persons of African ancestry with higher education socially permitted to whiten themselves statistically. Where "actual whites" predominate in a region (such as the South), there is little flexibility for persons of visible African ancestry to whiten themselves regardless of their skin shade or educational status. This pattern is even more stark for men of African ancestry than for the women of African ancestry, perhaps as a result of the sexualization of Afro-Brazilian women in combination with their deployment of feminine whitening grooming alterations of hair texture, face powder, and lip shape with lipstick.[74]

Similarly, the intergenerational whitening of children follows a specific racialized pattern. In a study of the 2005 Brazilian national household survey (collected by the Brazilian Institute of Geography and Statistics – the agency also responsible for the census) it was found that a nonwhite parent with secondary school or primary school education is unlikely to whiten his or her child from a marriage to a white person.[75] It is primarily among the infrequent intermarriages between those with higher education that a child is often statistically whitened. Intermarriage alone does not enable the "one drop of white blood" to whiten a mixed-race child. Rather, it is the educational status within a mixed marriage that facilitates whitening.

What all these studies of the malleability of racial/color categories in Brazil demonstrate is that while factors other than racial ancestry

[74] Kia Lilly Caldwell, *Negras in Brazil: Re-envisioning Black Women, Citizenship, and the Politics of Identity* (New Brunswick, NJ: Rutgers University Press, 2007), pp. 59–65, 90–106.

[75] Luisa Farah Schwartzman, "Does Money Whiten? Intergenerational Changes in Racial Classification in Brazil," *American Sociological Review* 72 (December 2007), 940–63.

influence the selection of census color categories, the actual practice of racial fluidity is restricted to lighter-skinned persons with higher education. For those with unambiguous white and black pigmentation and features, racial classification is more fixed and polarized. Indeed, even those studies that have examined the plethora of informal color categories that exist in Brazil have concluded that in practice the variation is all centered on denoting racial mixture, while maintaining the polarities in meaning of whiteness and blackness.[76]

For that reason, Brazilian social justice activists mounted a 1991 Brazilian census campaign for the elimination of the brown/*pardo* mixed-race color category in favor of a specific African-ancestry race question.[77] Although the request to eliminate the mixed-race category was refused, the organizers also mounted a publicity campaign to encourage respondents to move away from the mixed-race category by checking the black category instead. This campaign was entitled "Don't Let Your Color Pass into White: Respond with Good Sense." The Brazilian Institute for Social and Economic Analysis (IBASE), a nongovernmental organization that systematically compiles and distributes statistics regarding racial disparities in the labor market, helped organize the campaign. The campaign was motivated by the concern that Brazilians often lie about their color by selecting a lighter color because they are embarrassed to have African origins. The campaign for greater numbers of persons to check the black category accurately was mounted to produce more reliable socioeconomic data on blacks and thereby assist in mobilizing a racial justice movement. Although the campaign was successful in raising awareness of the political content of racial identification, persons of African descent did not overwhelmingly flock to the black category on the census. The inability to gain access to the census enumerators for a training session on politics and social etiquette of asking the race/color question may have also hindered the census campaign.

---

[76] Roger Sanjek, "Brazilian Racial Terms: Some Aspects of Meaning and Learning," *American Anthropologist* 73 (October 1971), 1126–43; Nelson do Valle Silva, "*Morenidade: Modo de Usar,*" *Estudos Afro-Asiáticos* 30 (1996), 79–95.

[77] Melissa Nobles, *Shades of Citizenship: Race and the Census in Modern Politics* (Stanford, CA: Stanford University Press, 2000), pp. 146–62.

The 1991 census results reflected a slight increase in the number of Brazilians using the brown category in comparison to the 1980 census numbers, and a slight decrease in the numbers using the white category. The black category maintained roughly the same numbers.[78] Although by quantitative measures the campaign was only negligibly successful, its proponents claimed a victory in inducing the Brazilian census officials to state publicly that they would rethink the color categories for future census years in order to reflect the number of persons of African ancestry more accurately.[79]

While the 2000 census again retained the same color categories as in previous years, for the first time in five decades the brown/*pardo* population numbers decreased while the white and black population numbers increased. In 2010, the black and brown/*pardo* population numbers continued to increase. The black population increased from 6.2 percent to 7.6 percent of the population, while the brown/*pardo* population rose from 38.4 percent to 43.1 percent. In contrast, the white population numbers decreased for the first time in Brazil census-taking history, from 53.7 percent of the population in 2000 to 47.7 percent of the population in 2010. The sociologist Edward Telles suggests that the census shifts in color category percentages indicate that the "Brazilian racial classification system is becoming increasingly bipolar" through the influence of the black movement and the globalization of black culture with the worldwide circulation of African diasporic music and films that encourage an unambiguous identification with blackness.[80] Telles's reflection is also borne out by recent ethnographic studies demonstrating the growing inclination persons of African ancestry in Brazil have for identifying as black/*negro* as a political choice that recognizes the formation of a specifically racial identity in response to the awareness of racial discrimination.[81]

[78] IBGE Informaçoes Estatísticas e Geocientíficas, Censo Demográfico de 1991, at http://www.ibge.gov.br/ibge/estatistica/populacao/censodem/default.shtm.
[79] Telephone interview with Melissa Nobles, Professor of Political Science, Massachusetts Institute of Technology (November 6, 1997).
[80] Telles, *Race in Another America*, p. 101.
[81] Caldwell, *Negras in Brazil*, pp. 107–30; Livio Sansone, *Blackness without Ethnicity: Constructing Race in Brazil* (New York: Palgrave Macmillan, 2003), p. 40; Santos Silva, "Negros Com Renda Média," 69; Ricardo Franklin Ferreira, "O Brasileiro, O Racismo Silencioso e a Emancipação do Afro-descendante," *Psicologia & Sociedade,*

Furthermore, the promotion of a political black racial identity is not solely the work of the black social justice movement. For instance, the progressive wing of the Catholic Church in Brazil identified as the Black Pastoral is involved in creating a problack, antiracist Catholic conscious-ness, via theology, liturgy, pastoral practice, training, workshops, and the media.[82] Even within Protestant communities that are commonly viewed as hostile to black pride invocations, ethnographers have found communities of poor Afro-descended Protestant devotees of the slave Anastácia, who formulate a black identity empowered by the historical figure of a saintly slave[83] and the equality discourse within the Pentecostal church.[84] Furthermore, ethnographers in the shanty towns (favelas) of Brazil have also documented not only the existence of a vibrant black racial consciousness among the residents, but also a binary rather than fluid approach to racial classification as epitomized by the statement "If you don't pass for white, you are black." In fact, the use of variable color categories was explained by the favela residents as simply a universally understood etiquette for maintaining racial harmony even in the midst of the implicit understanding that "there are only two races."[85]

As one Brazilian scholar has so frankly stated:

> There is no insurmountable difficulty in establishing a functional and standard system of racial classification in Brazil because we voluntarily classify ourselves as black, white, pardo, yellow and indigenous when interviewed by census officials and are also eas-ily identified as such by fellow citizens, the police, and the justice system. We have no problem knowing who is black, pardo, white, yellow, or indigenous.[86]

---

14 (January/June 2002), 69–86; Ayana Hosten, "Tornar-Se Negro and Thinking Beautiful," Study Abroad Program thesis, Claremont McKenna College (2007), pp. 21–9, http://digitalcollections.sit.edu/isp_collections/244/.

[82] John Burdick, *Legacies of Liberation: The Progressive Catholic Church in Brazil at the Start of a New Millennium* (Hampshire: Ashgate, 2004), pp. 19, 48–53.

[83] Robin E. Sheriff, *Dreaming Equality: Color, Race and Racism in Urban Brazil* (New Brunswick, NJ: Rutgers University Press, 2001), p. 10.

[84] John Burdick, *Blessed Anastácia: Women, Race, and Popular Christianity in Brazil* (New York: Routledge, 1998), pp. 127–47, 161–80.

[85] Sheriff, *Dreaming Equality*, p. 58.

[86] Sales Augusto dos Santos, "Who Is Black in Brazil? a Timely or a False Question in Brazilian Race Relations in the Era of Affirmative Action?" *Latin American Perspectives* 33 (July 2006), 30–48, 43.

It would thus appear that claims regarding the contemporary Brazilian resistance to racial identity have been overstated.

While it is certainly true that Brazil's Latin American racial ideology extols the virtues of the presumed ability to have flexibility about claiming a color and racial identity, it coexists with the ability to impose social consequences on those identified as nonwhite. Seth Racusen has aptly stated that "if numerous public and private actors can routinely make discretionary determinations for discriminatory purposes, how could it be impossible to make determinations for the purpose of anti-discrimination policies?"[87] Racusen's point is that while there can be variation as to how nonwhites who look the same might racially identify (black versus brown), what is most salient for the administration of an affirmative action policy is a social structure that differentiates between whiteness and nonwhiteness in ways that influence social status and opportunity. This is because what an affirmative action policy centrally seeks to do is to intervene in the status quo exclusions of the racial ordering. The fluidity of the categories is immaterial as compared to the significance of the particular racial hierarchy in which the categories align themselves. Indeed, Brazilian officials have managed to administer affirmative action programs that creatively operate in the midst of racial fluidity by using various combinations of nonwhite race proxies such as public secondary school attendance and low-income status, along with racial self-declarations of being black or brown, photographs, and interviews for determining program participation. Hence the claim that affirmative action is a U.S. imperialist import that cannot effectively be applied in a Latin American race context like Brazil has not been borne out. As such, the Brazilian experience thus far should serve as an important guidepost for the rest of Latin America.

---

[87] Seth Racusen, "Fictions of Identity and Brazilian Affirmative Action," pp. 89, 92.

7 CONCLUSION: THE UNITED STATES–LATIN AMERICA CONNECTIONS

> Just as racism has become an international thing, the fight against it is also becoming international. We believe that it is one struggle.
>
> Malcolm X[1]

As in Latin America, the racial justice movement in the United States today has reached an important turning point. While the formal mechanisms for addressing racial inequality have long been in place, there is a growing societal belief that it is no longer necessary for the government to be proactively engaged in ensuring racial equality. A racial hierarchy continues to exist alongside a deteriorated social commitment to race-based programs. The early U.S. civil rights movement was astonishingly successful at making the goal of racial equality a stated national norm and catalyzing government programs designed to provide concrete access to jobs and education. However, the movement's very success contributes to the notion that blacks and other persons of color no longer require legal assistance in accessing equal opportunity. Indeed, President Obama's election in 2008 is viewed as the culmination of U.S. racial transcendence, so that now the United States presents itself as "racially innocent" in much the same way Latin America has long claimed to be. At the same time, systemic racism has not been eradicated, as evidenced by the long-standing institutional racial disparities in employment, educational attainment, access to health care and capital, residential segregation, and disparate incarceration and execution rates.

---

[1] Manning Marable, *Malcolm X: A Life of Reinvention* (New York: Viking, 2011), p. 415.

Thus, despite the differences in historical particularities, demo-graphic variations, legal structures, and mode of governance, the Americas share the commonality of struggling with the enduring leg-acy of slavery and postabolition regimes of discrimination. Moreover, the Americas now centrally share a rhetoric of racial progress uttered in the midst of systemic racial hierarchy. In other words, the success-ful civil rights movement struggle against Jim Crow segregation now places racial minorities in the United States in a situation comparable to that of Afro-descendants in Latin America – struggling against racial hierarchy without formal legal discrimination as a target. Furthermore, U.S. postracialism undermines the commitment to racial equality laws and policies because it disregards manifestations of racial inequality in its celebration of formal equality and pursues a color blindness that equates the articulation of racial concerns with an act of racism.[2] This most certainly resonates with what has long been the Latin American approach to matters of race. Because Latin America is a region that has long claimed that all racial distinctions were abandoned with the abolition of slavery, a comparison to the Latin American racial democ-racy version of "postracialism" is an instructive platform from which to assess the viability of contemporary assertions of postracialism in the United States – a rhetoric that contends that racism has already been largely transcended.[3] As the longtime scholar of comparative race relations Anani Dzidzienyo notes, examining the Latin American racial context "can provide insights for Afro-Americans who are today having to confront the mainstream's assumptions concerning 'the end of racism' in a post–Civil Rights U.S. society."[4]

The examination of the Latin American context may also be help-ful to the U.S. racial justice movement today given what the sociologist Eduardo Bonilla-Silva terms the growing "Latin Americanization" of race in the United States.[5] By "Latin Americanization," Bonilla-Silva

[2] Kimberlé Williams Crenshaw, "Twenty Years of Critical Race Theory: Looking Backward to Move Forward," *Connecticut Law Review* 43 (2011), 1253, 1256.
[3] Sumi Cho, "Post-Racialism," *Iowa Law Review*, 94 (2009), 1589–1649.
[4] Anani Dzidzienyo, "The Changing World of Brazilian Race Relations?" in Dzidzienyo and Oboler (eds.), *Neither Enemies nor Friends: Latinos, Blacks, Afro-Latinos* (Houndmills: Palgrave Macmillian, 2005), pp. 137–55, 144.
[5] Eduardo Bonilla-Silva, "We Are All Americans! The Latin Americanization of Racial Stratification in the USA," *Race & Society* 5 (2002), 3–16.

refers to what he perceives as the growing U.S. use of a "pigmentocratic logic" color-based method for reorganizing the U.S. racial stratification scheme that is slowly shifting from a biracial black/white structure to a triracial structure loosely organized into the general categories of white, honorary white, and collective black. The honorary white category is envisioned as an intermediary category like coloreds in apartheid South Africa, or mulattoes in Latin America for nonwhites able to distinguish themselves from African Americans but excluded from the category of whiteness. Honorary whites would be accorded an elevated status above the most socially derided category of collective blacks. Bonilla-Silva predicts that as in Latin America, U.S. residents will grow to embrace racial identities based on a Eurocentric preference for lightness, while proclaiming that race does not matter. While a number of scholars have challenged the details of Bonilla-Silva's predictions, the value of his analysis lies in his call to examine what in the changing U.S. attitudes toward race and racism resonates with preexisting Latin American constructs.[6]

The Latin American notion that racial mixture transcends race and that racial fluidity breaks down racial barriers has been noted in the contemporary U.S. "postracial" racial discourse particularly with regard to census taking and the identity movements of multiracial persons. To be specific, growing rates of immigration, intermarriage, and mixed race children are now routinely touted as both the proof and the reason why race-conscious remedial programs are no longer needed. Indeed, the growing acceptance of race mixture and, more particularly, multiracial racial identities is viewed as completely challenging the U.S. notion of race that was so implicitly central to the early civil rights movement. Today, there is a growing scholarly acknowledgment that race is a socially constructed concept and that African ancestry may not necessarily lead an individual either to embrace a black racial identity or to view race as socially salient.

---

[6] Christina Sue, "An Assessment of the Latin Americanization Thesis," *Ethnic & Racial Studies* 6 (2009), 1058–70; "Symposium on Bonilla-Silva's Latin Americanization of Race Relations Thesis," *Race & Society* 5 (2002), 17–102; Eduardo Bonilla-Silva, "Are the Americas 'Sick with Racism' or Is It a Problem at the Poles? a Reply to Christina A. Sue," *Ethnic and Racial Studies* 32 (July 2009), 1071–82.

The U.S. reconsideration of race is reflected in a growing transformation from the belief that racial categories are static and hence that racial identification is self-evident and straightforward, to a belief that race mixture will dissolve the rigidity of those categories and, in and of itself, instill societal racial harmony and even eradicate the need to refer to one another by race.[7] The U.S. Census Bureau's decision to permit people to claim multiple racial designations on the 2000 and 2010 census forms rather than its traditional insistence on single-box checking, is a striking example of the evolving changes in U.S. race ideology. Some demographers and sociologists have concluded that the more nuanced racial identification permitted by checking multiple racial designations may help break down racial barriers. The notion is that recognition of a multiracial identity has the presumed benefit of blurring color lines and thus reducing racial animus.[8] Long-disputed Latin American attitudes toward race are disconcertingly echoed in U.S. multiracial discourse. For instance, the belief that racial mixture will destroy racism has been featured prominently in the promotion of a mixed-race census count. Leaders for the recognition of a "multiracial" census category frequently posit that multiracial persons are a "unifying force"[9] on the theory that multiracial persons "as a group may be the embodiment of America's best chance to clean up race relations."[10] Indeed, the equating of racial mixture with racial harmony is often quite explicit.

> I contend that society should embrace, as a transitory vehicle, multiple racial categories that expressly recognize and acknowledge products of mixed-race unions as distinct from both blacks and whites. I assert that this will have the effect of creating a type of

---

[7] Ronald Fernández, *America beyond Black and White: How Immigrants and Fusions Are Helping to Overcome the Racial Divide* (Ann Arbor: University of Michigan Press, 2007).

[8] Bijan Gilanshah, "Multiracial Minorities: Erasing the Color Line," *Law & Inequality Journal* 12 (1993), 183, 199.

[9] *Review of Federal Measurements of Race and Ethnicity: Hearings before the Subcomm. on Census, Statistics and Postal Personnel of the House Comm. on Post Office and Civil Service*, 103d Cong. 171 (1993) (testimony of Carlos Fernández, president, Association of MultiEthnic Americans).

[10] Ramona E. Douglass, "Multiracial People Must No Longer Be Invisible," *New York Times*, July 12, 1996, p. A26.

"shade confusion" which will eventually destroy the black/white dichotomy that currently exists, ultimately reducing race to a meaningless category, as it should be.[11]

Even the Harvard sociologist Orlando Patterson has agreed that "if your object is the eventual integration of the races, a mixed-race or middle group is something you'd want to see developing. ... The middle group grows larger and larger, and the races eventually blend."[12] The multiracial discourse narrative is thus that "mixing away" racism will absolve the nation from having to address entrenched racial disparities in socioeconomic opportunity.[13]

Yet, an even greater demonstration of the U.S. reconsideration of race is the manner in which the public has received and fixated on the Census 2000 population results. Although only 2.4 percent of the population actually chose to select more than one racial category,[14] the public clamor regarding the potential to do so is a striking indicator of how the Census Bureau and the rhetoric about the census had an influence on public perception. For instance, in observing the increasing racial diversity of many cities that was reported by the Census Bureau, news entities typically noted that the demographic shift "will not only transform the city but will also alter how Americans think about race, helping them move beyond simple concepts of whiteness and blackness."[15] Kenneth Prewitt, the former director of the Census Bureau, concluded that the availability of multiple racial categories to an increasingly mixed-race demographic is "a very healthy sign that barriers are breaking down. ... It's an indication of not only the complexity but the fluidness of our population makeup."[16] In addition,

---

[11] Alex M. Johnson Jr., "Destabilizing Racial Classifications Based on Insights Gleaned from Trademark Law," *California Law Review* 84 (1996), 887–952, 891.

[12] Tom Morganthau, "What Color Is Black?" *Newsweek*, February 13, 1995, pp. 63, 65.

[13] Jim Chen, "Unloving," *Iowa Law Review* 80 (1994), 145.

[14] Nicholas A. Jones and Amy Symens Smith, "The Two or More Races Population: 2000, Census 2000 Brief," (Washington, DC: U.S. Dept. of Commerce, Economics and Statistics Admin., U.S. Census Bureau, Nov. 2001), p. 1, http://www.census.gov/prod/2001pubs/c2kbr01–6.pdf.

[15] Andrew Friedman, "Behind the Big Numbers, a Million Little Stories," *New York Times*, March 18, 2001, sec. 14, p. 6.

[16] Mae M. Cheng, "'The Face of America': New Census Acknowledges City's Multiracial Residents," *Newsday*, March 16, 2001, p. E6 (quoting Prewitt).

Prewitt's predecessor, Martha Farnsworth Riche, commented that the Census 2000 results mark "the beginning of the end of the overwhelming role of race in our public life."[17]

Nor have some civil rights activists been immune to jumping to the conclusion that the demographic changes immediately mean "we're moving beyond a black-white paradigm of race,"[18] and that "the more mixed we are, the more likely it is that we will be sensitive to each other."[19] Similarly, some demographers and sociologists have concluded that "the more nuanced" racial identification permitted by checking multiple racial designations "may help break down racial barriers."[20] Furthermore, in a national poll conducted after the public release of the Census 2000 data, 64 percent of respondents stated that it "would be 'good for the country' to have more Americans 'think of themselves as multiracial rather than as belonging to a single race.'"[21] Reporting on the poll, *USA Today* observed: "Racial lines may blur until the 'melting pot' idealized by playwright Israel Zangwill in 1908 becomes a harmonious, 'we-are-the-world' reality."[22] That observation was then followed by a police officer's reaction: "Who'll be left to hate?" Thus, the U.S. reconsideration of race is reflected in a growing transformation from the belief that racial categories are static and hence that racial identification is self-evident and straightforward, to a belief that race mixture will dissolve the rigidity of those categories and, in and of itself, instill societal racial harmony and even eradicate the need to refer to one another by race.

The emergence of a Latin American–style postracial discourse in the United States is also suggested both by the growing numbers of

[17] Martin Kasindorf and Haya El Nasser, "Impact of Census' Race Data Debated," *USA Today*, March 13, 2001, p. 1A (quoting Riche).

[18] Eric Schmitt, "For 7 Million People in Census, One Race Category Isn't Enough," *New York Times*, March 13, 2001, p. A1 (quoting Sonia M. Pérez, a deputy vice president at the National Council of La Raza, a Hispanic advocacy organization).

[19] Kasindorf and El Nasser, "Impact of Census' Race Data Debated," p. 1A (quoting Beatriz López-Flores, vice president of the Mexican-American Legal Defense and Educational Fund).

[20] Schmitt, "For 7 Million People in Census," p. A1.

[21] Kasindorf and El Nasser, "Impact of Census' Race Data Debated," p. 1A. *USA Today*/CNN/Gallup Poll surveyed 1,015 adults on March 9–10, 2001.

[22] Ibid.

individuals who no longer think that racism is a problem[23] and by the judiciary's own deflection from race in the pursuit of "color blindness" because race is a taboo subject whose mere referencing is an act of racism. Such views are embodied in the Supreme Court justice Scalia's statement "In the eyes of government, we are just one race here. It is American."[24] Furthermore, as with Latin America's various nation-building campaigns, U.S. citizens are being encouraged to view themselves as "simply American" rather than identifying along racial or ethnic lines, which practice is considered inherently divisive. Indeed, even attacks on race-conscious attempts to facilitate electoral political participation in redistricting have been articulated as being concerned with how they "stimulate[ ] public awareness of race" and thus "fan[ ] the flames of racial division."[25]

Yet thus far, the U.S. blurring of races is retaining a decidedly pejorative view of blackness that resonates with the Latin American derision of blackness in the midst of racial mixture celebrations. It is true that intermarriage rates in the United States have increased tremendously over the years with nearly one in seven marriages in 2008 interracial or interethnic, thereby representing double the intermarriage rate of the 1980s and six times the intermarriage rate of the 1960s.[26] Yet, white-black couples represented the fewest number of such marriages, and black females had the lowest intermarriage rate of all. While much has been made of the fact that the high incarceration rate of black males provides black females with fewer black male partners, it is also true that black females, followed by black men, are viewed as the least desirable marriage partners for other races

---

[23] Joe R. Feagin, *Racist America: Roots, Current Realities and Future Reparations* (New York: Routledge, 2000), p. 96.

[24] *Adarand Constructors, Inc. v. Pena*, 515 U.S. 200, 239 (1995) (Scalia, J., concurring in part and concurring in the judgment). Adarand held that federal affirmative action programs instituted to assist subordinated groups are subject to the same strict scrutiny standard as acts of discrimination against subordinated group members.

[25] Melissa L. Saunders, "Of Minority Representation, Multiple-Race Responses, and Melting Pots: Redistricting in the New America," *North Carolina Law Review* 79 (2001), 1367–82.

[26] Jeffrey Passel, Wendy Wang, and Paul Taylor, "Marrying Out: One-in-Seven New U.S. Marriages Is Interracial or Interethnic," *Pew Research Center Report*, June 4, 2010, http://pewresearch.org/pubs/1616/american-marriage-interracial-interethnic.

and ethnic groups.[27] Thus, even though a recent study indicates that Asian men are the least preferred Internet dating options of white women, the disproportionate disinclination for marriage with black men remains.[28] Furthermore, the disregard for black women also extends to Internet dating, where they are viewed as the least desirable option for white men.

Even when blacks partner in interracial relationships, their offspring meet with greater social resistance when asserting a multiracial identity than other racially mixed individuals identifying as multiracial. Specifically, in Lee and Bean's study of multiracial identity among mixed-race persons, it was found that multiracial identities are more readily accepted when expressed by Asian-white and Latino-white mixed-race persons than by black-white mixed-race persons.[29] In addition, they also received greater social acceptance to assert a white racial identity with or without a cultural ethnic identity. The study observed that Asian and Latino experiences with multiraciality are closer to those of European immigrants who were first racialized and then over time permitted to treat their affiliations as volitional ethnic choices. The context of Asian and Latino multiracials suggests an easing of racial boundaries for deciding if, when and how they will choose to racially identify, that is not available to black multiracials.

Furthermore, for many Latinos in the United States, who are often described as an inherently multiracial people, whiteness continues to be the racial category of choice.[30] For instance, when provided the ability to check as many census racial categories as apply on the 2010 census, 94 percent of Latinos still elected to choose a single racial category, and the single race chosen 53 percent of the time was white.[31]

---

[27] Ralph Richard Banks, *Is Marriage for White People? How the African American Marriage Decline Affects Everyone* (New York: Dutton, 2011).

[28] Cynthia Feliciano, Belinda Robnett, and Golnaz Komaie, "Gendered Racial Exclusion among White Internet Daters," *Social Science Research* 38 (March 2009), 39–54.

[29] Jennifer Lee and Frank D. Bean, "Reinventing the Color Line: Immigration and America's New Racial/Ethnic Divide," *Social Forces* 86 (December 2007), 561–86.

[30] William Darity Jr. et al., "Bleach in the Rainbow: Latin Ethnicity and Preference for Whiteness," *Transforming Anthropology* 13 (October 2005), 103–9; Haya El Nasser, "Hispanic Responses on Race Give More Exact Breakdown," *USA Today*, March 9, 2011.

[31] U.S. Census Bureau, Hispanic or Latino Population by Type of Origin and Race: 2010.

Those Latinos who selected the "Some Other Race" category 36.7 percent of the time appeared to do so as a mechanism for denoting their indigenous ancestry since the large majority of Latino "Some Other Race" category respondents were from Central America but may have felt excluded by the census racial category "American Indian" with its inquiry into registered tribal affiliations. Only 2.5 percent of Latinos selected the black racial category. When recent Latino immigrants are surveyed separately, 79 percent choose the single white category regardless of skin color.[32]

In contrast, the construct of race continues to be imposed upon black mixed-race persons such that Lee and Bean conclude that "it is not simply that race matters, but more specifically, that black race matters, consistent with the African-American exceptionalism thesis." This suggests that as in Latin America, the all-embracing rhetoric of multiracial postracialism continues to support racial hierarchy and antiblack bias. As discussed in Chapters 2 and 6, the presumed fluidity of Latin American racial identity is contradicted by its restriction to lighter-skinned persons with higher education. For those with unambiguous black pigmentation and African features, racial classification is more fixed and polarized.

Disturbingly, when racial mixture as a solution to racial conflict has been promoted in Latin America, the burden has been consistently placed on Afro-descendants to mix. In effect, assimilation of blacks into whiteness, not the mixture itself, has been an underlying goal of miscegenation racial democracy campaigns in Latin America. And the result has always been the maintenance of white supremacy. Indeed, as Chapter 2 illustrates, the Latin American promotion of a mixed-race class was motivated by the desire to "whiten" each country by having blacks disappear through a mixing of the races, with the census colors ranked hierarchically from the most positively valued color of white to the pejoratively viewed color of black. The whitening ideal "remains encoded and enmeshed in the language of 'a mixed people'

---

[32] Elizabeth M. Grieco, "Race and Hispanic Origin of the Foreign-Born Population in the United States: 2007," *American Community Survey Reports*, January 2010, http://www.census.gov/prod/2010pubs/acs-11.pdf; Reanne Frank, Ilana Redstone Akresh, and Bo Lu, "Latino Immigrants and the U.S. Racial Order: How and Where Do They Fit In?" *American Sociological Review* 75 (June 2010), 378–401.

which is generally taken to mean, a 'lighter' if not 'whiter' people."[33] Thus, Latin American postracialism has not led to a transcendence of race but instead to a reinforcement of a racial caste system in a region long touted as a racial democracy.

The legacy and continued support for the myth of racial democracy in Latin America have interfered with the government acknowledgment that collecting data by race can be a useful aid to pursuing racial equality. But growing pressure by Afro-descendant activists is beginning to make Latin American governments more receptive to race-conscious public policies. Indeed, the Latin American context also illustrates how resistance to postracialism can be possible even after decades of postracial rhetoric. Latin American states have shifted from defending the myth of racial democracy in nations with large populations of indigent Afro-descendants, or from marginalizing an invisible minority of Afro-descendants in largely indigenous "mestizo" nations, to slowly acknowledging the salience of race and racism.[34] In February 2008, Belize elected Dean Barrow, its first black prime minister. In 2007, Paola Moreno became the first Afro-Colombian cabinet member in five decades. In 2003, Brazil named its first black Supreme Court justice. In 1999, Venezuela elected the Afro-descendant Hugo Chávez president of the country. These Afro-descended positions of leadership are particularly noteworthy because the officials openly identify themselves as Afro-descendants. This is in great contrast to the Latin American history of having leaders of color who others suspected of having African ancestry but who never explicitly racially identified themselves as such (like the Colombian president Juan José Gil, January–July 1861; the Cuban president Fulgencio Batista, 1952–9; the Dominican president Rafael Trujillo, 1942–52; the Dominican president Leonel Fernández Reyna, 1996–2000 and 2004–present; the Honduran president Manuel Bonilla Chirinos, 1903–7 and 1912–13; the Mexican president Vicente Guerrero, April–December 1829; and the Peruvian president Luis Miguel Sánchez Cerro, 1930–1). The prominence of individuals who are now able to assert African ancestry

---

[33] Melissa Nobles, "'Responding with Good Sense': The Politics of Race and Censuses in Contemporary Brazil," Ph.D. dissertation, Yale University (1995), p. 112.

[34] Mala Htun, "From 'Racial Democracy' to Affirmative Action: Changing State Policy on Race in Brazil," Latin American Research Review 39 (2004), 60–89.

affirmatively and counter long-standing derogatory racial stereotypes by occupying positions of leadership is a significant milestone of racial progress in Latin America. Yet the racialized discourse that continues to be embedded in the articulation of opposition to leaders such as Hugo Chavez suggests that much more work needs to be done before true racial equality is broadly achieved.

Because North and South America share the same battle against insidious systems of racial hierarchy, it is sensible for both Americas to look beyond the facial differences of their legal histories and instead focus upon the commonality of the historical legacy of slavery and its outgrowth in the continuing societal efforts to maintain privilege as veiled by the discourse of merit, self-reliance, and culture. It is perhaps by the strategically combined efforts of peoples of African descent in the Americas that racial justice can be effectuated in the contemporary landscape of presumably color-blind lawmaking within the complex reality of racial disparity. This book can provide clarity about the ways in which racial hierarchy can be maintained even with seemingly different racial ideologies and approaches. Moreover, the comparative examination of the Afro-descendant struggle against racism may be helpful to U.S. racial justice advocates in confronting their own "postracial" contemporary version of Latin American–like racial democracy ideology. Specifically, U.S. activists may be better able to pierce the veil of postracialism with the knowledge of how similar rhetoric in the rest of the Americas facilitated racial inequality. This reflects the current governmental interests in transnational cooperative efforts to pursue racial justice as memorialized in the U.S. State Department's 2010 U.S.-Colombia Action Plan on Racial and Ethnic Equality and its 2008 U.S.-Brazil Joint Action Plan to Eliminate Racial Discrimination. Because as the Brazilian social justice activist and educator Paulo Freire once stated, "Ninguém liberta ninguém, ninguém se liberta sozinho. Os homens se libertam en comunhão."[35] [No one liberates anyone else, no one can liberate themselves alone. People liberate themselves in community with others.]

---

[35] Paulo Freire, *Pedagogia do Oprimido* (Rio de Janeiro: Paz e Terra, 1987).

APPENDIX A. AFRO-DESCENDANT ORGANIZATIONS IN LATIN AMERICA

ARGENTINA

Asociación Civil "África y su Diáspora para la Defensa de los Derechos Humanos"
asociacionafricaysudiaspora@yahoo.com.ar
www.africaysudiaspora.com.ar

Asociación Civil África Vive
pochalamadrid@yahoo.com.ar

Asociación Civil y Religiosa Ile Ase Osun Dayo
info@doyo.com.ar
www.doyo.com.ar

Asociación Misibamba. Comunidad Afro Argentina de Buenos Aires
jsuaque@yahoo.com.ar
bakongocandombe@gmail.com

Casa de la cultura Indo-afroamericana
indoafro@hotmail.com
indoafroamericana@yahoo.com.ar

Sociedad de Socorros Mutuos Unión Caboverdeana
sociedadcaboverdeana@yahoo.com.ar

BOLIVIA

Centro Afro boliviano para el Desarrollo Integral y Comunitario – CADIC

jorgemedina_bol@yahoo.com
contactos@cadic.org.bo
www.cadic.org.bo

Fundación de Afrodescendientes Pedro Andaverez Peralta FUNDAFRO
P.A.P.
fundafro@hotmail.com

Movimiento Cultural Saya Afro boliviano – MOCUSABOL
afrobolivia88@yahoo.es
www.afrobolivia.org.bo

BRAZIL

Agentes de Pastoral Negros do Brasil
apnsbrasil@yahoo.com.br
www.apnsbrasil.com.br

AQUILOAFROS – Irmandade dos Quilombolas Afrodescendentes do Quilombo Santacruz
aquiloafros@hotmail.com
vandelip@hotmail.com

Articulação de Mulheres Negras
amnb@uol.com.br
http://www.amnb.org.br/site/

Articulação Política de Juventudes Negras
apjnbrasil@yahoo.com.br
www.apjnbrasil.blogspot.com

Associação Brasileira de Pesquisadores(as) Negros(as)
adpn@adpn.org.br
www.adpn.org.br

Associação Vida Inteira
francgunzo@gmail.com
http://associacaovidainteira.wordpress.com/

Casa da Cultura da Mulher Negra
ccmnegra@uol.com.br
www.casadeculturadamulhernegra.org.br

Centro de Estudos e Pesquisa de Intercambio da Cultura Africana – Centro
Cultural Africano
cca@centroculturalafricano.org
www.centroculturalafricano.org.br

CONNEB – Congresso Nacional de Negras e Negros do Brasil
conneb.org.br

Coordenação das Associações das Comunidades Remanescentes de
Quilombos do Pará
malungupara.org.br
malungu.pa@hotmail.com

CRIOLA
criola@criola.org.br
www.criola.org.br

Educafro
freidavid@gmail.com
www.educafro.org.br

Escola de Educação Percussiva Integral – EEPI
eepipercussiva@gmail.com
http://www.myspace.com/escolapercussiva

Fala Preta Organização de Mulheres Negras
deisebenedicto45@yahoo.com.br
falapret@uol.com.br

Forum Estadual de Juventude Negra do Espírito Santo – FEJUNES
Fejunes_es@yahoo.com.br
www.fejunes.blogspot.com

Fundação Baobá – Fund for Racial Equity
baoba@baoba.org.br
www.baoba.org.br

Geledes Instituto da Mulher Negra
geledes@geledes.org.br
www.geledes.org.br

Ilú Oba De Min – Educação, Cultura e Arte Negra
iluobademin@yahoo.com.br
www.iluobademin.com.br

www.myspace.com/bandafemininadepercussoliobdemin

Instituto AMMA Psique e Negritude

ammapsi@uol.com.br

Instituto de Assessoria a Projetos e Pesquisas em Educação e Etnia Odoya

edevaldoed@gmail.com

edevaldoj@vivax.com.br

Instituto de Mulheres Negras do Amapá

imenamacapa@yahoo.com.br

Instituto Negra do Ceará – INEGRA

inegra.ce@gmail.com

inegrace.wordpress.com

KOINONIA Presença Ecumênica e Serviços

koinonia@koinonia.org.br

www.koinonia.org.br

Maria Mulher – Organização de Mulheres Negras

mariamulher@mariamulher.org.br

www.mariamulher.org.br

Mundo Negro

www.mundonegro.com.br

Núcleo de Resgate e Preservação da Cultura Afro-Brasileira – Omi-dudu

Artes

bartolomeudc@yahoo.com.br;

joseliaomidudu@yahoo.com.br

www.nucleoomidudu.org.br

Povo Kalunga

coordenacao@povokalunga.org.br

Rede Afro Brasileira Sócio-Cultural

redeafro@hotmail.com

http://redeafro.ning.com

Rede Mulheres Negras do Paraná

redemulheresnegras@yahoo.com.br

www.redemulheresnegraspr.org.br

UNEGRO

http://www.unegro.org.br/site/

YLË AXÉ OPÔ OMIM I – Associação Casa Caminho da Alegria
yleaxeopoomin@hotmail.com
casacaminhoalegria@yahoo.com.br
casacaminhoalegria.blogspot.com

CHILE

Organización Cultural y Social de Afrodescendientes Chilenos Lumbanga
organizacionlumbanga@yahoo.es
afrochileno@yahoo.es
www.afrochileno.blogspot.com

Organización No Gubernamental Oro Negro de Afrodescendientes Chilenos
martavictoriasalgado619@hotmail.com
afrochile@gmail.com
www.ong-oronegro.blogspot.com

COLOMBIA

AFROLIDER – Fundación para la Formación de Líderes Afrocolombianos
fundafrolider@etb.net.com

Asociación de Afrocolombian@s en Itagui
Socorro3384@hotmail.com

Asociación de Alcaldes de Municipios con Población Afrodescendiente – AMUNAFRO
contacto@amunafro.com
www.amunafro.com

Asociación Colombiana de Peluqueros y Peinadores Afrodescendientes
asocolppa@gmail.com
www.asocolppa.blogspot.com

Asociación para el desarrollo integral de las comunidades afrocolombianas
KUMANANÁ

kumana.pcn@renacientes.net

www.renacientes.org

Asociación de ecoturismo del Bajo Anchicaya Los Tucán

hvallecillac@gmail.com

herlmer1972@hotmail.es

Asociación para el Fomento de la integración de las negritudes – AFIN

afin85@hotmail.com

Asociación para las investigaciones culturales del Choco – ASINCH

asinch.choco@gmail.com

www.asinch.blogspot.com

Asociación Mutual para el desarrollo de la Afrocolombianidad y el Cooperativismo

afromutual@gmail.com

www.fundartecp.com

Asociación Nacional de Afrocolombianos Desplazados – AFRODES

afrodescolombia@gmail.com

www.afrodes.org

Centro de documentación cultural afrocolombianas

bikookib@hotmail.com

CIMARRON

cimarronnacional@movimientocimarron.org

http://www.movimientocimarron.org/

Consejo Comunitario de la Comunidad Negra del Río Cajambre

cccajambre@yahoo.com

Consejo Comunitario de la comunidad negra del río Naya

consejocomunitariorionaya@yahoo.es

Consejo Comunitario Cuenca del Río

luzdalmi@yahoo.com.ar

Consejo Comunitario de la Cuenca del rió Mayorquin

Mayorevan@hotmail.com

Corporación Cultural Afro Colombiana Sankofa

www.sankofadanzaafro.wordpress.com

sankofadanzafro@hotmail.com

Corporación para el Desarrollo Social y Empresarial de los Pueblos
Afrocolombianos – ECODESARROLLO
info@ecodesarrollo.org.co
www.ecodesarrollo.org.co

Corporación para el Fomento de la Investigación Etnoeducativa,
Sociocultural, Económica y Ambiental Afrocolombiana Ancestros-
Corporación Ancestros
corpoancestro@yahoo.com
www.renacientes.org

Corporación Identidad Cultural – CORPIDENCU
corpidencu@gmail.com
www.corpidencu.net

ECOTAMBOR
ecotambor@yahoo.com

Federación Afroamérica XXI
rosacv2003@yahoo.com
www.afroamerica21.org

Fundación Afroamericana para la educación cultura y desarrollo – FUNDAFRO
Fundafro001@yahoo.com

Fundación Afroguajira – FUNAGUA
yohanis_mejia@hotmail.com
fundación-afroguajira@hotmail.com

Fundación Arte y Cultura del Pacífico – FUNDARTECP
fundartecp@yahoo.es
www.fundartecp.com

Fundación Assim Bonanga
gmakanaky@hotmail.com

Fundación Instituto para el Desarrollo Cultural y Educativo de las Etnias – FUNIDESCUDET
funidescudet@hotmail.com
funidescudet.jimdo.com

Fundación valores de nuestra etnia
cambindo75@hotmail.com

Kilombo Organizativo para la Reivindicación Afrodescendiente – KORA
griots_0000000001@hotmail.com

Organización Social de Comunidades Negras Ángela Davis
organizacionangeladavis@gmail.com
Malawi@yahoo.com
www.organizacionsocialangeladavis.com

PCN – Processo de Comunidades Negras
http://www.renacientes.org/

Red Nacional de Mujeres Afrocolombianas Kambirí
auradalia@yahoo.com
redmujerafro@hotmail.com
redmujerafro.tripod.com

Unidad Fraternal Palenque – UFP
ufplibre@hotmail.com

COSTA RICA

Asociación para el Desarrollo de la Mujer Negra Costarricense
mujerdp@ice.co.cr
http://mujeresafrocostarricenses.blogspot.com

Asociación Proyecto Caribe
asociación.proyectocaribe@hotmail.com
procarib@ice.co.cr
www.proyectocaribe.org

Red de Mujeres Afro Latinoamericanas y Afro Caribeñas
www.movemientos.org/mujerafro

CUBA

AfroCuba
director@afrocuba.org
www.afrocuba.org

Cofradía de la Negritud – CONEG
afrocubaweb.com/coneg/coneg.htm

Comisión de Lucha Contra el Racismo y la Discriminación, de la UNEAC (Union of Artists & Writers)
www.afrocubaweb.com/uneaccommissionracism.htm

DOMINICAN REPUBLIC

Centro Cultural Dominico-Haitiano – CCDH
Ccdhjulio1982@gmail.com
http://www.ccdh.org.do

Fundación Étnica Integral – LA FEI
Ong.fei@gmail.com

Movimiento de Mujeres Dominico Haitiana – MUDHA
mudhaong@hotmail.com

ECUADOR

Acción y Desarrollo Comunitario – ACDECOM
Adecom.ecuador@yahoo.es
adecom@uio.satnet.net
acdecom.wordpress.com/contactos

Asociación Presencia Negra Ecuatoriana – ANPNE
afroec98anpne@hotmail.com

Asociación social y cultural para la Integración de la Raza Negra del Ecuador – ASCRINE
ascirne@hotmail.com
www.ascirneafroecuatoriana.org

Centro Internacional de Esmeraldas para la Diversidad Cultural Afroindoamericana y el Desarrollo Humano.
mindapanibal@yahoo.es

Centro Cultural Afroecuatoriano
cca@centroafroecuatoriano.com
www.centroafroecuatoriano.com

Confederación Nacional Cultural Africanos en la Diáspora para la Defensa y Desarrollo Integral del Ser Humano y su Entorno – CONCADISHE
concadishe@yahoo.com
www.concadishe.org

Coordinadora Nacional de Mujeres Negras. CONAMUNE
mujeresnegras@coopi.org
conamune.org

Federación de Comunidades e Organizaciones Negras de Imbabura y Carchi – FECONIC
info@feconic.org
http://www.feconic.org/

Federación de Organizaciones y Grupos Negros del Guayas
vidal38leones@hotmail.com

Fundación Cimarrón Siglo XXI Ecuador
cimarronxxi@gmail.com
ibsen8@gmail.com

Fundación Cultural y Artesanal Afroecuatoriana Ochún
afromosquera@yahoo.es

Fundación de Desarrollo Social y Cultural Afroecuatoriana Azucar
info@azucarafroe.com
www.azucarafroe.com

Fundación de Integración, Desarrollo y Acción Social (I.D.E.A.S.)
Funideas05@hotmail.com

GUATEMALA

Centro de Investigaciòn Afrocaribe Wadeimalu Garifuna
wadimalu.centro@gmail.com

HONDURAS

Asociación de Micro, Pequeños y Medianos Empresarios Afro-Hondureños – CAMAFROH cedecoxxi@yahoo.com

rguevara@hondumail.net

Comité de Emergencia Garífuna de Honduras

Afro_cagah@yahoo.com

www.cegah.org

ECOSALUD

ecosalud98@yahoo.com

ecosalud.org

Fundación Luagu Hatuadi Wduheñu "Por la Salud de Nuestros Pueblos"

Fhatuadiw@yahoo.es

www.atuadi.org

Organización Afrohondureña de la juventud – OAFROHJU

oafrohju@hotmail.com

Organización de desarrollo étnico comunitario – ODECO

odeco@caribe.hn

clavarez@caribe.hn

www.odeco.org

Organización Fraternal Negra Hondureña – OFRANEH

ofraneh@yahoo.com

www.ofraneh.org

Organización Negra Centroamericana – ONECA

odeco@caribe.hn

clavares@caribe.hn

Fundación Hondureña para la Defensa de la Cultura Garifunas y Centro de

Cultura Garinagu de Honduras – CENCUGLAR

garinagu@cablecolor.hn

MEXICO

Africa A. C.

I_reyes_larrea@hotmail.com

colectivo_africa@hotmail.com

colectivoafrica.blogspot.com

Centro de Derechos Humanos, Ciudadanos y Autonómicos – CEDEHCA
información@cedehcanicaragua.com
www.cedehcanicaragua.com

Colectivo Regional para la Defensa de los Pueblos Indígenas y Negros de Oaxaca México – COLECTIVO PINOTEPA
colectivopinotepa@gmail.com
www.colectivopinotepa.blogspot.com

México Negro AC
gynmexneg@hotmail.com
mexiconegroac.blogspot.com

NICARAGUA

Nicaribbean Black People Association – NBPA
duhindo@yahoo.com
bush-black@hotmail.com

Red de Mujeres Afrolatinoamericanas, Afrocaribeñas y de la Diáspora
mafroni@cablenet.com.ni
www.mujeresafro.org

PANAMA

Asociación de Puertos Obaldieños Unidos
apou@cwpanama.net
apou@cableonda.net

Asociación Respuesta Afropanameña
ellen_greaves99@yahoo.com

Centro de Estudios Afropanameños – CEDEAP
gmaloneyf@hotmail.com
nerebet_470@hotmail.com

Centro de la Mujer Panameña – CEMP
cemp76@hotmail.com

Consejo Nacional de Etnias Negras – CONEN
http://conenpanama.com

Comisión de la etnia negra de Colón
cgarnesafro@msn.com
selviamillerpalmaresselviam@panama.net
la_negra@hotmail.com

Coordinadora Nacional de las Organizaciones Negras Panameñas – CONEGPA
eunice108@hotmail.com
diadelaetnia.homestead.com/coordinadora.html

Fundación Bayano
fundaba@cwpanama.net
www.fundacionbayano.org/panama

Fundación para la Gestión del Arte Afrodescendiente – FUGAA
proyectofuga@walla.com

Fundación de Mujeres Afrodescendientes Trabajando para la Comunidad – FUMUAFRO
horowe@pancanal.com
hortensiarowe@yahoo.com

Grupo Congo de Panamá "Tradiciones de mi raza"
pcongodepanama@gmail.com

Sociedad de Amigos del Museo Afroantillano de Panamá – SAMAAP
info@samaap.org
www.samaap.org

PARAGUAY

Asociación Afro paraguaya Kamba Cua – AAPKC
morenada01@hotmail.com

Comisión Cultural Afro-descendiente Kamba Kokue virgen del rosario
susiarce1@gmail.com

PERU

Ashanti – Red Nacional de Jóvenes Afroperuanos
ashanti-reddejovenes@hotmail.com

ashanti-peru.blogspot.com

Asociación Civil Raíces Afroperuana
vickyzega@hotmail.com
raices_afroperuana@hotmail.com

Asociación Cultural de Promoción y Desarrollo "Todas las Sangres"
todaslassangres@hotmail.com
agztodaslassangres@yahoo.es
www.cimarrones-peru.org/todaslas.htm

Asociación Negra de Defensa y Desarrollo de la Mujer y Juventud Chinchana – Margarita
margaritachinchaafro@hotmail.com
www.cimarrones-peru.org/marga.htm

Asociación Negra de Defensa y Promoción de los Derechos Humanos – ASONDEH
asondeh@asondeh.com
www.asondeh.com

Centro de Desarrollo Étnico – CEDET
cedetdir@ec-rec.com
www.cedet.net

Centro de Desarrollo de la Mujer Negra Peruana – CEDEMUNEP
cedemunep@hotmail.com
www.cedemunep.org

Centro Para el Desarrollo Urbano y Rural – CEPDUR
MPRO_cepdur@speedy.com.pe

Cimarrones
www.cimarrones-peru.org

CUMANA – Asociación Afro peruana comprometida con el Desarrollo
Sostenible
cumanapiura@gmail.com

Grupo Cultural Afroperuano Las Sabu de Isamar
lasabuisamar@hotmail.com

LUNDU Centro de Estudios y Promoción Afroperuanos
lundu@lundu.org.pe

www.lundu.org.pe

Makungu para el Desarrollo
perumakungu@gmail.com
perumakungu.blogspot.com

Organización Afro peruana para el Desarrollo Étnico de Cañete – Ña Catita
afrocatitasanluis@hotmail.com

Songorocosongo
afrosongo@hotmail.com

URUGUAY

Asociación Afro Iberoamericana – AFRIB
afroaii@gmail.com
cgalloso@adinet.com.uy

Asociación Civil Africanía
toliverach@hotmail.com
www.bantuuruguay.com

Centro Cultural por la Paz y la Integración – CECUPI
cecupi.org@hotmail.com
www.cecupi.blogspot.com

Escuela De Candombre de Cerro Largo
Candombe101@adinet.com.uy

Federación IFA del Uruguay (Instituciones Federadas Afroumbandistas)
Atabaque
ifadeluruguay@hotmail.com
www.atabaque.com.uy

Grupo Cultural Afrogama
afrogama@hotmail.com
www.afrogama.blogspot.com

Mizangas – Mujeres Jóvenes Afrodescendientes
reuniondemizangas@gmail.com

Nzinga. Artesanías étnicas
intiartesana@gmail.com

http://ancestralesafro.blogspot.com
http://afroarte.blogspot.com
http://nzinga.winnernet.net

Organizaciones Mundo Afro
mundoafro@gmail.com
www.mundoafro.org

Organización Social Salvador Por un Movimiento Afrouruguayo
http://organizacionsocialsalvador.blogspot.com/

UAFRO
uafro@adinet.com.uy
aliciaesqui@gmail.com

VENEZUELA

Fundación Afro-América
www.fundacionafroamerica.com

APPENDIX B: TYPOLOGY OF LATIN AMERICAN RACIAL ANTIDISCRIMINATION MEASURES

Nation	Multicultural Constitutions	Land Rights	Penal Code	Const. Equality	Public Accommodations	Employment	Education	Hate Speech
Argentina			X	X	X			X
Bolivia	X	X	X	X				X
Brazil		X	X	X	X	X	X	X
Chile				X				
Colombia	X	X		X	X	X	X	
Costa Rica			X	X	X	X	X	X
Cuba			X	X				X
Dom. Rep.				X				
Ecuador	X	X	X	X			X	X
El Salvador				X				
Guatemala	X	X	X	X			X	X
Honduras	X	X		X				
Mexico	X		X	X	X	X		X
Nicaragua	X	X		X		X		
Panama			X	X	X	X		
Paraguay	X			X				
Peru			X	X	X	X	X	X
Uruguay			X					X
Venezuela	X		X	X				X

BIBLIOGRAPHY

Primary Sources

Decrees, Statutes, Rules, and Constitutions

Anais da Câmara dos Deputados de São Paulo, vol. 1, 1928, 13 Sessão Ordinária em 31 julho.

Código Penal [Penal Code] art. 140, § 3 (Braz.).

Constitución Nacional (Arg.) (1853).

Constitución Nacional of 1994 (Arg.), *available at* http://pdba.georgetown.edu/Constitutions/Argentina/argentina.html.

Constituíção da República Dos Estados Unidos do Brasil de 16 julho de 1934.

Constituíção da República Dos Estados Unidos do Brasil de 18 septembro de 1946.

Constituíção da Republica Federativa do Brasil 5 de Octubro de 1988.

Constituíção Federal [C.F.] [Constitution] (Braz.).

Constitución (1992) (Cuba), in Inter-Univ. Assocs., Inc., Republic of Cuba, 5 *Constitutions of the Countries of the World*, Release 2000–1 (2000).

Constitución de la República Dominicana (2002), *available at* http://pdba.georgetown.edu/Constitutions/DomRep/dominicanrepublic.htm.

Constitución (El Sal.), in Inter-Univ. Assocs., Inc., Republic of El Salvador, in 6 *Constitutions of the Countries of the World*, Reka Koerner (trans.), Release 98–5 (1998).

Constitución, (Hond.), in Gisbert H. Flanz and Jefri Jay Ruchti, in 8 *Constitutions of the Countries of the World, Republic of Honduras*, Reka Koerner (trans.), Release 97–2 (1997).

Constitución de la Confederación Argentina (1853).

Constitución Del Ecuador, *available at* http://www.asambleanacional.gov.
ec/documentos/constitucion_de_bolsillo.pdf.

Constitución Política (2008) (Ecuador), http://pdba.georgetown.edu/
Constitutions/Ecuador/ecuador08.html#mozTocId666824.

Constitución Política (Panama), in Jorge Fábrega P. and Jefri Jay Ruchti,
Republic of Panama, in *14 Constitutions of the Countries of the World*,
Jorge Fábrega P. (trans.), Release 95–8 (1995).

Constitución Política de Colombia.

Constitución Política de Colombia, in Gisbert H. Flanz, in *4 Constitutions
of the Countries of the World*, Release 95–4, Peter B. Heller & Marcia
W. Coward (trans.) (1995).

Constitución Política de la República de Chile.

Constitución Política de la República de Nicaragua.

Constitución Política de la República de Nicaragua, in Inter-Univ. Assocs.,
Inc., Republic of Nicaragua, *13 Constitutions of the Countries of the
World*, Anna I. Vellvé Torras (trans.), Release 98–5 (1998).

Constitutión de la República Dominicana (2002), *available at* http://
pdba.georgetown.edu/Constitutions/DomRep/dominicanrepublic.
html.

Constitución Política de los Estados Unidos Mexicanos (1917 with 2008
reforms), *available at* http://pdba.georgetown.edu/Constitutions/
Mexico/textovigente2008.pdf.

Constitución Política de la República de Chile, art. 19 (1980 with 2005
reforms), *available at* http://pdba.georgetown.edu/Constitutions/
Chile/chile05.html.

Constitución de la República Oriental del Uruguay.

Constitución Política (Peru), in Peter B. Heller, Peru, in *14 Constitutions of
the Countries of the World*, Release 95–1 (1995), p. 113; Constitución,
tit. III, ch. 1, art. 21, cl. 1 (Venez.), in Gisbert H. Flanz, Bolivarian
Republic of Venezuela, in *20 Constitutions of the Countries of the World*,
Release 2000–3 (2000).

Constitution of Paraguay (1992), *available at* http://pdba.georgetown.edu/
Constitutions/Paraguay/paraguay.html.

Corte Constitucional, Sentencia T-025 (2004).

Criminal Code, Art. 36.5 (Nicaragua).

Decree No. 1122, 18 Junio 1998 (Colombia).

Decreto 20.921, de 25 August 1931, Diario Oficial dos Estados Unidos
do Brasil, pp. 13, 552–8.

Decreto No. 428 (2005) (Venezuela).

Decree No. 4247, art. 5, de 6 janeiro 1921, Diario Oficial Da União
[D.O.U.] (Brazil).

Decreto No. 43007, de 6 de Junho de 2011 (Brazil).

Decreto Supremo No. 003–97-TR (Peru), *available at* www.mpfn.gob.pe/descargas/texto_unico_ordenado_ds_03–97-tr.pdf.

Decreto Ley No. 25868, Ley De Organización y Funciones Del Instituto Nacional De Defensa De La Competencia y De La Protección De La Propiedad Intelectual (INDECOPI) (November 6, 1992), *available at* http://www.concytec.gob.pe/infocyt/25868.html.

Executive Decree 09–2007 (Honduras).

Immigration Act of 1917, ch. 29, 39 Stat. 874 (1917).

Immigration Act of 1924, ch. 190, 43 Stat. 153 (1924).

Law No. 641, Criminal Code, Art. 427, 428 (Nicaragua).

Law No. 7.347, de 24 Julho 1985, D.O.U. of 25 Julho 1985, as amended by Law Nos. 8.078 of 11 Setembro 1990; 8.884 de 11 Junho 1994; 9.494 de 10 setembro 1997 (Brazil).

Law No. 12.288/10 (Brazil).

Law No. 12.288, de 20 Julio 2010, *available at* http://www.portaldaigualdade.gov.br/.arquivos/Estatuto%20em%20ingles.pdf (Brazil).

Lei Número 9 394 de 20 de dezembro de 1996 (Brazil).

Lei Número 1.390, de 3 Julho 1951 (Brazil).

Lei Número 7.716 de 5 de Janeiro de 1989 (Brazil).

Lei Número 8.081, de 21 de Setembro de 1990 (Brazil).

Lei Número 9.459 de 1997 (Brazil).

Ley 115 de Febrero 8 de 1994, Art. 160, §10 (Colombia).

Ley Contra Actos de Discriminación, Ley No. 27270 (2000), *available at* http://www.ilo.org/dyn/natlex/docs/WEBTEXT/56275/65196/S00PER02.htm (Peru).

Ley No. 24–97, Párrafo III, Art. 9 (Dominican Republic), *available at* http://www.iin.oea.org/badaj/docs/l24–97do.htm#Texto.

Ley No. 26772 (1997) *modified by* Ley No 27270 (2000) *available at* http://www.congreso.gob.pe/comisiones/2002/discapacidad/leyes/26772.htm (Peru).

Ministro Rui Barbosa, Circular No. 29, 14 de maio 1891 (Brazil).

Public Law 3708/2001, State of Rio de Janeiro, *available at* http://www.alerj.rj.gov/top_leis_ordinairas.htm.

Public Law 3524/2000, State of Rio de Janeiro, *available at* http://www.alerj.rj.gov/top_leis_ordinairas.htm.

Public Law 4151/2003, State of Rio de Janeiro, *available at* http://www.alerj.rj.gov.br/processo2.htm.

Provisional Measure No. 2.102–28 de 23 February 2001 (Brazil).

Regulamento para o Serviço de Imigração da Província de São Paulo (São Paulo: Tipografia do Correio Paulistano, 1887), art. 17.

Resolución Suprema No. 010–2009-MIMDES, 27 noviembre 2009 (Peru).

República de Bolivia Constitución Política del Estado, art. 6 (2009), *available at* http://pdba.georgetown.edu/Constitutions/Bolivia/bolivia.html.

Rules of Procedure of the Inter-American Court of Human Rights, *reprinted in* Basic Documents Pertaining to Human Rights in the Inter-American System, OEA/Ser.L/V/I.rev.9 (2003).

International Convention on the Elimination of All Forms of Racial Discrimination, March 7, 1966, in force January 4, 1969, *available at* http://treaties.un.org/Pages/ViewDetails.aspx?src=TREATY&mtdsg_no=IV-2&chapter=4&lang=en#EndDec.

Case Law

Ação Direta De Inconstitucionalidade 3.197 Rio de Janeiro, Decisão de 19 de março 2012, Relator: Min. Celso de Mello (Brazil).

Adarand Constructors, Inc. v. Peña, 515 U.S. 200, 239 (1995).

Case of the Mayagna (Sumo) Awas Tingni Community v. Nicaragua, 2001 Inter-Am. Ct. H.R. (ser. C) No. 79 (Aug. 31, 2001).

Christiansburg Garment Co. v. EEOC, 434 U.S. 412, 420 (1978).

De Almeida v. Brazil, Case No. 12.440, Inter-Am. Comm'n Report No. 73/06 (2006).

Diniz v. Brazil, Case 12.001, Inter-Am. Comm'n Report No. 83/04 (2004).

Ghen v. Rich, 8 F 159 (D. Mass. 1881).

S.T.F., RE No. 597285, Relator: Min. Ricardo Lewandowski, 09.10.2009, 191 DJe 1479 (Brazil).

T.J.R.J., Dir. Inc. No. 2009.007.0009, Relator: Des. José Carlos S. Murata Ribeiro, 25.05.2009 (Brazil).

T.J.R.J., Embargos Infringentes No. 2005.005.00060, CEAP v. Sony Music Entertainment Brasil, 11 Câmara Cível do Tribunal de Justiça do Estado do Rio De Janeiro, Acórdão 14.12.2005 (Brazil).

T.J.R.J. Representação Por Inconstitucionalidade No. 2009.007.00009, Relator: Des. Sérgio Cavalieri Filho, 18.11.2009 (Brazil).

Newspapers and Magazines

"15 Abogados Afroecuatorianos se Especializan," CODAE, May 13, 2011, http://www.codae.gob.ec/index.php?option=com_k2&view=it em&id=137:15-abogados-afroecuatorianos-se-especializan.

"Alan García pidió perdón a pueblo afroperuano en ceremonia oficial," El Comercio, December 7, 2009, http://elcomercio.pe/politica/378597/n oticia-presidente-garcia-pidio-perdon-pueblo-afroperuano-ceremoni a-oficial.

Jaime Alves, "Ouro de Tolos: O Estatuto da Igualdade e a Submissão Política Negra II," Ìrohìn, June 21, 2010, http://www.irohin.org.br/onl/new.php?sec=news&id=8090.

"Aprodeh Señala Que Hay Más Discriminación Racial en Lima, Cusco y Arequipa," El Comercio, March 10, 2005.

Marina Ari, "Argentina: Empanada, Asado de Vaca y Mucho Racismo," Kaos En La Red, May 22, 2010, http://www.kaosenlared.net/noticia/argentina-empanada-asado-vaca-mucho-racismo.

T. Avellaneda, "Manifestaciones del Racismo en Cuba: Varias Caras de Un Viejo Mal," Revista Digital Consenso, 2005, http://www.desde-cuba.com/02/articulos/11_01.shtml.

"Becas y Maestrías," CODAE, May 2011, http://www.codae.gob.ec/index.php?option=com_content&view=article&id=194:beca s-y-maestrias&catid=1.

Madison Smartt Bell, "A Hidden Haitian World," New York Review of Books, July 17, 2008, p. 41.

"Brazil's Unfinished Battle for Racial Democracy," The Economist, April 22, 2000, p. 31.

"Casi dos millones de argentinos tienen sus raíces en el Africa negra," Clarín, June 9, 2006, http://www.clarin.com/diario/2006/06/09/sociedad/s-03801.htm.

Mae M. Cheng, "'The Face of America': New Census Acknowledges City's Multiracial Residents," Newsday, March 16, 2001, p. E6.

Diego Cevallos, "Latin America: Afro-Descendants Marginalized and Ignored," Inter Press Service News, May 19, 2005, http://ipsnews.net/africa/interna.asp?idnews=28752.

Lino D'Ou, "El fantasma histriónico," Labor Nueva, February 27, 1916.

Ramona E. Douglass, "Multiracial People Must No Longer Be Invisible," New York Times, July 12, 1996, p. A26.

Patricio Downes, "Casi dos Millones de Argentinos Tienen Sus Raíces en el Africa Negra," Clarín, June 9, 2006, http://edant.clarin.com/diario/2006/06/09/sociedad/s-03801.htm.

Patricia Duarte, "Negros São Maiores Vítimas do Trabalho Infantil no País," O Globo, November 18, 2006.

Haya El Nasser, "Hispanic Responses on Race Give More Exact Breakdown," USA Today, March 9, 2011.

"Entidades Criticam 'Racismo Institucional'," Correio de Sergipe, November 20, 2008, http://correiodesergipe.com/lernoticia. php?noticia=30545.

Andrew Friedman, "Behind the Big Numbers, a Million Little Stories," New York Times, March 18, 2001, sec. 14, p. 6.

Rosario Gabino, "¿Hay Negros en Argentina?" BBC Mundo, March 16, 2007, http://news.bbc.co.uk/hi/spanish/specials/2007/esclavitud/ newsid_6455000/6455537.stm.

César Rodríguez Garavito, "En Defensa de las Acciones Afirmativas," El Espectador, July 13, 2009, http://www.elespectador.com/columna150 499-defensa-de-acciones-afirmativas.

Antônio Gois, "Brasileiros Vêem Cota Como Essencial e Humilhante, Revela Datafolha," Folha de São Paulo Online, November 23, 2008, http://www1.folha.uol.com.br/folha/brasil/ult96u470649.shtml.

Wagner Gomes, "Negros São Minoria Na Igreja," O Globo, May 14, 2007, p. 3.

"Iberoamérica, ¿una región racista?" (Ibero-America: A Racist Region?) BBC Mundo, 13 October 2005, http://news.bbc.co.uk/go/pr/fr/-/hi/ spanish/latin_america/newsid_4331000/4331708.stm.

Rafael Duharte Jiménez and Elsa Santos García, "'No Hay Negro Bueno Ni Tamarindo Dulce:' Cuba, 118 Años Después de la Abolición de la Esclavitud," Matices, http://www.matices.de/18/18pcuba.htm.

Martin Kasindorf and Haya El Nasser, "Impact of Census' Race Data Debated," USA Today, March 13, 2001, p. 1A.

Abraham Lama, "Market Reforms Come at a Cost to Education," Inter Press Service, October 9, 1997, p. 1.

Roberta Lopes, "Discriminação Racial Pode Fazer Com Que Brasil Não Cumpra Metas do Milênio," Agência Brasil, November 23, 2006, http://www.agenciabrasil.gov.br/noticias/2006/11/23/ materia.2006-11-23.6429391562/view.

Carlos Salinas Maldonado, "Alta Hooker Rectora de la Uraccan 'El Chamán es Sólo la Punta del Iceberg'," Diario de la Prensa, February 22, 2009, http://archivo.laprensa.com.ni/archivo/2009/febrero/22/ suplementos/domingo/313375.shtml.

Telma Marotto, "Brazilian Secret 93 Million Don't Want to Talk about Is Racism," Bloomberg.com News, June 26, 2008, http://www.bloomberg. com/apps/news?pid=20601109&refer=news&sid=aIezjRWRd5Tk.

Alonso Mata, "Epsy Campbell se Mantendrá en el PAC," Nacion. com, June 2, 2009, http://wvw.nacion.com/ln_ee/2009/junio/02/ pais1983157.html.

Maiá Menezes, "Vítimas de racismo perdem 57.7% das ações," O Globo, November 20, 2008, http://oglobo.globo.com/pais/noblat/post.asp?t=vitimas_de_racismo_perdem_57_7_das_acoes&cod_Post=141465&a=111.

Tom Morganthau, "What Color Is Black?" Newsweek, February 13, 1995, pp. 63, 65.

"Negras Recembem Menos Anesthesia do Que Brancas," O Globo, November 26, 2006.

Carlos Neri, "Un Grupo Argentino Exterminación de los Negros de Mierda Indigna en Facebook," Moebius, March 2, 2008, http://enmoebius.com.ar/?p=972.

Mario Osava, "Brazil: Race Quotas – Accused of Racism," Inter Press Service News, July 26, 2006, http://ipsnews.net/news.asp?idnews=34111.

Bryce Pardo, "Member of Congress Discuss Challenges Facing Afro-Descendants in Latin America," Inter-American Dialogue, April 9, 2008.

Jeffrey Passel, Wendy Wang and Paul Taylor, "Marrying Out: One-in-Seven New U.S. Marriages is Interracial or Interethnic," Pew Research Center Report, June 4, 2010, http://pewresearch.org/pubs/1616/american-marriage-interracial-interethnic.

"Piden que Un Libro Infantil que Fomenta El Racismo sea Quitado de Circulación," MDZ Online, May 27, 2010, http://www.mdzol.com/mdz/nota/212497.

José Alfredo Andaluz Prado, "Prácticas Racistas y Discriminatorias Es Castigada Con Prisión," Diario Correo, 6 July 2009, http://www.diariocorreo.com.ec/archivo/2009/07/06/practicas-racistas-y-discriminatorias-es-castigada-con-prision.

Ronald Soto Quirós, "Desafinidad Con La Población Nacional: Discursos y Políticas de Inmigración en Costa Rica," Istmo, July 24, 2003.

Fernando Ravsberg, "Advierten Sobre Racismo en Cuba," BBC Mundo, February 13, 2003, http://news.bbc.co.uk/hi/spanish/latin_america/newsid_2759000/2759775.stm.

Catalina Gallo Rojas, "Igualdad Sin Cuotas," El Tiempo, July 12, 2009, p. 7.

Hernando Salazar, "Colombia Contra el Racismo," BBC Mundo, May 23, 2008, http://news.bbc.co.uk/hi/spanish/latin_america/newsid_7415000/7415897.stm.

Eric Schmitt, "For 7 Million People in Census, One Race Category Isn't Enough," New York Times, March 13, 2001, p. A1.

Gonzalo Vega Sfrani, "Universidad Reserva La Mitad de sus Cupos Para Negros y Desata Polémica," El Mercurio, October 22, 2006, http://www.ifcs.ufrj.br/~observa/noticias/elmercurio/discriminacion_22.htm.

Maria Aparecida Silva Bento, "A Mulher Negra No Mercado de Trabalho," Observatório Social, March 2004, p. 29.

Calvin Sims, "Peru's Blacks Increasingly Discontent With Decorative Role," New York Times, August 17, 1996, p. 2.

K.W. Stephenson, "Michael Campbell: El Racismo Está Enraizado en la Sociedad Nicaragüense," La Brújula Digital, February 25, 2011, http://www.labrujula.com.ni/noticia/159.

"STF declared the constitutionality of the quota system at the University of Brasilia," STF Internacional (Federal Supreme Court of Brazil news portal), April 26, 2012, http://www2.stf.jus.br/portalStfInternacional/cms/destaquesClipping.php?sigla=portalStfDestaque_en_us&idConteudo=207138.

"Supremo declara constitucionalidade do ProUni," Secretaria de Políticas de Promoção da Igualdade Racial, Últimas Notícias, May 4, 2012, http://www.seppir.gov.br/noticias/ultimas_noticias/2012/05/supremo-declara-constitucionalidade-do-prouni.

Frederico Vasconcelos, "Situações de Discriminação Só Tive No Brasil, Diz Ministro do STF," Folha de São Paulo Online, November 23, 2008, http://www1.folha.uol.com.br/folha/brasil/ult96u470662.shtml.

Márcia Vieira, "Médicos da Uerj Põem á Prova Sistema de Cotas," O Estado de São Paulo, May 8, 2011.

Wilfredo Ardito Vega, "Discriminación en los servicios turísticos," La Insignia, December 5, 2006, http://www.lainsignia.org/2006/diciembre/ibe_011.htm.

Other Primary Sources

Joel Zito Araújo, A Negação do Brasil: O Negro na Telenovela Brasileira (Documentary 2000).

Review of Federal Measurements of Race and Ethnicity: Hearings before the Subcomm. on Census, Statistics and Postal Personnel of the House Comm. on Post Office and Civil Service, 103d Cong. 171 (1993) (testimony of Carlos Fernández, President, Association of MultiEthnic Americans).

Interviews

Interview with Joaquim Barbosa (May 14, 2007) (transcript in Tanya K. Hernández's possession).

Telephone Interview with Melissa Nobles, Professor of Political Science, Massachusetts Institute of Technology (November 6, 1997).

Secondary Sources

Books and Publications

Actualidad Afrodescendiente en Iberoamérica: Estudio Sobre Organizaciones Civiles y Políticas de Acción Afirmativa, (Madrid: Secretaria General Iberoamericana, July 2010), *available at* http://segib.org/publicaciones/files/2010/07/Actualidad-Afrodescendiente-Iberoamerica.pdf.

Orlando Albornoz, *Education and Society in Latin America* (Pittsburgh: Macmillan, 1993).

George Reid Andrews, *The Afro-Argentines of Buenos Aires, 1800–1900* (Madison: University of Wisconsin Press, 1980).

Afro-Latin America, 1800–2000 (New York: Oxford University Press, 2004).

Blackness in the White Nation: A History of Afro-Uruguay (Chapel Hill: University of North Carolina Press, 2010).

Victor Tau Anzoátegui, *El Poder de la Costumbre: Estudios Sobre el Derecho Consuetudinario en América Hispana Hasta La Emancipación* (Buenos Aires: Instituto de Investigaciones de Historia del Derecho, 2001).

Eunice Aparecida de Jesus Prudente, *Preconceito Racial e Igualdade Jurídica No Brasil* (Campinas: Julex Livros, 1989).

Kiran Asher, *Black and Green: Afro-Colombians, Development, and Nature in the Pacific Lowlands* (Durham, NC: Duke University Press, 2009).

Ralph Richard Banks, *Is Marriage for White People? How the African American Marriage Decline Affects Everyone* (New York: Dutton, 2011).

Roger Bastide, *The African Religions of Brazil: Toward a Sociology of the Interpenetration of Civilizations*, Helen Sebba (trans.) (Baltimore: Johns Hopkins University Press, 1978).

David J. Bederman, *Custom as a Source of Law* (Cambridge: Cambridge University Press, 2010).

Leslie Bethell (ed.), *Latin America: Politics and Society since 1930* (New York: Cambridge University Press, 1998).

"Between the Law and Their Land: Afro-Brazilian Quilombo Communities' Struggle for Land Rights" (Austin, TX: Bernard and Audre Rapoport Center for Human Rights and Justice, September 22, 2008), *available at* http://www.utexas.edu/law/centers/humanrights/projects_and_publications/brazil-report.pdf.

Harold A. Bierck, Jr. (ed.), *Selected Writings of Bolivar, Volume I: 1800–1822,* Lewis Betrand (trans.) (New York: Colonial Press, 1951).

Allan R. Brewer-Carías, *Constitutional Protection of Human Rights in Latin America: A Comparative Study of Amparo Proceedings* (Cambridge: Cambridge University Press, 2009).

Daniel M. Brinks, *The Judicial Response to Police Killings in Latin America: Inequality and the Rule of Law* (Cambridge: Cambridge University Press, 2008).

Alison Brysk, *From Tribal Village to Global Village: Indian Rights and International Relations in Latin America* (Stanford, CA: Stanford University Press, 2000).

Marisa Bucheli and Wanda Cabela, *Encuesta Nacional de Hogares Ampliada 2006: Perfil demográfico y socioeconómico de la población uruguaya según su ascendencia racial* (Montevideo: Instituto Nacional de Estadística, 2006), p. 2, *available at* http://www.ine.gub.uy/enha2006/Informe%20 final%20raza.pdf.

John Burdick, *Blessed Anastácia: Women, Race, and Popular Christianity in Brazil* (New York: Routledge, 1998).

Legacies of Liberation: The Progressive Catholic Church in Brazil at the Start of a New Millenium (Aldershot: Ashgate, 2004).

Richard W. Burkhardt, *The Spirit of the System: Lamarck and Evolutionary Biology* (Cambridge, MA: Harvard University Press, 1977).

Kim D. Butler, *Freedoms Given, Freedoms Won: Afro-Brazilians in Post-Abolition São Paulo and Salvador* (New Brunswick, NJ: Rutgers University Press, 1998).

Kia Lilly Caldwell, *Negras in Brazil: Re-envisioning Black Women, Citizenship, and the Politics of Identity* (New Brunswick, NJ: Rutgers University Press, 2007).

Fernando Henrique Cardoso and Octavio Ianni, *Censo de Puerto Rico: 1935 Población y Agricultura* (Washington, DC: Adminstración de Reconstrucción de Puerto Rico, 1938).

Côr e mobilidade social em Florianópolis: Aspectos das relaçoes entre negros e brancos numa comunidade do Brasil meridional (São Paulo: Companhia Ed. Nac., 1960).

Costa Rica, Country Reports on Human Rights Practices 2006 (Washington, DC: Department of State, Bureau of Democracy, Human Rights, and Labor, March 6, 2007), *available at* http://www.state.gov/g/drl/ rls/hrrpt/2006/78886.htm.

Raquel Cesar, "Açoes afirmativas no Brasil: e agora, doutor?" *Ciencia Hoje,* 33 (July 2003).

Congresso Agrícola do Rio de Janeiro (Rio de Janeiro: Tipografia Nacional, 1878).

Martin Chanock, *Law, Custom and Social Order: The Colonial Experience in Malawi and Zambia* (Portsmouth, NH: Heinemann, 1985).

María Dakolias, *The Judicial Sector in Latin America and the Caribbean: Elements of Reform* (Washington, DC: International Bank of Reconstruction and Development, 1996).

Jerry Dávila, *Diploma of Whiteness: Race and Social Policy in Brazil, 1917–1945* (Durham, NC: Duke University Press, 2003).

Warren Dean, *Rio Claro: A Brazilian Plantation System, 1820–1920* (Stanford, CA: Stanford University Press, 1976).

Fernando de Azevedo, *Brazilian Culture: An Introduction to the Study of Culture in Brazil*, William Rex Crawford (trans.) (New York: Macmillan, 1950).

Thales de Azevedo, *Democracia Racial* (Petrópolis: Editora Vozes, 1975).

Manuel de Jesús Galván, *Enriquillo* (Santo Domingo: G. Hermanos, 1882).

Felipe de la Barra, *Invasiones militares de Lima: desde la Conquista hasta la República* (Austin: University of Texas Press, 2008) (digitized 1959 manuscript).

Carlos de la Torre, *Afroquiteños: Cidadanía y Racismo* (Quito: Centro Andino de Acción Popular, 2002).

Daniela Patti do Amaral and Fátima Bayma de Oliveira, "*O ProUni e a conclusão do ensino superior: questões introductórias sobre os egressos do programa na zona oeste do Rio de Janeiro*," *Ensaio: Aval. Pol. Públ. Educ.* 19 (March 2011).

Petrônio Domingues, *Uma História Não Contada: Negro, racismo, e branqueamento em São Paulo pós-abolição* (São Paulo: Editora Paz e Terra, 2004).

Paul W. Drake and Mathew D. McCubbins, *The Origins of Liberty: Political and Economic Liberalization in the Modern World* (Princeton, NJ: Princeton University Press, 1988).

Estudos de estatística teórica e aplicada, contribuções para o estudo da demográfica do Brasil (Rio de Janeiro: Instituto Brasileiro de Geográfia e Estatística, 1970).

El Derecho a la Educación: La Educación en la Perspectiva de los Derechos Humanos (Bogotá: Procuraduría General de la Nación, 2006).

Robert C. Ellickson, *Order without Law: How Neighbors Settle Disputes* (Cambridge, MA: Harvard University Press, 1991).

Joe R. Feagin, *Racist America: Roots, Current Realities and Future Reparations* (New York: Routledge, 2000).

M. Fennema and T. Lowenthal, *La Construcción de raza y nación en la República Dominicana* (Santo Domingo: Editora Universitaria, 1987).

Florestan Fernandes, *The Negro in Brazilian Society*, Jacqueline D. Skiles, A. Brunel, and Arthur Rothwell (trans.) (New York: Simon & Schuster, 1971).

Forum on Poverty Alleviation for Minority Communities: Communities of African Ancestry in Costa Rica, Honduras, Nicaragua, Argentina, Colombia, Ecuador, Peru, Uruguay, Venezuela (Washington, DC: Inter-American Development Bank, 1996).

Paul Finkelman and Joseph C. Miller (eds.), *Macmillan Encyclopedia of World Slavery*, vol. 1, p. xlvii (New York: Macmillan Reference USA, 1998).

Paulo Freire, *Pedagogia do Oprimido* (Rio de Janeiro: Paz e Terra, 1987).

Gilberto Freyre, *Casa Grande e Senzala* (Rio de Janeiro: Maia & Schmidt, 1933).

Sobrados e Mucambos: Decadência do Patriarchado Rural no Brasil (São Paulo: Companhia Editora Nacional, 1936).

Fundo de Desenvolvimento das Nações Unidas para a Mulher, & Secretaria Especial de Políticas para as Mulheres, Retrato das desigualdades de gênero e raça, 3rd ed. (Brasília: Instituto de Pesquisa Econômica Aplicada, September 2008).

Francis Galton, *Hereditary Genius* (London: Macmillan, 1869).

César Augusto Rodríguez Garavito, Tatiana Andrea Alfonso Sierra, and Isabel Cavelier Adarve, *El Derecho a no Ser Discriminado: Primer Informe Sobre Discriminación Racial y Derechos de la Población Afrocolombiana* (Versión Resumida) (Bogotá: Universidad de Los Andes, 2008).

Iliana Paris García, *Ideología y Proceso de Blanqueamiento Una Aproximación Construccionista a su Posible Influencia en la Identidad y la Autoimagen de Tres Mujeres Negras Venezolanas* (Caracas: Fondo Editorial de Humanidades y Educación, 2002).

Henry Louis Gates, Jr., *Black in Latin America* (New York: New York University Press, 2011).

Tanya María Golash-Boza, *Yo Soy Negro: Blackness in Peru* (Gainesville: University of Florida Press, 2011).

Donna M. Goldstein, *Laughter Out of Place: Race, Class, Violence, and Sexuality in a Rio Shantytown* (Berkeley: University of California Press, 2003).

Nuno Espinosa Gomes da Silva, *História Do Direito Português* (Lisboa: Fundacão Calouste Gulbenkian, 1991).

Peter Goodrich, *Reading the Law: A Critical Introduction* (London: Basil Blackwell, 1986).

Richard Gott, *Cuba: A New History* (New Haven, CT: Yale University Press, 2005).

Doreen S. Goyer and Eliane Domschke, *The Handbook of National Population Censuses: Spanish America and the Caribbean, North America, and Oceania* (Westport, CT: Greenwood Press, 1983).

Antonio Sérgio Guimarães, *Preconceito e Discriminaçaõ: Queixas de Ofensas e Tratamento Desigual dos Negros no Brasil* (Salvador: Novos Toques, 1998).

Linn A. Hammergren, *The Politics of Justice and Justice Reform in Latin America* (Boulder, CO: Westview Press, 1998).

Aline Helg, *Our Rightful Share: The Afro-Cuban Struggle for Equality, 1886–1912* (Chapel Hill: University of North Carolina, 1995).

Jens R. Hentschke, *Reconstructing the Brazilian Nation: Public Schooling in the Vargas Era* (Baden-Baden: Nomos, 2007).

Rosana Heringer, "*Diversidade Racial e Relações de Gênero no Brasil Contemporâneo*," in *CEPIA* (ed.), *O Progresso Das Mulheres No Brasil* (Brasilia: UNIFEM, 2006).

Juliet Hooker, *Race and the Politics of Solidarity* (Oxford: Oxford University Press, 2009).

Mala N. Htun, *Dimensions of Political Inclusion and Exclusion in Brazil: Gender and Race*, Technical Papers (Washington, DC: Inter-American Development Bank, December 2003), appendix A, table A.

Dimensiones de la inclusión y exclusión política en Brasil: Género y raza, Serie de informes técnicos del Departamento de Desarrollo Sostenible (Washington, DC: Banco Interamericano de Desarrollo, 2004), *available at* http://www.iadb.org/IDBDocs.cfm?docnum=361865.

David Howard, *Coloring the Nation: Race and Ethnicity in the Dominican Republic* (Oxford: Signal Books, 2001).

Herbert Felix Jolowicz, *Historical Introduction to the Study of Roman Law* (Cambridge: Cambridge University Press, 1967).

Nicholas A. Jones and Amy Symens Smith, "The Two or More Races Population: 2000, Census 2000 Brief" (Washington, DC: U.S. Dept. of Commerce, Economics and Statistics Admin., U.S. Census Bureau, Nov. 2001), http://www.census.gov/prod/2001pubs/c2kbr01-6.pdf.

"The Judicial System and Racism against People of African Descent: The Cases of Brazil, Colombia, the Dominican Republic and Peru" (Justice

Studies Center of the Americas, March 2004), *available at* http://www.
cejamericas.org/portal/index.php/es/biblioteca/biblioteca-virtual/
cat_view/43-documentos/66-informes-comparativos.

Robert Kaufmann and Stephan Haggard, *Development, Democracy and
Welfare States: Latin America, East Asia and Eastern Europe* (Princeton,
NJ: Princeton University Press, 2008).

Ali Kamel, *Não Somos Racistas: Uma Reação Aos Que Querem Nos
Transformar Numa Nação Bicolor* (São Paulo: Nova Fronteira, 2006).

Lúcio Kowarick, *Trabalho e Vadiagem: A Origem Do Trabalho Livre No Brasil*
(São Paulo: Editora Paz e Terra, 1987).

*La Discriminación en el Perú: Problemática, Normatividad y Tareas
Pendientes* (Perú: Defensoría del Pueblo, República del Perú, 2007).

Americo Jacobina Lacombe, Francisco de Assis Barbosa, and Eduardo da
Silva, *Rui Barbosa E a Queima Dos Arquivos* (Rio de Janeiro: Fundação
Casa de Rui Barbosa, 1988).

Linda Larach, *Secondary Education Profile: A Summary of "Secondary
Education: Time to Move Forward,"* Human Development Network
Secondary Education Series Brazil (Washington, DC: World Bank,
2001), p. 7, *available at* http://www.wds.worldbank.org/servlet/
WDSContentServer/WDSP/IB/ 2002/09/07/000094946_02082104
033872/Rendered/PDF/multi0page.pdf.

Magdalena León and Jimena Holguín, *Acción Afirmativa Hacia Democracias
Inclusivas: Colombia* (Santiago: Fundación Equitas, March 2005),
pp. 208–11, *available at* http://www.fundacionequitas.org/archivo.
aspx?cod_idioma=ES&id=29 (Chart 9 describes all the affirmative
action programs, including admissions).

Brian D. Lepard, *Customary International Law: A New Theory with Practical
Applications* (Cambridge: Cambridge University Press, 2010).

Christopher H. Lutz, *Santiago de Guatemala 1541–1773/ City, Caste, and
the Colonial Experience* (Norman: University of Oklahoma Press,
1994).

Yvonne Maggie, *Medo do Feitiço: Relações Entre Magia e Poder no Brasil*
(Rio de Janeiro: Arquivo Nacional, Orgão do Ministério da Justiça,
1992).

Daniel Bonilla Maldonado, *La Constitución Multicultural* (Bogotá: Siglo
del Hombre Editores, 2006).

Manning Marable, *Malcolm X: A Life of Reinvention* (New York: Viking,
2011).

Cecilia Maria Marinho de Azevedo, *Onda Negra, Medo Branco: O Negro No Imaginário Das Elites Século XIX* (São Paulo: AnnaBlume, 1987).

Gustavo Márquez et al., *OUTSIDERS? The Changing Patterns of Exclusion in Latin America and the Caribbean* (Washington, DC: Inter-American Development Bank, 2007).

José Martí, Deborah Shnookal (ed.), and Mirta Muñiz (ed.) *José Martí Reader: Writings on the Americas* (Melbourne: Ocean Press, 1999).

Anthony W. Marx, *Making Race and Nation: A Comparison of South Africa, The United States, and Brazil* (Cambridge: Cambridge University Press, 1998).

Daniel M. Masterson and Sayaka Funada-Classen, *The Japanese in Latin America* (Urbana: University of Illinois Press, 2004).

Teresa A. Meade, *"Civilizing" Rio: Reform and Resistance in a Brazilian City, 1889–1930* (University Park: Pennsylvania State University Press, 1996).

John Henry Merryman and Rogelio Pérez-Perdomo, *The Civil Law Tradition: An Introduction to the Legal Systems of Europe and Latin America*, 3rd ed. (Stanford, CA: Stanford University Press, 2007).

Samantha Ribeiro Meyer-Pflug, *Liberdade de Expressão e Discurso do ódio* (São Paulo: Editora Revista dos Tribunais, 2009).

Marilyn Grace Miller, *Rise and Fall of Cosmic Race: The Cult of Mestizaje in Spanish America* (Austin: University of Texas Press, 2004).

S. W. Mintz, *Caribbean Transformations* (Chicago: Aldine, 1974).

M. C. Mirow, *Latin American Law: A History of Private Law and Institutions in Spanish America* (Austin: University of Texas Press, 2004).

Gustavo Enrique Mustelier, *La Extinción del Negro: Apuntes Político-Sociales* (Havana: Imprenta y Papelería de Rambla, Bouza y Cía, 1912).

Joaquim Nabuco, *Discursos Parlamentares* (Brasília: Câmara dos Deputados, Centro de Documentacão e Informacão, Coordenacão de Publicacões, 1983).

Elisa Larkin Nascimento, *The Sorcery of Color: Identity, Race, and Gender in Brazil* (Philadelphia: Temple University Press, 2007).

Rogelio Pérez-Perdomo, *Latin American Lawyers: A Historical Introduction* (Stanford, CA: Stanford University Press, 2006).

Fernando Pinto, *A Presença do Costume e Sua Força Normativa* (Rio de Janeiro: Editora Liber Juris, 1982).

David N. Plank, *The Means of Our Salvation: Public Education in Brazil, 1930–1995* (Boulder, CO: Westview Press, 1996).

Pueblos Indígenas y Afrodescendientes de América Latina y el Caribe: Información Sociodemográfica para Políticas y Programas (New York: Comisión Económica para América Latina y el Caribe, 2006).

Thomas H. Reynolds and Arturo A. Flores, *Foreign Law: Current Sources of Codes and Basic Legislation in Jurisdictions of the World, Brazil* (Littleton, CO: Fred B. Rothman, 1989 & August 2004 Release), vol. I.

Right to Education of Afro-descendant and Indigenous Communities in the Americas, Report Prepared for a Thematic Hearing before the Inter-American Commission on Human Rights (Washington, DC: Robert F. Kennedy Memorial Center for Human Rights, March 12, 2008), p. 3, *available at* http://scm.oas.org/pdfs/2008/CP21371E.pdf.

George Rutherglen, *Employment Discrimination Law:Visions of Equality in Theory and Doctrine*, 3rd ed. (New York: Foundation Press, 2010).

J. L. Salcedo-Bastardo (ed.), Simón Bolívar, *The Hope of the Universe* (Paris: UNESCO, 1983).

Enrique Sánchez and Paola García, *"Más Allá de los Promedios: Afrodescendientes en América Latina"* (Washington, DC: ACNUR, 2006), pp. 16 and 38, *available at* www.acnur.org/biblioteca/pdf/4558. pdf.

Margarita Sánchez and Maurice Bryan, *Afro-descendants, Discrimination and Economic Exclusion in Latin America* (London: Minority Rights Group International, May 2003), available at http://www.minorityrights.org/933/macro-studies/afrodescendants-discrimination-and-economic-exclusion-in-latin-america.html.

Persons of African Descent, Discrimination and Economic Exclusion in Latin America (London: Minority Rights Group International, 2003), pp. 3–4, tbl.1, *available at* http://www.minorityrights.org/933/macro-studies/afro-descendants-discrimination-and-economic-exclusion-in-latin-america. html.

Livio Sansone, *Blackness without Ethnicity: Constructing Race in Brazil* (New York: Palgrave Macmillan, 2003).

Gevanilda Santos and Maria Palmira da Silva (eds.), *Racismo No Brasil: Percepções Da Discriminação E Do Preconceito Racial Do Século XXI* (São Paulo: Fundação Perseu Abramo, 2005).

Mark Q. Sawyer, *Racial Politics in Post-Revolutionary Cuba* (Cambridge: Cambridge University Press, 2006).

Leon Sheleff, *The Future of Tradition: Customary Law, Common Law and Legal Pluralism* (London: Frank Cass, 1999).

Robin E. Sheriff, *Dreaming Equality: Color, Race and Racism in Urban Brazil* (New Brunswick, NJ: Rutgers University Press, 2001).

Rachel Sieder (ed.), *Multiculturalism in Latin America: Indigenous Rights, Diversity and Democracy* (Houndmills: Palgrave Macmillan, 2002).

Hédio Silva Jr., *Discriminação Racial nas Escolas: entre a lei e as práticas socias* (Brasília: UNESCO Brasil, 2002).

Fabiana Augusto Martins Silveira, *Da criminalização do racismo: aspectos jurídicos e sociocriminológicos* (Belo Horizonte: Del Rey, 2006).

Kimberly Elson Simmons, *Reconstructing Racial Identity and the African Past in the Dominican Republic* (Gainesville: University of Florida Press, 2009).

Thomas Skidmore, *Black Into White: Race and Nationality in Brazilian Thought* (New York: Oxford University Press, 1974).

Politics in Brazil 1930–1964: An Experiment in Democracy (New York: Oxford University Press, 1967).

D. A. Skinner, *Porto Rico: Report from Supervisor of the Census for the District of Porto Rico, to the Hon. E. Dana Durand, Director of the Census* (Washington, DC: United States Census Bureau, July 26, 1910).

Nancy Leys Stepan, *The Hour of Eugenics* (Ithaca, NY: Cornell University Press, 1991).

Carlos Augusto Taunay, *Manual do Agricultor Brasileiro* (São Paulo: Companhia das Letras, 2001).

Edward E. Telles, *Race in Another America: The Significance of Skin Color in Brazil* (Princeton, NJ: Princeton University Press, 2004).

José Homem Corréa Telles, *Comentário Crítico à Lei da Boa Razão* (Lisboa: 1824).

Hugh Thomas, *The Slave Trade: The Story of the Atlantic Slave Trade, 1440–1870* (New York: Simon & Schuster, 1997).

France Winddance Twine, *Racism in a Racial Democracy: The Maintenance of White Supremacy in Brazil* (New Brunswick, NJ: Rutgers University Press, 1998).

"Using the Inter-American System for Human Rights: A Practical Guide for NGOs," Global Rights Partners for Justice (2004).

Donna Lee Van Cott, *The Friendly Liquidation of the Past: The Politics of Diversity in Latin America* (Pittsburgh: University of Pittsburgh Press, 2000).

Teun A. van Dijk, *Racism and Discourse in Spain and Latin America* (Philadelphia: John Benjamins, 2005).

José Vasconcelos, *La Raza Cósmica: Misión de la raza Iberoamericana, Notas de Viajes a la América del Sur* (Paris: Agencia mundial de librería, 1920).
The Cosmic Race: A Bilingual Edition, Didier T. Jaén (trans.), 2nd ed. (Baltimore: Johns Hopkins University Press, 1997).
Luis Fernando Verissimo, *O Mundo é Bárbaro – E o que Nós Temos a Ver Com Isso* (Rio de Janeiro: Objetiva, 2008).
Sir Paul Vinogradoff, *Custom and Right* (Cambridge, MA: Harvard University Press, 1925).
Peter Wade, *Blackness and Race Mixture: The Dynamics of Racial Identity in Colombia* (Baltimore: Johns Hopkins University Press, 1993).
Race and Sex in Latin America (London: Pluto Press, 2009).
Peter Wade, Fernando Urrea Giraldo, and Mara Viveros Vigoya (eds.), *Raza, Etnicidad y Sexualidades: Ciudadanía y Multiculturalismo en América Latina* (Bogotá: Universidad Nacional de Colombia, 2008).
Thomas Glyn Watkin, *An Historical Introduction to Modern Civil Law,* Law of the Nations Series (Aldershot: Ashgate, 1999).
Laurence Wolff and Claudio de Moura Castro, *Secondary Education in Latin America and the Caribbean: The Challenge of Growth and Reform* (Washington, DC: Inter-American Development Bank, 2000).

Articles and Book Chapters

Sérgio Adorno, "*Discriminação Racial e Justiça Criminal em São Paulo,*" *Novos Estudos CEBRAP* 43 (November 1995).
Luis E. Aguilar, "Cuba, c. 1860–c. 1930," in Leslie Bethell (ed.), *Cuba: A Short History* (Cambridge: Cambridge University Press, 1993).
Ana María Alonso, "Conforming Disconformity: 'Mestizaje,' Hybridity, and the Aesthetics of Mexican Nationalism," *Cultural Anthropology* 19 (2004).
José E. Álvarez, "Promoting the 'Rule of Law' in Latin America: Problems and Prospects," *George Washington Journal of International Law & Economics* 25 (1991).
Raquel Álvarez de Flores, "Evolución Histórica de las Migraciones en Venezuela: Breve Recuento," *Aldea Mundo* 22 (November 2006–April 2007).
George Reid Andrews, "Black and White Workers: São Paulo, Brazil, 1888–1928," *Hispanic American Historical Review* 68 (August 1988).
"Brazilian Racial Democracy, 1900–90: An American Counterpoint," *Journal of Contemporary History* 31 (1996).

John P. Augelli, "Cultural and Economic Changes of Bastos, a Japanese Colony on Brazil's Paulista Frontier," *Annals of the Association of American Geographers* 48 (March 1958).

Kif Augustine-Adams, "Making Mexico: Legal Nationality, Chinese Race, and the 1930 Population Census," *Law and History Review* 27 (2009).

Sales Augusto dos Santos, "Who Is Black in Brazil? A Timely or a False Question in Brazilian Race Relations in the Era of Affirmative Action?" *Latin American Perspectives* 33 (July 2006).

Sales Augusto dos Santos and Laurence Hallewell, "Historical Roots of the 'Whitening' of Brazil," *Latin American Perspectives* 29 (January 2002).

Jeferson Bacelar, "Black in Salvador: Racial Paths," in Larry Crook and Randal Johnson (eds.), *Black Brazil: Culture, Identity, and Social Mobilization* (Los Angeles: UCLA Latin American Center, 1999).

Samuel L. Baily, "The Adjustment of Italian Immigrants in Buenos Aires and New York, 1870–1914," *American Historical Review* 88 (April 1983).

Taunya Lovell Banks, "*Mestizaje* and the Mexican Mestizo Self: *No Hay Sangre Negra*, So There Is No Blackness," *Southern California Interdisciplinary Law Journal* 15 (2006).

Scott H. Beck, Kenneth J. Mijeski, and Meagan M. Stark, "*¿Qué es Racismo? Awareness of Racism and Discrimination in Ecuador*," *Latin American Research Review* 46 (2011).

Homi K. Bhabha, "Of Mimicry and Man: The Ambivalence of Colonial Discourse," *October* 28 (1984).

Christina Biebesheimer, "Justice Reform in Latin America and the Caribbean: The IDB Perspective," in Pilar Domingo & Rachel Sieder (eds.), *Rule of Law in Latin America: The International Promotion of Judicial Reform* (2001).

Peter Blanchard, "The Language of Liberation: Slave Voices in the Wars of Independence," *Hispanic American History Review* 82 (2002).

Adriana Bolívar et al., "Discourse and Racism in Venezuela: A 'Café con Leche' Country," in van Dijk, *Racism and Discourse in Latin America* (2009).

Eduardo Bonilla-Silva, "Are the Americas 'Sick with Racism' or Is It a Problem at the Poles? A Reply to Christina A. Sue," *Ethnic and Racial Studies* 32 (July 2009).

"We Are All Americans!: the Latin Americanization of Racial Stratification in the USA," *Race & Society* 5 (2002).

Woodrow Borah, "Race and Class in Mexico," *Pacific Historical Review* 23 (1954).

Pierre Bourdieu and Loic Wacquant, "Sobre as Artimanhas de Razão Imperialista," *Estudos Afro-Asiáticos* 1 (2002).

André Brandão and Ludmila Gonçalves da Matta, "Avaliação da Política de Reserva de Vagas na Universidade Estadual do Norte Fluminense: Estudos dos Alunos Que Ingressarem em 2003," in André Augusto Brandão (ed.), *Cotas Raciais no Brasil: A Primeira Avaliação* (Rio de Janeiro: DP&A, 2007).

Alejandro Guzmán Brito, "El Régimen de la Costumbre en las Codificaciones Civiles de Hispanoamérica y España Emprendidas Durante el Siglo XIX," http://www.restudioshistoricos.equipu.cl/index.php/rehj/article/view/161/155.

Diana DeG. Brown, "Power, Invention, and the Politics of Race: Umbanda Past and Future," in Larry Crook and Randal Johnson (eds.), *Black Brazil: Culture, Identity, and Social Mobilization* (Los Angeles: UCLA Latin American Center, 1999).

Kia Lilly Caldwell, "Look at Her Hair": The Body Politics of Black Womanhood in Brazil," *Transforming Anthropology* 11 (2004).

Kirsten Matoy Carlson, "Notice: Premature Predictions of Multiculturalism?" *Michigan Law Review* 100 (May 2002).

Lourdes Casal, "Race Relations in Contemporary Cuba," in Anani Dzidzienyo and Lourdes Casal (eds.), *The Position of Blacks in Brazilian and Cuban Society* (London: Minority Rights Group, 1979).

Ignazio Castellucci, "Law v. Statute, Ius v. Lex: An Analysis of a Critical Relation in Roman and Civil Law," *Global Jurist* 8 (2008).

Marjorie Jiménez Castro, "Las Máscaras del Chiste Racista," *InterSedes: Revista de las Sedes Regionales* 2 (2001).

Sueann Caulfield, "Interracial Courtship in the Rio de Janeiro Courts, 1918–1940," in Nancy P. Applebaum, Anne S. Macpherson, and Karin Alejandra Rosenblatt (eds.), *Race and Nation in Modern Latin America* (Chapel Hill: University of North Carolina Press, 2003).

Sidney Chalhoub, "Medo Branco de Almas Negras: Escravos, Libertos e Republicanos na Cidade do Rio," *Revista Brasileira de Historia* 8 (1988).

Martin Chanock, "Law, State and Culture: Thinking about 'Customary Law' after Apartheid," *Acta Juridica*, 1991 (1991).

"Neither Customary nor Legal: African Customary Law in an Era of Family Law Reform," *International Journal of Law and the Family* 3 (1989).

Jim Chen, "Unloving," *Iowa Law Review* 80 (1994).

Sumi Cho, "Post-Racialism," *Iowa Law Review*, 94 (2009).

Convenio de Cooperación Interinstitucional Entre La Corporación de Desarrollo Afroecuatoriano-CODAE y El Ilustre Municipio Del Cantón Ibarra (Quito: CODAE, 2010), *available at* http://www.codae.gob.ec/ images/stories/transparencia/proyectos /convenio%20ibarra.pdf.

Rebecca J. Cook, "Overcoming Discrimination: Introduction," in Juan E. Méndez, Guillermo O'Donnell and Paulo Sérgio Pinheiro (eds.), *The (Un)Rule of Law and the Underprivileged in Latin America* (Notre Dame, IN: University of Notre Dame Press, 1999).

Ethel Correa, "*Indios, Mestizos, Negros y Blancos en un municipio de la Costa Chica, Oaxaca a través de un censo de 1890*," *Suplemento del Boletín Diario de Campo* (March–April 2007).

"Cotas No Brasil: Um Panorama do Aplicação de Políticas Afirmativas Nas Universidades Públicas,"*Revista Adusp* 43 (July 2008).

Corina Courtis et al., "Racism and Discourse: A Portrait of the Argentine Situation," in Teun A. van Dijk (ed.), *Racism and Discourse in Latin America* (Lanham: Lexington Books, 2009).

William Darity Jr. et al., "Bleach in the Rainbow: Latin Ethnicity and Preference for Whiteness," *Transforming Anthropology* 13 (October 2005), 103–9.

Jose Alberto Magno de Carvalho et al., "Estimating the Stability Of Census-Based Racial/Ethnic Classifications: The Case of Brazil," *Population Studies* 58 (2004).

José Jorge de Carvalho, "As Propostas de Cotas Para Negros e O Racismo Acadêmico No Brasil," *Sociedade e Cultura*, 4 (July/December 2001).

Kimberlé Williams Crenshaw, "Twenty Years of Critical Race Theory: Looking Backward to Move Forward," *Connecticut Law Review* 43 (2011).

Alejandro de la Fuente, "Race and Inequality in Cuba, 1899–1981," *Journal of Contemporary History* 30 (1995).

Carlos de la Torre, "Afro-Ecuadorian Responses to Racism: Between Citizenship and Corporatism," in Anani Dzidzienyo and Suzanne Oboler (eds.), *Neither Enemies nor Friends: Latinos, Blacks, Afro-Latinos* (New York: Palgrave Macmillan, 2005).

Kwame Dixon, "Transnational Black Social Justice Movements in Latin America: Afro-Colombians and the Struggle for Human Rights," in Richard Stahler-Sholk, Harry E. Vanden, and Glen David Kuecker (eds.), *Latin American Social Justice Movements in the Twenty-First Century: Resistance, Power, and Democracy* (Lanham: Rowman & Littlefield, 2008).

Abdias do Nascimento and Elisa Larkin Nascimento, "Dance of Deception: Reading of Race Relations in Brazil," in Charles V. Hamilton, Lynn Huntley, Neville Alexander, Antonio Sérgio Alfredo Guimarães, and Wilmot James (eds.), *Beyond Racism: Race and Inequality in Brazil, South Africa, and the United States* (Boulder, CO: Lynne Rienner, 2001).

Nelson do Valle Silva, "Morenidade: Modo de Usar," *Estudos Afro-Asiáticos* 30 (1996).

Nelson do Valle Silva and Carlos A. Hasenbalg, "Race and Educational Opportunity in Brazil," in Rebecca Reichmann (ed.), *Race in Contemporary Brazil: From Indifference to Inequality* (University Park: Pennsylvania State University Press, 1999).

Ariel E. Dulitzky, "A Region in Denial: Racial Discrimination and Racism in Latin America," in Anani Dzidzienyo and Suzanne Oboler (eds.), *Neither Enemies nor Friends: Latinos, Blacks, Afro-Latinos* (New York: Palgrave Macmillan, 2005).

Anani Dzidzienyo, "The Changing World of Brazilian Race Relations?" in Anani Dzidzienyo and Suzanne Oboler (eds.), *Neither Enemies nor Friends: Latinos, Blacks, Afro-Latinos* (New York: Palgrave Macmillan, 2005).

Stanley L. Engerman and Kenneth L. Sokoloff, "The Evolution of Suffrage Institutions in the New World," *Journal of Economic History* 65 (December 2005).

Dario A. Euraque, "The Banana Enclave, Nationalism and Mestizaje in Honduras, 1910s-1930s," in Avi Chomsky & Aldo Lauria (eds.), *At the Margins of the Nation-State: Identity and Struggle in the Making of the Laboring Peoples of Central America and the Hispanic Caribbean, 1860–1960* (Durham, NC: Duke University Press, 1998).

Jorge L. Esquirol, "The Failed Law of Latin America," *American Journal of Comparative Law* 56 (Winter 2008).

Cynthia Feliciano, Belinda Robnett and Golnaz Komaie, "Gendered Racial Exclusion among White Internet Daters," *Social Science Research* 38 (March 2009).

Ronald Fernández, *America beyond Black and White: How Immigrants and Fusions Are Helping to Overcome the Racial Divide* (Ann Arbor: University of Michigan Press, 2007).

Ricardo Franklin Ferreira, "O Brasileiro, O Racismo Silencioso e a Emancipação do Afro-descendente," *Psicologia & Sociedade*, 14 (January/June 2002).

Angela Figueiredo, "'Out of Place:' The Experience of the Black Middle Class," in Bernd Reiter and Gladys L. Mitchell (eds.), *Brazil's New Racial Politics* (Boulder, CO: Lynne Rienner, 2010).

Peter Fitzpatrick, "Traditionalism and Traditional Law," *Journal of African Law* 28 (1984).

Nicola Foote, "Race, State and Nation in Early Twentieth Century Ecuador," *Nations and Nationalism* 12 (2006).

Reanne Frank, Ilana Redstone Akresh, and Bo Lu, "Latino Immigrants and the U.S. Racial Order: How and Where Do They Fit In?" *American Sociological Review* 75 (June 2010).

Peter Fry, Sérgio Carrara, and Ana Luiza Martins-Costa, "Negros e Brancos no Carnaval da Velha Republica," in João José Reis (ed.), *Escravidão e a Invencão da Liberdade: Estudos sobre o Negro no Brasil* (São Paulo: Brasiliense, Brasilia: CNPQ, 1988).

Alejandro M. Garro, "Access to Justice for the Poor in Latin America," in Juan E. Méndez, Guillermo O'Donnell, and Paulo Sérgio Pinheiro (eds.), *The (Un)Rule of Law and the Underprivileged in Latin America* (Notre Dame, IN: University of Notre Dame Press, 1999).

Joseph L. Gastwirth, "Issues Arising in the Use of Statistical Evidence in Discrimination Cases," in Joseph L. Gastwirth (ed.), *Statistical Science in the Courtroom* (New York: Springer, 2000).

Pablo Gentili, "Educación y Ciudadanía: Un Desafio para América Latina," in Jenny Assael et al. (eds.), *Reforma Educativa y Objetivos Fundamentales Transversales* (Santiago: Programa Interdisciplinario de Investigaciones en Educación, 2003).

Bijan Gilanshah, "Multiracial Minorities: Erasing the Color Line," *Law & Inequality Journal* 12 (1993).

Isar Godreau, Hilda Lloréns, and Carlos Vargas-Ramos, "Employing Incongruence at Work: Employing U.S. Census Racial Categories in Puerto Rico," *Anthropology News* (May 2010).

Joaquim Barbosa Gomes, "O Debate Constitucional Sobre as Ações Afirmativas," in Antonio Sérgio Alfredo Guimarães et al. (eds.), *Ações Afirmativas: Políticas Públicas Contra as Desigualdades Raciais* (Rio de Janeiro: DP&A Editora, 2003).

Olivia Maria Gomes da Cunha, "The Stigmas of Dishonor: Criminal Records, Civil Rights, and Forensic Identification in Rio de Janeiro, 1903–1940," in Sueannn Caulfield and Sarah C. Chambers (eds.), *Honor, Status, and Law in Modern Latin America* (Durham, NC: Duke University Press, 2005).

Eliezer Gomes da Silva and Ivonei Sfoggia, "O Crime de Raçismo na Legislação Penal Brasileira: Passado, Presente e Futuro," *Igualdade: Revista Trimestral do Centro de Apoio Operacional das Promotorias da Criança e do Adolescente* 5 (January/March 1997).

Mónica Treviño González, "Opportunities and Challenges for the Afro-Brazilian Movement," in Bernd Reiter and Gladys L. Mitchell (eds.), *Brazil's New Racial Politics* (Boulder, CO: Lynne Rienner, 2010).

Richard Gott, "Spanish America as a White Settler Society," *Bulletin of Spanish American Research* 26 (2007).

Claudio Grossman, "The Inter-American System of Human Rights: Challenges for the Future," *Indiana Law Journal* 83 (2008).

Alicia Castellanos Guerrero et al., "Racist Discourse in Mexico," in Teun A. van Dijk (ed.), *Racism and Discourse in Latin America* (Lanham: Lexington Books, 2009).

Gema R. Guevara, "Inexacting Whiteness: Blanqueamiento as a Gender-Specific Trope in the Nineteenth Century," *Cuban Studies Journal* 36 (2005).

Antonio Sérgio Alfredo Guimarães, "Ações Afirmativas Para a População Negras Nas Universidades Brasileiras," in Renato Emerson dos Santos and Fatima Lobato (eds.), *Ações Afirmativas: Políticas Públicas Contra As Desigualdades Racias* (Rio de Janeiro: Programa Políticas da Cor na Educação Brasileira, 2003).

Emmanuel Gustavo Haddad, "O Costume Como Parâmetro da Aplicação da Justiça e da Criação da Lei," *Jus Navigandi* 11 (February 6, 2007).

Ronald N. Harpelle, "Ethnicity, Religion and Repression: The Denial of African Heritage in Costa Rica," *Canadian Journal of History* 29 (April 1994).

"The Social and Political Integration of West Indians in Costa Rica: 1930–50," *Journal of Spanish American Studies*, 25 (February 1993).

Aline Helg, "Race and Black Mobilization in Colonial and Early Independent Cuba: A Comparative Perspective," *Ethnography* 44 (1997).

"Race in Argentina and Cuba, 1880–1930: Theory, Policies, and Popular Reaction," in Richard Graham (ed.), *The Idea of Race in Spanish America, 1870–1940* (Austin: University of Texas Press, 1990).

Castro Heredia et al., "Un breve acercamiento a las políticas de Acción Afirmativa: orígenes, aplicación y experiencia para grupos étnico-raciales en Colombia y Cali," *Revista Sociedad y Economía*

169 (January 2009), *available at* http://redalyc.uaemex.mx/redalyc/pdf/996/99612491009.pdf.

Rosana Heringer, "Ação Afirmativa e Promoção da Igualdade Racial no Brasil: O Desafio da Prática," in Angela Randolpho Paiva (ed.), *Ação Afirmativa na Universidade: Reflexão Sobre Experiências Concretas Brasil-Estados Unidos* (Rio de Janeiro: Editora-PUC Rio, 2004).

Harry Hoetink, "The Dominican Republic in the Nineteenth Century: Some Notes on Stratification, Immigration, and Race," in Magnus Mörner (ed.), *Race and Class in Spanish America* (New York: Columbia University Press, 1970).

Thomas P. Holloway, "Immigration and Abolition: The Transition from Slave to Free Labor in the São Paulo Coffee Zone," in Dauril Alden and Warren Dean (eds.), *Essays Concerning the Socioeconomic History of Brazil and Portuguese India* (Gainesville: University Press of Florida, 1977).

Juliet Hooker, "Afro-descendant Struggles for Collective Rights in Latin America: Between Race and Culture," *Souls* 10 (2008).

Mala N. Htun, "From 'Racial Democracy' to Affirmative Action: Changing State Policy on Race in Brazil," *Latin American Research Review* 39 (February 2004).

Mala N. Htun and Mark Jones, "Engendering the Right to Participate in Decisionmaking: Electoral Quotas and Women's Leadership in Latin America," in N. Craske and M. Molyneux (eds.), *Gender and the Politics of Rights and Democracy in Latin America* (London: Palgrave Macmillan, 2002).

Alexandra Isfahani-Hammond, "Introduction: Who Were the Masters in the Americas?" in Alexandra Isfahani-Hammond (ed.), *The Masters and the Slaves: Plantation Relations and Mestizaje in American Imaginaries* (New York: Palgrave Macmillan, 2004).

Alex M. Johnson Jr., "Destabilizing Racial Classifications Based on Insights Gleaned from Trademark Law," *California Law Review* 84 (1996), 887–952, 891.

Paul Christopher Johnson, "Law, Religion, and 'Public Health' in the Republic of Brazil," *Law and Social Inquiry* 26 (Winter 2001).

Samuel Kilsztajn et al., "Concentração e Distribuição do Rendimento por Raça No Brasil," *Revista de Economia Contemporânea* 9 (May/August 2005).

James F. King, "The Case of José Ponciano de Ayarza: A Document on Gracias al Sacar," *Hispanic American History Review* 31 (1951).

Herbert S. Klein, "The Integration of Italian Immigrants into the United States and Argentina: A Comparative Analysis," *American Historical Review* 88 (April 1983).

Jennifer Lee and Frank D. Bean, "Reinventing the Color Line: Immigration and America's New Racial/Ethnic Divide," *Social Forces* 86 (December 2007).

David Lehmann, "Gilberto Freyre: The Reassessment Continues," *Latin American Research Review* 43 (2008).

Jeffrey Lesser, "Immigration and Shifting Concepts of National Identity in Brazil during the Vargas Era," *Luso-Brazilian Review* 31 (Winter 1994).

Saul Litvinoff, "Moral Damages," *Louisiana Law Review* 38 (1977).

Peggy A. Lovell, "Gender, Race, and the Struggle for Social Justice in Brazil," *Latin American Perspectives* 27 (November 2000).

"Race, Gender, and Work in São Paulo, Brazil, 1960–2000," *Latin American Research Review* 41 (October 2006).

"Women and Racial Inequality at Work in Brazil," in Michael Hanchard (ed.), *Racial Politics in Contemporary Brazil* (Durham, NC: Duke University Press, 1999).

Mara Loveman and Jerónimo O. Muñiz, "How Puerto Rico Became White: Boundary Dymanics and Intercensus Racial Reclassification," *American Sociological Review* 72 (December 2007).

Samuel H. Lowrie, "O elemento negro na população de São Paulo," *Revista do Arquivo Municipal* 48 (junho 1938).

"The Negro Element in the Population of São Paulo, a Southernly State of Brazil," *Phylon* 3 (1942).

"Racial and National Intermarriage in a Brazilian City," *American Journal of Sociology* 44 (March 1939).

Marcelo Sabino Luiz, "A Mulher Negra No Mercado de Trabalho: A Pseudoequidade, Marcada Pela Discriminação da Sociedade E a Mídia No Século," *Partes* 21 (September 9, 2010), *available at* http://www.partes.com.br/politica/mulhernegranotrabalho.asp.

Mary Ann Mahony, "Afro-Brazilians, Land Reform, and the Question of Social Mobility in Southern Bahia, 1880–1920," in Hendrik Kraay (ed.), *Afro-Brazilian Culture and Politics: Bahia, 1790's to 1990's* (Armonk, NY: M. E. Sharpe, 1998).

Tomoko Makabe, "Ethnic Hegemony: The Japanese Brazilians in Agriculture, 1908–1968," *Ethnic and Racial Studies* 22 (July 1999).

Marylee Mason Mandiver, "Racial Classifications in Spanish American Censuses," *Social Forces* 28 (December 1949).

Sheldon L. Maram, "Labor and the Left in Brazil, 1890–1921: A Movement Aborted," *Hispanic American Historical Review* 57 (1977).

"Urban Labor and Social Change in the 1920's," *Luso-Brazilian Review* 16 (1979).

Luis Gerardo Martínez Miranda, "Desde Adentro: una aproximación al tema de Verdad, Justicia y Reparación a partir de las víctimas afrocolombianas," in Claudia Mosquera Rosero-Labbé and Luiz Claudio Barcelos (eds.), *Afro-reparacions: Memorias de la Esclavitud y Justicia Reparativa para Negros, Afrocolombianos y Raizales* (Bogotá: Universidad Nacional de Colombia, 2006).

Lourdes Martínez-Echazábal, "Mestizaje and the Discourse of National/ Cultural Identity in Spanish America, 1845–1959," *Spanish American Perspectives* 25 (May 1998).

Frederic Martínez, "Apogeo y Decadencia del Ideal de la Inmigración Europea en Colombia, siglo XIX," *Boletín Cultural y Bibliográfico* 34 (1998).

Francisco Martins, "Racism in Brazilian Aquarelle – the Place of Denying," *International Journal of Migration, Health and Social Care* 4(2) (October 2008).

Marianne Masferrer and Carmelo Mesa-Lago, "The Gradual Integration of the Black in Cuba: Under the Colony, the Republic, and the Revolution," in Robert Brent Toplin (ed.), *Slavery and Race Relations in Spanish America* (Westport, CT: Greenwood Press, 1974).

Michael J. Mitchell and Charles H. Wood, "Ironies of Citizenship: Skin Color, Police Brutality, and the Challenge to Democracy in Brazil," *Social Forces* 77 (March 1999).

Graziella Moraes da Silva and Elisa P. Reis, "Perceptions of Racial Discrimination among Black Professionals in Rio de Janeiro," *Latin American Research Review* 46 (2011).

James Bernard Murphy, "Habit and Convention at the Foundation of Custom," in Amanda Perreau-Saussine and James Bernard Murphy (eds.), *The Nature of Customary Law: Legal, Historical and Philosophical Perspectives* (Cambridge: Cambridge University Press, 2007).

Álvaro Pereirado Nascimento, "Um Reduto Negro: Cor e Cidadania na Armada (1870–1910)," in Olívia Maria Gomes da Cunha and Flávio dos Santos Gomes (eds.), *Quase-cidadão: Histórias e Antropologias da Pós-Emancipação no Brasil* (Rio de Janeiro: Editora FGV, 2007).

Elisa Larkin Nascimento, "Aspects of Afro-Brazilian Experience," *Journal of Black Studies* 11 (1980).

"It's in the Blood: Notes on Race Attitudes in Brazil from a Different Perspective," in Charles V. Hamilton, Lynn Huntley, Neville Alexander, Antonio Sérgio Alfredo Guimarães, and Wilmot James (eds.), *Beyond Racism: Race and Inequality in Brazil, South Africa, and the United States* (Boulder, CO: Lynne Rienner, 2001).

Carmen Nava, "Lessons in Patriotism and Good Citizenship: National Identity and Nationalism in Public Schools during the Vargas Administration, 1937–1945," *Luso-Brazillian Review* 35 (Summer 1998).

Moisés González Navarro, "*Mestizaje* in Mexico during the National Period," in Magnus Mörner (ed.), *Race and Class in Spanish America* (New York: Columbia University Press, 1970).

Laura Beth Nielsen, Robert L. Nelson, and Roy Lancaster, "Individual Justice or Collective Legal Mobilization? Employment Discrimination Litigation in the Post Civil Rights United States," *Journal of Empirical Legal Studies* 7 (June 2010).

Melissa Nobles, *Shades of Citizenship: Race and the Census in Modern Politics* (Stanford, CA: Stanford University Press, 2000).

Suzanne Oboler, "The Foreignness of Racism: Pride and Prejudice among Peru's Limeños in the 1990s," in Anani Dzidzienyo and Suzanne Oboler (eds.), *Neither Enemies nor Friends: Latinos, Blacks, Afro-Latinos* (New York: Palgrave Macmillan, 2005).

Marcelo Paixão, Irene Rossetto, Fabiana Montovanele, and Luiz M. Carvano, *Relatório Anual das Desigualdades Raciais no Brasil; 2009–2010* (Rio de Janeiro: Editora Garamond Ltda., 2010).

Renato H. L. Pedrosa et al., "Academic Performance, Students' Background and Affirmative Action at a Brazilian University," *Higher Education Management and Policy* 19 (2007).

Yesilernis Peña, Jim Sidanius, and Mark Sawyer, "Racial Democracy in the Americas: A Latin and U.S. Comparison," *Journal of Cross-Cultural Psychology* 35 (November 2004).

Amanda Perreau-Saussine and James Bernard Murphy, "The Character of Customary Law: An Introduction," in Amanda Perreau-Saussine and James Bernard Murphy (eds.), *The Nature of Customary Law: Legal, Historical and Philosophical Perspectives* (Cambridge: Cambridge University Press, 2007).

Louis A. Pérez, Jr., "Politics, Peasants, and People of Color: The 1912 'Race War' in Cuba Reconsidered," *Hispanic American History Review* 66 (1986).

Hanne Petersen, "Reclaiming 'Juridical Tact'? Observations and Reflections on Customs and Informal Law as (Pluralist) Sources of Polycentric Law," in Hanne Petersen and Hendrik Zahle (eds.), *Legal Polycentricity: Consequences of Pluralism in Law* (Aldershot: Dartmouth, 1995).

Paulo Sérgio Pinheiro, "The Rule of Law and the Underprivileged in Latin America: Introduction," in Juan E. Méndez, Guillermo O'Donnell and Paulo Sérgio Pinheiro (eds.), *The (Un)Rule of Law and the Underprivileged in Latin America* (Notre Dame, IN: University of Notre Dame Press, 1999).

Antônio Pitanga, Larry Crook (ed.), and Randal Johnson (ed.), *Where Are the Blacks?* in *Black Brazil: Culture, Identity, and Social Mobilization* (Los Angeles: UCLA Latin American Center, 1999).

Plan Plurinacional Para Eliminar la Discriminación Racial y la Exclusión Étnica y Cultural (Quito: CODAE, September 2009), *available at* http://www.codae.gob.ec/index.php?option=com_content&view=article&id=188%3Aplan-plurinacional-para-eliminar-la-discriminacion-racial-y-la-exclusion-etnica-y-cultural&catid=27&Itemid=63.

Jeanny Posso, "Mecanismos de Discriminación Étnico-Racial, Clase Social y Género: La Inserción Laboral de Mujeres Negras en el Servicio Doméstico de Cali," in María del Carmen Zabala Arguelles (ed.), *Pobreza, Exclusión Social y Discriminación Étnico-Racial en América Latina y el Caribe* (Bogotá: Siglo del Hombre Editores y Clasco, 2008).

Delcele Mascarenhas Queiroz and Jocelio Teles dos Santos, "Sistema de Cotas: Um Debate: Dos Dados a Manutençao de Privilegios e de Poder," *Educação e Sociedade* 27 (2006).

Seth Racusen, "Fictions of Identity and Brazilian Affirmative Action," *National Black Law Journal* 21 (2009).

"Making the 'Impossible' Determination: Flexible Identity and Targeted Opportunity in Contemporary Brazil," *Connecticut Law Review* 36 (2004).

Jean Muteba Rahier, "Blackness and the 'Racial' Spatial Order, Migration, and Miss Ecuador 1995–1996," *American Anthropologist* 100 (1998).

"Soccer and the (Tri-)Color of the Ecuadorian Nation: Visual and Ideological (Dis)Continuities of Black Otherness from Monocultural Mestizaje to Multiculturalism," *Visual Anthropology Review* 24 (2008).

Carlos M. Rama, "The Passing of the Afro-Uruguayans from Caste Society into Class Society," in Magnus Mörner (ed.), *Race and Class in Spanish America* (New York: Columbia University Press, 1970).

Bernd Reiter, "Inequality and School Reform in Bahia, Brazil," *International Review of Education* 55 (2009).

Andrew Juan Rosa, "El Que No Tiene Dingo, Tiene Mandingo: The Inadequacy of the 'Mestizo' as a Theoretical Construct in the Field of Spanish American Studies – the Problem and Solution," *Journal of Black Studies* 27 (1996).

Angel Rosenblat, *La Población Indígena y el Mestizaje en América*, Vol. II (Buenos Aires: Editorial Nova, 1954).

Carlos Rosero, "Los Afrodescendientes y el Conflicto Armado en Colombia: La Insistencia en lo Propio Como Alternativa," in Claudia Mosquera, Mauricio Pardo, and Odile Hoffman (eds.), *Afrodescendientes en las Américas: Trayectorias Sociales e Identitarias, 150 Años de la Abolición de la Esclavitud en Colombia* (Bogotá: Universidad Nacional de Colombia, 2002), pp. 547–59.

Cesar Rossato, Verônica Gesser, and Eliane Cavalleiro (ed.), "A Experiencia da Branquitude Diante de Conflitos Racias: Estudos de Realidades Brasileiras e Estadunidenses," in *Racismo E Anti-Racismo Na Educaçao: Repensando nossa Escola* (São Paulo: Selo Negro, 2001).

José Antonio Saco, *Colección de Papeles Científicos, Históricos y Políticos Sobre la Isla de Cuba*, vol. 3 (Paris: Impr. de d'Aubusson y Kugelmann, 1858).

Helen I. Safa, "Racial and Gender Inequality in Latin America: Afro-Descendant Women Respond," *Feminist Africa Diaspora Voices* (2007), *available at* http://www.feministafrica.org.

Frank Safford, "Race, Integration, and Progress: Elite Attitudes and the Indian in Colombia, 1750–1870," *Hispanic American Historical Review* 71 (1991).

Roger Sanjek, "Brazilian Racial Terms: Some Aspects of Meaning and Learning," *American Anthropologist* 73 (October 1971).

Rosembert Ariza Santamaría, "Usos y costumbres en el procedimiento administrativo: una Administración al servicio de sociedades pluriculturales," in *Procedimiento y Justicia Administrativa en América Latina* (Mexico City: Fundación Konrad Adenauer, 2009).

Melissa L. Saunders, "Of Minority Representation, Multiple-Race Responses, and Melting Pots: Redistricting in the New America," *North Carolina Law Review* 79 (2001).

Ruth Sautu, "Poverty, Psychology, and Dropouts," in Laura Randall and Joan B. Anderson (eds.), *Schooling for Success: Preventing Repetition and Dropout in Latin American Primary Schools* (Armonk, NY: M. E. Sharpe, 1999).

German Savastano, "Custom as a Source of Law: Argentinean and Comparative Legal Systems," *ILSA Journal of International and Comparative Law* 15 (2009).

Luisa Farah Schwartzman, "Does Money Whiten? Intergenerational Changes in Racial Classification in Brazil," *American Sociological Review* 72 (December 2007).

Renato Sêrgio de Lima, Alessandra Teixeira, and Jacqueline Signoretto, "Mulheres Negras: As Mais Punidas Nos Crimes de Roubo," *Boletín del Núcleo de Pesquisas IBCCRIM* 125 (April 2003).

Rachel Sieder, "Conclusions: Promoting the Rule of Law in Latin America," in Pilar Domingo and Rachel Sieder (eds.), *Rule of Law in Latin America: The International Promotion of Judicial Reform* (London: Brookings Institution Press, 2001).

María Aparecida Silva Bento, "Silent Conflict: Discriminatory Practices and Black Responses in the Workplace," in Rebecca Reichmann (ed.), *Race in Contemporary Brazil: From Indifference to Inequality* (University Park: Pennsylvania State University Press, 1999).

Thomas E. Skidmore, "Racial Ideas and Social Policy in Brazil, 1870–1940," in Richard Graham (ed.), *The Idea of Race in Latin America, 1870–1940* (Austin: University of Texas Press, 1990).

Donald Hugh Smith, "Civil Rights: A Problem in Communication," *Phylon* 27 (1966).

Christina Sue, "An Assessment of the Latin Americanization Thesis," *Ethnic & Racial Studies* 6 (2009).

Jorge Correa Sutil, "Judicial Reforms in Latin America: Good News for the Underprivileged?" in Juan E. Méndez, Guillermo O'Donnell, and Paulo Sérgio Pinheiro (eds.), *The (Un)Rule of Law and the Underprivileged in Latin America* (Notre Dame, IN: University of Notre Dame Press, 1999).

"Symposium on Bonilla-Silva's Latin Americanization of Race Relations Thesis," *Race & Society* 5 (2002).

Edward Telles, "Residential Segregation by Skin Color in Brazil," *American Sociological Review* 57 (1992).

Edward E. Telles, "Racial Ambiguity among the Brazilian Population," *Ethnic and Racial Studies* 25 (May 2002), 415–41.

Arlene Torres, "La Gran Familia Puertorriqueña 'Ej Preita de Beldá,'" in Arlene Torres and Norman E. Whitten, Jr. (eds.), *Blackness in Spanish America and the Caribbean*, vol. 2 (Bloomington: Indiana University Press, 1998).

Michael R. Trochim, "The Brazilian Black Guard," *Americas* 44 (January 1988).

Jorge A. Vargas, "Moral Damages under the Civil Law of Mexico: Are These Damages Equivalent to U.S. Punitive Damages?" *University of Miami Inter-American Law Review* 35 (2004).

João H. Costa Vargas, "When a Favela Dared to Become a Gated Community: The Politics of Race and Urban Space in Rio de Janeiro," *Latin American Perspectives* 33 (July 2006).

Mário C. Vásquez, "Immigration and Mestizaje in Nineteenth-Century Peru," in Magnus Mörner (ed.), *Race and Class in Spanish America* (New York: Columbia University Press, 1970).

Bobby Vaughn, "Afro-Mexico: Blacks, Indígenas, Politics, and the Great Diaspora," in Anani Dzidzienyo and Suzanne Oboler (eds.), *Neither Enemies nor Friends: Latinos, Blacks, Afro-Latinos* (Houndmills: Palgrave Macmillian, 2005).

Jacques Velloso, "Curso e Concurso: Rendimento No Universidade e Desempenho en um Vestibular Com Cotas da UnB," *Cadernos de Pesquisa* 39 (2009).

Peter Wade, "Afro-Latin Studies: Reflections on the Field," *Latin American and Caribbean Ethnic Studies* 1 (April 2006).

Alan Watson, "An Approach to Customary Law," *University of Illinois Law Review* 1984 (1984).

Barbara Weinstein, "Racializing Regional Difference: São Paulo versus Brazil, 1932," in Nancy P. Applebaum, Anne S. Macpherson, and Karin Alejandra Rosenblatt (eds.), *Race and Nation in Modern Latin America* (Chapel Hill: University of North Carolina Press, 2003).

Jurema Werneck, "The Beautiful and the Pure? Racism, Eugenics and New (Bio)technologies," in Alejandra Rotania and Jurema Werneck (eds.), *Under the Sign of Biopolitics: Critical Voices from Civil Society Reflections in Brazil*, vol. 1 (Rio de Janeiro: E-papers, 2004).

John Valery White, "The Activist Insecurity and the Demise of Civil Rights Law," *Louisiana Law Review* 63 (2003).

Norman Whitten, Jr., "El *Mestizaje*: An All Inclusive Ideology of Exclusion," in Norman Whitten, Jr. (ed.), *Cultural Transformation and Ethnicity in Modern Ecuador* (Urbana: University of Illinois Press, 1981).

Patricia J. Williams, "Spare Parts, Family Values, Old Children, Cheap," *New England Law Review* 28 (1994).

Laurence Wolff and Claudio de Moura Castro, *Secondary Education in Latin America and the Caribbean: The Challenge of Growth and Reform* (Washington, DC: Inter-American Development Bank, 2000).

Charles H. Wood, José Alberto Magno de Caravalho, and Cláudia Júlia Guimarães Horta, "The Color of Child Mortality in Brazil, 1950–2000," *Latin American Research Review* 45 (2010).

Winthrop R. Wright, "Café con Leche: A Brief Look at Race Relations in Twentieth Century, Venezuela," *Maryland Historian* (1970).

"Elitist Attitudes toward Race in Twentieth-Century Venezuela," in Robert Brent Toplin (ed.), *Slavery and Race Relations in Spanish America* (Westport, CT: Greenwood Press, 1974).

"Race, Nationality, and Immigration in Venezuelan Thought, 1890–1937," *Canadian Review of Studies in Nationalism* 6 (1979).

Jonas Zoninsein, "The Economic Case for Combating Racial and Ethnic Exclusion in Latin America and the Caribbean Countries," in Mayra Buvinic, Jacqueline Mazza, and Ruthanne Deutsch (eds.), *Towards a Shared Vision of Development* (Washington, DC: Inter-American Development Bank, 2001).

Theses, Dissertations, Presentations, and Working Papers

Sam C. Adamo, "Race, Health, and Justice in Rio de Janeiro, 1890–1940," PhD dissertation, University of New Mexico (1983).

Marco Antonio I. Aguirre, "Los Grupos Étnicos en los Censos de Guatemala," presentation at "Todos Contamos: Los Grupos Étnicos en los Censos," Cartagena de Indias, Colombia (November 2000) (on file with the Interamerican Development Bank, Washington, DC).

Donald Allen, "La Experiencia de Costa Rica," presentation at "Todos Contamos: Los Grupos Étnicos en los Censos," Interamerican Development Bank, Cartagena de Indias, Colombia (November 2000).

Mary Elizabeth Bletz, "Whiteness of a Darker Color: Narratives of Immigration and Culturation in Brazil and Argentina, 1890–1930," PhD dissertation, New York University (2003).

Yolanda Bodnar, "Colombia: Apuntes sobre la diversidad cultural y la información sociodemográfica disponible en los pueblos indígenas," presentation at "Pueblos indígenas y afrodescendientes de América

Latina y el Caribe: relevancia y pertinencia de la información socio-demográfica para políticas y programas," United Nations Economic Commission for Spanish America and the Caribbean, Santiago de Chile (April 2005), p. 14, *available at* http://www.eclac.cl/mujer/noticias/noticias/5/27905/YBodnar.pdf.

Deyanira Áviles Bosquez, "Los Grupos Étnicos en los Censos: Experiencia de Panamá," presentation at "Todos Contamos: Los Grupos Étnicos en los Censos," Cartagena de Indias, Colombia, November 2000 (on file with the Interamerican Development Bank, Washington, DC).

Fernando Lobo Braga, "Discriminação No Mercado de Trabalho: Diferenças Racias e Por Sexo No Ano de 2003," Master's dissertation, Universidade Católica de Brasília (2005).

"Brief Summary of the Status of the Negotiations of the Working Group Organized to Elaborate a Draft of an Inter-American Convention against Racism and All Forms of Discrimination and Intolerance," Organization of American States International Law Department (May 28, 2009), *available at* http://scm.oas.org/doc_public/SPANISH/HIST_09/CP22305S04.doc.

Claudete Batista Cardoso, "Efeitos da Política de Cotas na Universidade de Brasília: Uma Análise do Rendimento e da Evasão," Master's dissertation, University of Brasilia (2008).

Raquel Coelho Lenz Cesar, "Acesso A Justiça Para Minorias Racias no Brasil: É a Açao Afirmativa o Melhor Caminho? Riscos e Açertos no Caso da UERJ," PhD dissertation, State University of Rio de Janeiro (2003).

Rosana Aparecida Peronti Chiarello, "Preconceitos E Discriminações Racias: Um Olhar de Professoras Sobre Seus (Suas) Alunos (as) Negros (as)," Master's thesis, Federal University of São Carlos (2003).

Darién J. Davis, "The Mechanism of Forging a National Consciousness: A Comparative Approach to Modern Brazil and Cuba, 1930–1964," PhD dissertation, Tulane University (1992).

Allison L. C. de Cerreno and Cassandra A. Pyle, "Educational Reform in Latin America P7," Working Paper, Council on Foreign Relations (1996), *available at* http://www.ciaonet.org/wps/cea01/.

Alexandre do Nascimento, "Movimentos Sociais, Educação E Cidadania: Um Estudo Sobre os Cursos Pré-Vestibulares Populares," Master's thesis, State University of Rio de Janeiro (1999).

Fernando Urrea Giraldo and Héctor Fabio Ramírez Echeverry, "Cambios en el Mercado de Trabajo de Cali (Colombia), Reestructuración Económica y Social del Empleo de la Población Negra en la

Década del 90: Un Análisis de Segregación Socio-Racial a Partir de las Transformaciones Más Recientes del Mercado de Trabajo," Presentation, Third Latin American Congress on the Sociology of Work, Buenos Aires, Argentina (May 2000), p. 1, *available at* http://www.alast.org/PDF/Marshall2/MT-Urrea.PDF.

Gema Rosa Guevara, "Founding Discourse of Cuban Nationalism: La Patria, Blanqueamiento and La Raza de Color," PhD dissertation, U.C. San Diego (2000).

Ayana Hosten, "Tornar-Se Negro & Thinking Beautiful," Study Abroad Program Thesis, Claremont McKenna College (2007), *available at* http://digitalcollections.sit.edu/isp_collections/244/.

Clara (Kaya) Ford, "The Impact of Socioeconomic Quotas on Student Retention: The Case of a Brazilian University," PhD dissertation, Capella University (2011).

Magdalena León and Jimena Holguín, "La Accíon Afirmativa en La Universidad de los Andes: el caso del programa 'Oportunidades para talentos nacionales,'" *Revista de Estudios Sociales* 19 (December 2004), *available at* http://res.uniandes.edu.co/view.php/405/indexar.php? c=Revista+No+18.

Jeffrey Lesser, "Negotiating National Identity: Middle Eastern and Asian Immigrants and the Struggle for Ethnicity in Brazil," Working Paper No. 8, Center for Comparative Immigration Studies Working Papers University of California, San Diego (April 2000).

Marina Jacob Lopes da Silva, "Igualdade e Ações Afirmativas Sociais e Raciais no Ensino Superior: O Que se Discute no STF?" Research Monograph, Sociedade Brasileira de Direito Público (2009).

Cláudia Margarida Ribas Marinho, "O Racismo no Brasil – Uma análise do desenvolvimento histórico do tema e da eficácia da lei como instrumento de combate à discriminação racial," Undergraduate thesis in law, Universidade Federal de Santa Catarina (July 1999).

"The Need for a Narrow-Focused Inter-American Convention against Racial Discrimination," Position Paper No. 1, University of Texas School of Law Human Rights Clinic (May 2009), http://www.utexas.edu/law/clinics/humanrights/work/Paper1-Narrow-focused-convention.pdf.

Melissa Nobles, "'Responding with Good Sense':The Politics of Race and Censuses in Contemporary Brazil," PhD dissertation,Yale University (1995).

Elizabeth Cezar Nunes, "Discriminação da Criança Negra no Processo de Adoção," J.D. dissertation, Centro Universitário de Brasilia (2008).

Isabel Rodas Núñez, "Identidades y la Construcción de la Categoría Oficial 'Ladino' en Guatemala," Working Paper No. 29, Centre for Research on Inequality, Human Security and Ethnicity (October 2006).

"Quest for Inclusion: Realizing Afro-Latin Potential," Organization of Africans in the Americas, Position Paper vol. 1 (2000).

"Political Feasibility Assessment: Country Potential for New Research on Race in Latin America," presentation at "International Conference, Todos Contamos: Los Grupos Étnicos en los Censos," Inter-American Development Bank, Cartagena de Indias (November 8–10, 2000).

Seth Racusen, "A Mulato Cannot Be Prejudiced: The Legal Construction of Racial Discrimination in Contemporary Brazil," PhD dissertation, Massachusetts Institute of Technology (2002).

Susana Schkolink and Fabiana del Popolo, "Los censos y los pueblos indígenas en América Latina: Una metodología Regional," presentation at "Pueblos indígenas y afrodescendientes de América Latina y el Caribe: relevancia y pertinencia de la información sociodemográfica para políticas y programas," United Nations Economic Commission for Spanish America and the Caribbean, Santiago de Chile (April 2005), p. 12, *available at* http://www.eclac.cl/celade/noticias/paginas/7/21237/FdelPopolo-SScholnick.pdf.

Cleusa Simão, "Mulher Negra: Identidade e Exclusão Social," Master's dissertation, Universidade São Marcos (2004).

Santos Silva, "Negros Com Renda Média No Bairro da Pituba," Master's thesis, Universidade Salvador-UNIFACS (2007).

Wilfredo Ardito Vega, "Las ordenanzas contra la discriminación," Working Paper No. 13, Pontificia Universidad Católica del Perú (2009), *available at* http://departamento.pucp.edu.pe/derecho/images/documentos/Cuaderno%2013.pdf.

Internet Sites

"10 Year Currency Converter," Bank of Canada, http://www.bankofcanada.ca/en/rates/exchform.html.

"1999 Country Reports on Human Rights Practices," U.S. Department of State, Bureau of Democracy, Human Rights, and Labor, February 25, 2000, http://www.state.gov/www/global/human_rights/1999_hrp_report/peru.html.

"Americas Barometer 2010," Ethnicity Module of the Project on Ethnicity and Race in Latin America (PERLA) in the 2010 America's

Barometer, Latin American Public Opinion Project of Vanderbilt University, *available at* www.AmericasBarometer.org.

"Afrocolombianos Desplazados, un Drama Sin Tregua," Consultoría Para los Derechos Humanos y el Desplazamiento, May 22, 2008, http://www.codhes.org/index.php?option=com_content@task=view@id=157.

"Annual Report: Peru (2000)," Inter-American Commission on Human Rights, *available at* http://www.cidh.oas.org/annualrep/2000eng/annex.htm.

"Compilation of Final Observations of the Committee for the Elimination of Racial Discrimination Regarding the Countries of Latin America and the Caribbean: 1970–2006 (June 2006)," United Nations High Commission for Human Rights, Latin America and the Caribbean Regional Representation, *available at* http://www2.ohchr.org/english/bodies/cerd/index.htm.

"Concluding Observations of the Committee on the Elimination of Racial Discrimination: Colombia," United Nations, August 20, 1999, *available at* http://www.unhchr.ch/tbs/doc.nsf/(Symbol)/c318bd791cc8a6 ea8025686b0043560f?Opendocument.

"Dados Socioculturais 2010," Vestibular UERJ, www.vestibular.uerj.br.

"Desplazamiento Forzado y Enfoques Diferenciales," Doc. No. 9, Consultoría Para los Derechos Humanos y el Desplazamiento, *available at* http://www.codhes.org/images/stories/publicaciones/enfoque%20dif_thumb.JPG.

"Examples of Cases Studied by the Project (Peru, 1995–2000)," International Development Research Centre, http://www.idrc.ca/en/ev-112282-201-1-DO_TOPIC.html.

Elizabeth M. Grieco, "Race and Hispanic Origin of the Foreign-Born Population in the United States: 2007," American Community Survey Reports, January 2010, http://www.census.gov/prod/2010pubs/acs-11.pdf

"Instituto Colombiano de Crédito Educativo y Estudios Técnicos en el Exterior," ICETEX, *available at* http://www.icetex.gov.co/portal/Default.aspx?tabid=275.

"Inter-American Commission on Human Rights Release Report on Afro-Descendants in Colombia," Inter-American Commission on Human Rights (May 15, 2009) *available at* http://www.cidh.org/Comunicados/English/2009/28–09eng.htm.

Joaquim B. Barbosa Gomes, "Discriminação Racial: Um Grande Desafio Para o Direito Brasileiro," Adami Advogados Associado, *available at* http://www.adami.adv.br/raciais/19.asp.

"Labor Rights Report 31 (September 2007)," Bureau of International Labor Affairs, Department of Labor, Peru, *available at* http://www. dol.gov/ilab/media/reports/usfta/PLRReport.pdf.

"Latin America: Promoting the Rights of Colombia's Afro-Descendants," Global Rights Partners for Justice, *available at* www.globalrights.org.

"Listo Proyecto Para Prohibir Discriminación Laboral en las Ofertas de Empleo," Jóvenes a la Obra, Programa Nacional de Empleo Juvenil (2010), *available at* http://www.projoven.gob.pe/noticia.php?id=32.

"Report on the Situation of Human Rights in Brazil," Inter-American Commission on Human Rights, http://www.cidh.oas.org/countryrep/ brazil-eng/Chaper%209%20.htm.

Amy Erica Smith, "Who Supports Affirmative Action in Brazil," LAPOP Americas Barometer 2010 Insights No. 49 (Oct. 4, 2010), http:// www.vanderbilt.edu/lapop/insights/I0849en.pdf.

"Síntese de Indicadores Socias: Uma Análise das Condiçoes de Vida da População Brasileira," Instituto Brasiliero de Geografia e Estatística, *available at* http://www.ibge.gov.br/home/estatistica/populacao/condi- caodevida/indicadoresminimos/sinteseindicsociais2010/default.shtm.

"Síntese de Indicadores Socias 2006, Estudos & Pesquisas: Informação Demográfica e Socioeconômica num. 19," Instituto Brasiliero de Geografia e Estatística, 2006, Table 9.7, *available at* http://www.ibge. gov.br/home/estatistica/populacao/condicaodevida/indicadoresmini- mos/sinteseindicsociais2006/default.shtm.

"Síntese de Indicadores Socias 2008, Estudos & Pesquisas: Informação Demográfica e Socioeconômica num. 23," Instituto Brasiliero de Geografia e Estatística, 2008, *available at* http://www.ibge.gov.br/ home/estatistica/populacao/condicaodevida/indicadoresminimos/sin- teseindicsociais2008/default.shtm.

Michael Smith, "Educational Reform in Latin America: Facing a Crisis," International Development Research Center Report, February 19, 1999, *available at* http://web.idrc.ca/en/ev-5552–201–1-DO_TOPIC. html.

INDEX

CPSIA information can be obtained at www.ICGtesting.com
Printed in the USA
LVOW070118190613

339217LV00002B/2/P